INCOME DETERMINATION THEORY: An accounting framework

INCOME DETERMINATION

NORTON M. BEDFORD

Department of Accountancy, University of Illinois

THEORY: An accounting framework

ADDISON-WESLEY · READING, MASSACHUSETTS

To Helen, Mark, and Martha

Preface

*"Philosophical and psychological theories, historical doctrines and all sorts of speculations and discoveries, have changed, and keep changing, the lives of countless millions. . . . It is impossible to conceive of our world in terms of action alone."** *

The concept of income is in a state of flux. Old views of it are no longer adequate to meet the growing uses to which income measurements are being put in modern society, and new concepts, normally variations of older ideas, have come into being. Different concepts have been developed for different purposes, and the distinctions among various income notions which have been drawn to clarify each new concept have resulted in changes and variations in methods of determining income. In many instances the changes have been confined to changes in the measurement procedures, but in a few cases more fundamental distinctions have been involved.

In general, the income concept has grown in usefulness to society, and the changes reflect the growth of the ability to measure income as well as the growth of the profession concerned with income determination. One

---

* Erwin Panofsky, *Meaning in the Visual Arts* (New York: Doubleday, 1955), page 23.

should not, as some are prone to do, consider these developments a deterioration of the value of the income concept. Instead one should view the increasing number of income concepts as an expansion of means for guiding the operations of our society, and predict an expanded role for the income concept in modern democratic society.

The expanding nature of the income concept has resulted in considerable controversy both among accountants and in accounting literature. This has resulted in misunderstandings among lawmakers, in courts, and in economic society in general. In fact, until the new nature of the overall income concept is articulated and the situation is clarified, and until society understands the income concept more completely, we may expect even more conflict and confusion. This unpleasant forecast is based on the study of past social changes, changes to which some societies adjusted so slowly that there were disastrous results. Let us hope that this prediction will call attention to the need for an explanation of the modern nature of the income concept.

The nature of these emerging concepts of business income is the subject of this present text. Here is presented a theoretical framework upon which details will have to be nailed and plastered to complete the structure. The presentation is made with the conviction that change is certain, that the old theoretical structure of income determination is inadequate for the modern world, and that guidelines for the new income concepts are much needed at the present time. This conviction is based on the fact that business values have changed in the last 20 or 30 years. More important, people's capacity to use the income concept to advance the smooth operations of our society has increased phenomenally in that period of time. Add to these developments the advances in measurement methods, and a reasonable basis emerges for the thesis which we have stated as a conviction.

It is not contended that the details to be fastened to this framework are permanent, but rather that old details will constantly be replaced by new. There is need, however, for a basic structure of a general income concept to indicate the type of detail needed at different times for different income concepts. The makeup of human wants is a variable in the social process, not a constant, and this is of immense importance to accounting theory and practice in general, and to income determination in particular. Only if we understand possible changes in human wants and needs in terms of a meaningful theoretical structure will we be able to adjust to the constantly changing environment in which the accounting profession operates.

In a reorientation of the conventional way of viewing income, we have constructed an operational framework of accounting income determination theory to comply with the demands for new income measurements.

Here we review the constitutive concepts of income in the light of modern needs, find them lacking, and distinguish them from the operational concepts of income by relating the latter to the operations of business.

This material is intended for students and researchers interested·in accounting theory. Depending on the level of study, it may be used to acquaint advanced undergraduate students with problem areas of income determination. For graduate students, it may be used as a basic text, supplemented by the appended bibliography, for a course or seminar on income determination. But the basic objective of the book is to provide a framework useful to practicing accountants, educators, businessmen, and regulatory agencies in developing the accounting discipline.

It is impossible to enumerate all those who have contributed to this study. Particular acknowledgment is due Professors Nicholas Dopuch of the University of Chicago and George Mead of Michigan State University. Their contributions have substantially influenced the structure of the entire book. In addition, graduate students, practicing accountants, and professors from several other universities have criticized, commended, and adjusted many drafts of the manuscript during the three-year period in which it was being written. Among those who contributed directly to the material in the book to such an extent that acknowledgment is appropriate are Professor Charles Weber of the University of Zurich, Switzerland, and Professor William J. Vatter of the University of California at Berkeley. Special thanks are due to Mrs. Dixie Schmisseur, who devoted many hours to typing and developing diagrams.

Urbana, Illinois   N.M.B.
July 1965

Contents

4   The Measurement of Income

5   An Operational Concept of Income

6   Measurement of Overall Operational Income

Chapter 1

Accounting Theory; Concepts Underlying Income Determination

1.1 THE ACCOUNTING DISCIPLINE

Accounting is a discipline with both a methodological and a substantive body of knowledge. Its methodology consists of technological means for measuring and communicating data. Included in this part of the discipline are the double-entry mechanism, reporting forms, certain types of charts and graphs, and an assortment of other measurement and communication techniques. Historically, this part of accounting owes its efficacy to an impressive list of mathematicians (George Boole, Arthur Cayley, Augustus DeMorgan, Robert Hamilton, Charles Hutton, Simon Stevin) [1] who were among the early contributors to the development of the discipline. Currently, mathematicians, statisticians, and logicians (Rudolph Carnap, C. West Churchman, George Dantzig, R. A. Fisher, Claude Shannon, John von Neumann) [1] may again be contributing to the further development of the methodology of accounting.

The substance of the accounting discipline, until a few years ago, consisted of financial data and to some extent other economic data. Recently the scope of the substance of accounting has expanded. Contributions to the theoretical substance of accounting, like contributions to its methodology, have come from those outside of accounting (Alex Bavelas, Kenneth E. Boulding, John Dewey, John M. Keynes, Paul Lazarsfeld, Herbert Simon), while developments in the substance of accounting practice have come from governmental agencies, corporate managements, society in general, and practicing accountants (in the form of certification of the accuracy of noneconomic data, the development of nonfinancial information on administrative performance, market research activities, management services, and national income accounting).

Accounting is neither methodology nor substance separately, for the scope of the accounting methodology is contained by the substance of the discipline and the substance of the field is limited by the methodology. It is possible to study either substance or methodology separately, but the development of accounting requires the balanced advance of both aspects.

1.2 SOURCES OF ACCOUNTING KNOWLEDGE

In both its methodological and its substantive content, the body of accounting knowledge is derived from two sources: the practical and the theoretical. In efforts to solve day-to-day problems, practitioners applying the discipline to business affairs develop new measurement techniques and enter new areas of activity. Thus they contribute data on specific accounting actions designed to meet specific needs.

Theoretical studies advance accounting by attempting to understand, adjust, and expand accounting actions. Theorists study developments in other disciplines (mathematics, psychology, sociology, economics, political science, statistics, logic), develop hypotheses for research from observations of current practice, and conduct research within the accounting discipline itself. It is thus impossible to say which source—theory or practice—is the more important.

As a discipline, accounting is an organized body of thought. "Organized" means that the various elements are arranged in such a manner as to reveal a general picture, map, or model of the whole that is accounting. As yet this organized body of knowledge is not well developed. Both the substance and the methodology are in a state of flux as they adjust to changing environmental conditions, although a general structure of the discipline does exist [2]. It might be thought of as the framework for the house of accounting now under construction. Some of the features of the structure (or thought organization) of the mass of techniques, procedures, assumptions, and objectives called accounting are described below.

1.2.1 The inductive nature of accounting knowledge

The discipline has an inductive characteristic in that its development was motivated by the need to meet the practical problems of commerce. As a result, theory was developed by generalizing the variety of practices followed by practitioners. This inductive process of going from specific procedures to generalized statements of theory, though it has contributed significantly to the development of the discipline, rests on the assumption that there exists in nature a body of knowledge that is accounting, and that the problem is to discover this knowledge. Discovery and organization of knowledge is the accepted objective of this process of theory formation. But the inductive approach has not been conducive to the creation of new accounting knowledge. Rather it has led merely to description, at the theory level, of past accounting practice. As a result, theory developed by the discovery process has not led to changes needed in the body of accounting knowledge if it is to adjust to a changing environment.

There is merit to the assumption that a given set of accounting principles does in fact exist, and that the discovery of these principles consists of selecting and combining those relations which underlie accounting practice. In the early stage of development of the discipline, this process of organizing accounting thought was most effective. It did provide a number of generalized statements of accounting theory. But as the discipline has developed, the concepts readily recognized by the induction process have proved inadequate to describe the contemporary body of accounting knowledge. Additional concepts are needed. Thus the formulation of new concepts is probably more important now to the accounting discipline than the inductive discovery of the principles.

1.2.2 Bases of accounting principles

Since the validity or accuracy of the underlying "facts" or evidence supporting the generalized statements of accounting principles is not of uniform quality, the discipline does not have a strong supporting information base. Accounting, unlike the physical sciences, does not yet rest on scientifically proved facts. In their eagerness to provide the overall framework or model of accounting thought, theorists have relied on evidence and facts which have varying degrees of reliability. As now constituted, the partially developed theory which is the framework of accounting thought is based on information having the following levels of validity:

(a) *Intuitions*, which are mere guesses or feelings as to what facts are. An example might be the feeling of some authorities that long-term leases are not assets. Because "an asset" has not been precisely and objectively defined, the only indication of whether or not leases are assets may be the opinion of certain authorities that intuitively they feel one way or the other. Until more dependable information is available, intuitively derived ideas will continue to be used in accounting thought, though different intuitions often cause conflicting theories.

(b) *Assumptions*, which are based on suppositions or general beliefs as yet unproved. The assumption that income is the sole objective of business operations is possibly the best illustration of this type of information. While there may be no valid data to prove this assumption, it is so widely assumed to be true that it is treated as basic information on which accounting theory may be based.

(c) *Evidence*, which represents information based on proved knowledge. Evidence is normally developed by a systematic empirical collection of facts marshaled to support and validate a statement.

1.2.3 The need for a consistent theory

The organized discipline does not present a uniform consistent pattern of thought throughout its theory. In fact, theoretical expressions that are contradictory and inconsistent are more typical of accounting theory than supporting and consistent utterances. Varying conditions, interests, and beliefs have resulted in a number of variations in the theoretical structure. Most of the variations, other than those due to differences in the underlying evidence, are due to the differing conditions and environment from which each theory was developed.

Since we lack a conceptual base of the same scope as the discipline, and thus lack a basic starting point, a good deal of accounting theory represents reasoned conclusion from selected and restricted evidence. The evidence is therefore suspect; for it may be purposely and consciously selected to induce a preconceived emotional conclusion, or it may be selected intuitively, without investigation, as appropriate for the issue involved. Consequently, inconsistent theoretical conclusions as to what constitutes proper accounting action, although these conclusions are all based on logical reasoning (which is theory), may be found in accounting literature. Littleton calls attention to the situation in the following terms:

> We seldom stop to think of it, but theory, like raw cotton, comes in a variety of grades, each with its own usefulness. Theory's explanation may be an account definition that will help us to know why a certain transaction fact must fall in one category rather than another. Explanation may show why some idea is or was generally accepted. Here explanation involves *justification*. If explanation shows why something should be thus and so, we have *persuasion*. If the verb is "might be" rather than "should be," explanation is *supposition*, a weaker form of theory and the one that commonly comes to mind at sight of the word theory.
>
> All gradations of theory are explanations, but not all explanations are equally good . . . [3]

Despite these limiting characteristics of the structure of accounting thought (the insistence on generalizing practice, the lack of scientifically proved facts as a base, and the tendency for theorists to reason to pre-conceived conclusions), there does exist a general mass of knowledge, ill structured but readily recognizable, and clustered around the concept of income, which is accounting thought.

1.3 THE NEED TO EXPAND THE SCOPE OF ACCOUNTING THEORY

Because the existing framework of accounting theory is not well structured, in that many of the component parts do not tie together well, it does not support nor explain the whole field of accounting. Thus we need a further development of the concepts on which the structure rests, mainly because of the multitude of formulas which, under the existing theoretical frame-work, are now used to determine income. In addition, many activities which are termed accounting processes (national income accounting, certain aspects of cost accounting, operations research analyses) are not explained by present accounting theory. In order to unify all account-ing under one theoretical structure, we shall ultimately need either new concepts or better articulation of existing ones. The immediate need is for concepts which will more closely link all the aspects of accounting. One part of this immediate need, the part dealing with income determina-tion, is what directly concerns us now.

It is not easy to develop new concepts, and it is impossible, as every scientist knows, to make rules to govern a creative process such as devel-oping concepts. Nevertheless, practical men have made few discoveries by the trial-and-error process, which should encourage us to broaden our methods of developing accounting concepts, and use every opportunity to advance the process until we achieve a method of reasoning and of logical proof similar to that used in science. (For an analysis of the belief that accounting can be studied scientifically, see [4].)

Establishing accounting concepts as a basis for the logical development of accounting theory is, practically speaking, most difficult. The inductive process—surveying what is done in practice—cannot help us now, for the new concepts needed in accounting theory are hard to envision. They must be created or formulated. Formulating new concepts is harder than merely discovering existing ones, because formulating concepts requires us to look in new ways at the world in which accounting operates or might operate. And it is most difficult to observe new actuality in the world and conjecture an improved view of civilization, because the scope of our imagination is dependent on our environment and on our necessarily limited experience. It is also difficult to communicate new concepts to others, because no one sees things except in terms of his own experiences. Hence we need a way to prove our new concepts, a method of proof which is more rigorous than that used to prove concepts arrived at inductively. While proof of formulated concepts may consist of confirming, by means of an appropriate investigation, that the concept does exist, this proof is merely the result of a search for confirming evidence and, at best, only supports the concept without proving it. Consequently, we need a better method of proving the validity of accounting concepts.

Those who discuss accounting theory are like the blind man who touched the side of an elephant and said the elephant was like a wall, then later touched its trunk and said the elephant was like a snake, and so forth. Similarly, although we used to be able to describe accounting as we observed it, we now realize that our observational capacities, like those of the blind man, are limited, and that we must examine the subject from as varied approaches as possible, so that we shall form new concepts instead of discovering existing ones.

However, it is easier to get people to accept a discovered concept than a new, unique one, since the discovered concept is intuitively observable from customary ways of viewing accounting, whereas the new one can be grasped only by looking at accounting from a different point of view. Therefore, if accounting theory is to develop further, we need new methods to prove the existence of the new concepts.

There are, of course, favorable aspects to this creative and formulative approach to theory development. For one thing, this approach overcomes the limitations we encounter when we derive concepts by the descriptive-inductive process (generalized statements regarding the nature of accounting practice), a method which necessarily limits accounting research to the scope of accounting practice. The formulation approach does not confine accounting research to such limits, since it may expand the scope of accounting research beyond the limits of what is done in practice, revealing new areas into which practice might or should expand (national income accounting, management advisory services). This possible extension of the boundaries of the field of accounting is not a justification for nor an objective of the concept-formulation approach. But neither should such an extension be a barrier to the scientific development of a theoretical structure of the accounting discipline. There is no reason why the search for concepts to explain the accounting discipline could not be extended into such areas as:

(a) The nature of human and organization behavior and motives (psychology and sociology)
(b) The determination of what human behavior should be (ethics)
(c) Measurement methods useful in disclosing activities of all types
(d) Communication methods
(e) Logical systems

(For an interesting discussion of basic areas into which accounting research could be conducted, see [5].)

A second advantage of the formulation approach is that the principles and rules of a theory developed from formulated concepts are likely to be based on deduction, partly because of efforts to relate accounting to scientific discoveries in other fields by rules of logic and systematic reasoning. But concepts formulated intuitively and subsequently proved by empirical investigation are equally valid, for the principles and rules are then derived from the concepts rather than from practice. Such principles and rules, if the basic formulated concepts are valid, are predictive in that they tell what should be done. Inductively derived principles, on the other hand, necessarily describe actual practice, and tend to support existing practice, even though conditions may have changed so that such practice is no longer optimum.

1.4 THE NATURE OF CONCEPTS

Theory exists when concepts exist. Recently, the idea has been advanced that a concept is merely an explanation of a "set of operations" and has validity only in the environment in which it exists. While a concept may have a constitutive or describable meaning, we can grasp its precise meaning only by referring to the set of operations it describes. For example, the concept of something being hot has meaning only in relative terms. "A hot fire" carries a different connotation from "a hot day." Coffee which is hot to one person may be merely warm to another. To describe the concept of "hot" operationally, we would have to describe the conditions and operations existing for each situation. Without a description of the set of operations surrounding it, a concept lacks precise meaning.

Henry Margenau points out that concepts should have two definitions: an operational one and a formal one. He states,

> "... it is necessary ... that every accepted scientific measurable quantity have at least two definitions, one formal and one instrumental. It is an interesting task to show how some sciences fail to become exact because they ignore this dual character of the definitory process. Omission of operational definitions leads to sterile speculation ... ; disregard of formal (or 'constitutive') definitions leads to that blind empiricism ..." [6]

The concept of income is an excellent illustration of the ambiguity which arises when a concept is defined in a constitutive sense only. There are many constitutive concepts of income, and there are shades of meaning to each constitutive definition. Therefore the concept of income may have precise meaning only if we can observe how income is created, measured, and used. After these operations have been clearly described, we can formulate a constitutive definition if we wish, but it will apply only when a similar set of income operations exists.

For accounting, the operational definition of the nature of concepts seems to be desirable because it implies that:

(1) Old concepts will be dropped when they cannot be described operationally. This will eliminate a number of nebulous notions.

(2) Concepts will be unambiguously defined and misunderstandings will be reduced. [By way of clarification, it should be noted that the term "operational definition" has been used incorrectly in certain accounting literature at various times. These ambiguous pseudo-operational definitions should not be confused with precise operational definitions.]

(3) Concepts will not be used in areas where they are not applicable.

If we hold to the operational definition of the nature of a concept, the "set of operations" which most adequately describes the process by which income is generated will be the income concept which accounting purports to measure and communicate. That is, income is the result of a set of operations, and it will have different meanings under different sets of operations. For example, income from the operation of a store is different from income from holding of property for price increases, even though both may be the same net dollar amount. Only if we described the set of operations in terms broad enough to cover both the buying and selling activities and the holding activities could we consider both types of gain income. This, of course, is now done, and it results in an imprecise notion of income. When we use a loose, general set of operations to describe a situation, we have a loose, general concept of income.

Thus the operational point of view encourages us to develop precise concepts of income appropriate for different purposes, and to recognize the limitations of a loose, general concept of income. The operational approach also suggests that the nature of the income concept will change both as the environment in which it operates changes and as the process for generating income changes. Conceivably it would be possible to construct a series of theoretical models of the nature of income determination, each model applicable to a different set of operations used to generate income. In reporting income, it would be necessary, of course, to set forth the set of operations from which income was computed.

The operational point of view does not imply that a single-valued overall concept of income cannot exist, nor does it imply that accounting income is just a member of a family of incomes which can be determined independent of each other. The fact is that there is a need for one overall general concept of income in our society. The formulation of the set of operations to be used in developing such a general concept of income is by far the most difficult aspect of such a process of theory formation. How do we know we have accurately observed the proper set of operations? Apparently the answer depends on the philosophical question of how one knows anything. In general, the sources of knowledge, including accounting knowledge, are:

(a) *Faith,* which represents a belief based on a faith supported or unsupported by evidence that the belief is true.
(b) *Authority,* which represents a belief because an authority has stated the belief as a fact.
(c) *Sense perception,* which represents a belief because the five senses have revealed existence by taste, smell, touch, sight, and sound.
(d) *Intuition,* which represents a "feeling" that a thing is so. This has at times been referred to as the sixth sense.
(e) *Scientific proof,* which represents facts that have withstood the test of scientific verification.

It would be highly desirable if the conceptual observations of the income-generation process were supported by scientifically proved fact. Unfortunately, this proof is not available and the concept of income generation proposed in this study rests on evidence no stronger than the commonsense perception of accountants. The concept is also based on a considerable number of experiments aimed at developing an appropriate set of operations to describe an income concept for general use.

REFERENCES

1. THOMAS H. WILLIAMS, *An Investigation of the Mathematical Dimension of Accountancy* (Ph.D. dissertation, University of Illinois, 1961)

2. A. C. LITTLETON, *Structure of Accounting Theory* (Columbus: American Accounting Association, 1953)

3. A. C. LITTLETON, *Structure of Accounting Theory,* pages 132–133

4. R. J. CHAMBERS, "Conditions of Research in Accounting," *Journal of Accountancy,* **90** (December 1960), pages 33–39

5. CARL T. DEVINE, "Research Methodology and Accounting Theory Formation," *Accounting Review,* **XXXV** (July 1960), pages 387–399

6. *The Validation of Scientific Theories,* P. G. Frank, editor (New York: Collier's Books, 1961), page 46

Chapter 2

The Role of Income in Society

The role of income in economic society has never been clearly set forth. Although its impact is undoubtedly felt in many places, there is no comprehensive treatise on where and how the concept influences the operation and development of society. (Attempts at such a treatise have been made: The *Five Monographs on Business Income* by the Study Group on Business Income is an example. These attempts, however, have concentrated on the uses of an income concept and not its function.) Such a study is sorely needed, for there is much misunderstanding of the uses to which the concept of income could or should be put and how the concept might be applied. The confusion should be dispelled as soon as possible before the ambiguity attached to the concept causes income measurements to lose much of their usefulness in our society. Reservations to the concept now exist, as evidenced by the authoritatively stated and widely accepted view that the income concept is a tool which breaks in one's hands upon close analysis. In fact, it has been suggested that much of the confusion surrounding the proper use of the income concept by society could be eliminated if it were recognized that income is not a single concept at all, but a family of concepts.

2.1 INCOME CONCEPTS

Underlying a great deal of the muddle is the existence of two distinct concepts, both described as income. Just as money may be described as a certain sum of gold or as a generally accepted medium of exchange, the acquisition of income may be described as the motivating force which causes man to engage in economic activity; or income may be said to be a computed amount used to direct and control the operations of society. One concept exists in the inborn or instinctive nature of man. The other is an invented or constructed measurement useful to the operation of society. Thus there is no reason why the two concepts must coincide or even be closely related.

The first and more basic concept of income has been with us as a recognized aspect of human nature for many ages. Buddha in his first sermon at Benares recognized it as the thirst or desire for pleasure, for existence, and for prosperity. Psychologists have spoken of it as a primary acquisitive drive or instinct. But sociologists, noting the extensive range and relevance of the exchange function in society, have tended to view income as a generalized means to gratify a variety of human needs. To sociologists income is a means to an end, while to some psychologists income is a desire to acquire and an end in itself. Sociologists concede, however, that over a period of time means acquire symbolic significance, in that income may become the symbol of achievement and of success, whether or not this income is used to gratify other needs. In this sense it becomes an end in itself. The basic notion of income as a means of exercising power takes on a rather special meaning; for income then refers to the means for gratifying not the economic needs of the possessor but the needs of others. This capability grants to the income-possessor the power to control others. To accountants, the significance of this concept is that income exists whether or not it is measured, for income is wealth and is the means to satisfy the wants, needs, or desires of man.

The second concept appears to have originated in the early Middle Ages, possibly as part of the bookkeeping calculation of profit and loss. It came into being, not as a distinct concept, but as a quantification of the basic concept of an increase in wealth, to meet the needs of men engaged in commerce and trade. The measurement was imperfect, but it was a reasonable approximation of the basic concept, and proved extremely useful to men of business when they had to decide which ventures to undertake. They no longer needed to balance subjectively a host of ill-conceived and unarticulated objectives and desires in making a decision, for all these were submerged into the one general measured amount of income. That is, income was considered a reasonable measure of the means for satisfying a host of man's desires and objectives. While intermediate between man's efforts and man's basic desires and objectives, measured income was recognized as an end in itself, so far as business planning was concerned.

The impact of the concept of measured income on the cultural, moral, and economic development of societies appears to be substantial. Income, as a measurable quantity, provided a clear-cut objective for economic endeavor. From the standpoint of culture, this concept is alleged to have caused people to think more precisely when they began to have to communicate by means of numbers rather than words. Furthermore, the resulting measurement enabled the modern audit concept to come into being, and this development was conducive to an improvement in moral conduct: people had to be honest. As an economic objective, the measurable-income concept crystallized the purpose of economic activity and facilitated the organization of economic effort. This gave business both a precise direction and a means to control its efforts. The basic income concept took on a new aspect: the means for disclosing not only whether income existed, but also how much of it existed, and whether the amount was more or less than that earned by someone else. It became possible to evaluate effort. And a host of situations arose in which the concept of measured income could be used to facilitate the operations of organized society.

As people began to employ the measured-income concept for this purpose, they became interested not only in its nature but in its sources. It became important whether the gain arose from a "capital" transaction or an "operating" transaction, whether it was stolen or earned, whether it was a gift or created, or whether it was made by producing or by investing. Unfortunately, users of the measured-income concept failed to disclose the fact that they were interested in only part of the "generalized means to gratify human needs," and the notion of income was restricted when people began to define income as being only the gain from specified sources. An example in today's context is that certain types of interest revenue from municipal bonds are excluded, for tax purposes, from income. The example is not precisely pertinent, but the point is that different sources of income enabled distinctions to be made among various types of income. The result was that different uses of the measured-income concept culminated in different concepts of measured income.

More recently interest has centered not on the use to which the concept is put but on the use to which income is put, and distinctions as to the use of income (not income concept) have been used to exclude certain "generalized means to gratify human needs" from the measured-income concept. For example, the Federal tax concept of income currently excludes gains made on the sale of a home if the gain is reinvested in another home.

2.2 USE OF INCOME CONCEPTS IN SOCIETY

Making distinctions among income items obtained from different sources or applied to different uses has led to a substantial expansion in the role of income concepts in society, but the distinctions have also caused confusion regarding the meaning of any one kind of measured income. This confusion is at times attributed to the crudeness of the accounting measurement, but society could adjust to the lack of precise measurement if the conceptual distinctions were clarified. In fact, most of the confusion relates to questions of concept rather than measurement.

Since much of the confusion arises from the different uses to which the income concept is put, any endeavor to clarify and correct this state of affairs—and that is the objective of this study—will have to begin by examining these different uses.

Itemizing all the roles of the income concept is probably not possible, but let us review some of the more frequently cited uses. George O. May's classic list of the major uses of financial accounts, given below, suggests certain functions performed by measured income [1]. According to May, a financial account may be used as:

(1) A report of stewardship
(2) A basis for fiscal policy
(3) A device to determine the legality of dividends
(4) A guide to wise dividend action
(5) A basis for the granting of credit
(6) Information for prospective investors in an enterprise
(7) A guide to the value of investments already made
(8) An aid to Government supervision
(9) A basis for price or rate regulation
(10) A basis for taxation

In addition, there is evidence that the role of accounting reports in general has become increasingly important in society, and that they are used in a variety of ways. John L. Carey, reporting on the conclusions of the Long Range Objectives Committee of the American Institute of Certified Public Accountants, has stated [1]:

Financial reports are now required for many purposes: for the information of stockholders and prospective investors; for the information of those considering acquisition or merger; for the information of banks and other credit grantors; to conform with the requirements of government agencies for a wide variety of purposes—loans, grants, insurance, compliance with statutes or regulations; to assure sound management of financial institutions; to determine costs as a basis for pricing under government procurement contracts; to assist in rate-making of regulated utilities and carriers; to determine whether monopolistic practices exist; to determine whether price discrimination exists, and, last but not least, to determine income subject to taxation. In addition, local government units render reports to taxpayers; health and welfare organizations make financial reports to contributors; parties to various types of contracts are required to make financial reports to each other. While generally not the recipients of special reports, labor unions have a deep interest in financial results of business operations. Finally, the public generally, as represented by students of the economy, financial writers, editors, legislators, and government officials, is displaying an increasing interest in the impact of corporate decisions and actions on the whole society, and the desire for more information about the affairs of the larger corporation is gaining momentum.

The Study Group on Business Income was concerned with the need for the income concept in society and Alexander [2] noted six uses of income, as follows:

(1) Income is used as the basis of one of the principal forms of taxation.
(2) Income is used in public reports as a measure of the success of a corporation's operations.
(3) Income is used as a criterion for the determination of the availability of dividends.
(4) Income is used by rate-regulating authorities for investigating whether those rates are fair and reasonable.
(5) Income is used as a guide to trustees charged with distributing income to a life tenant while preserving the principal for a remainderman.
(6) Income is used as a guide to management of an enterprise in the conduct of its affairs.

Economists have also been interested in the income concept; and in a general economic sense, income has been said to perform such functions as the following:

(1) The income objective tends to cause resources to be allocated to their most productive use, provided that competition is free.
(2) Measured past income may be used either by itself or in combination with other factors as a basis for computing the return on investment to evaluate the effectiveness of management, assuming that income is the primary objective of management.
(3) "Real" income may be used to evaluate the growth of a nation and the effectiveness, in an economic sense, of the political system under which the nation operates.

Finally, let us look at philosophy's viewpoint. Although philosophers have treated income in a rather broad manner, we can note certain generalizations and suggest that, in a philosophical sense, income appears to perform the following functions:

(1) It is a means to gratify mankind's physiological requirements (food, clothing, shelter, medicine), and enables man to consider both present and anticipated future needs.

(2) It is a means to satisfy the need for self-expression in the form of pursuit of noneconomic interests (religious, ethical, scientific, and esthetic).

(3) It is a means to satisfy the need for social recognition (power, prestige, and popularity).

For the mass of mankind, it is the first of these philosophically defined functions which is the significant role of income in organized society. The third function becomes significant only to those who have effectively satisfied their need for physical existence and self-expression.

These listings are more illustrative than comprehensive, for so wide are the possible influences of income that the variety of uses to which the concept is applied, is perhaps, beyond the comprehension of both accountants and other observers of society. Certainly one could expand any existing list of the uses of the income concept.

It is readily apparent that the measured-income concepts appropriate to each of the roles of income might differ markedly from one another. This fact should not be interpreted, as some observers are inclined to do, to mean that the several concepts of income are unrelated. It is true that "taxable income" may differ from "business income." These differences however, are related differences, in that the measured amounts differ from one another by identifiable basic income items which are either excluded or included when we measure income for a particular purpose. For those who deplore the development of these modified measured incomes, the future is bleak. For, if we can clarify the income concept, we may expect a greater number of these modified income measurements. This development will take place because the income concept lends itself, under a free-enterprise society, to a variety of uses.

2.3 THE ROLE OF BUSINESS INCOME

Our particular concern is with business income, for in a broad sense business income is the motivating force which directs economic society. That is, all economic activity is undertaken to acquire business income, directly or indirectly, and this compelling function is the main role of income in economic society. We know intuitively that it is realistic to say that the economic activities of an entire nation are directed toward the acquiring, or the spending, of business income. The concept gains strength as we reflect on it, for surely almost all of business is concerned with planning how to make income and controlling activities so that income will be made. This holds true even when the managers of a large company try to increase the price of the company's common stock in the market in order to increase the value of their stock options or to meet possible pressure from stockholders; for income still serves as the motivational force, in that the market price of stock is closely tied to earnings.

The motivational aspects of income extend in many directions. Even the education of much of the youth of the nation is directed, despite the lament of some professors of the liberal arts, toward developing capacities which will provide business income in the future. The Federal Government has noted the motivational aspects of business income and has effectively used the concept to channel economic activity into "preferred" areas. Because the Internal Revenue Department allows accelerated depreciation on facilities used to produce equipment for defense purposes, manufacturers have been motivated to produce such equipment, for higher after-tax business incomes were made possible by the higher depreciation allowances. Alternatively, high taxes have been used to reduce business income opportunities in "undesired" areas of activity, and the economy has responded because of the decreased business income motivation. Sociologists have suggested that the high economic standard of living in the United States may be accounted for by the intensity of the business income motivation. Possibly no other society in history has been so highly motivated to acquire business income as has our own. The fact that this motivation is universally felt by all members of our society is also significant. Yet, despite the considerable evidence supporting the existence of the motivational role of business income, there is no satisfactory explanation of the cause of the phenomenon. Thus there is a need for research to determine why our culture places so high a value on business income or why undeveloped areas are often not highly motivated by it.

In discussing the role of business income in society, a distinction should be made between income as an objective, or thing sought, and income as a result, or thing attained. It is as an objective that income serves as a motivating force, for it is the expectation of income, not its realization, which causes activity. Past income, of course, may offer assurance that future income can be made by repeating past activities, but as a motivating force it is the prospects of future income, however these prospects are determined, which cause activity. This does not mean that past income plays no significant role in our society. On the contrary, both future and past income perform many important functions. The primary role of attained or past business income is to provide a means for evaluating the effectiveness of managers or others seeking income. We might say that effective management was that management which attained the maximum business income in the situation in which it operated.

We might measure this in a number of ways. One way to reveal managerial success, which would disclose the relationship between future and past income, would be to compare income determined "before the fact" with income determined "after the fact." Variation between the two would indicate an inaccurate determination of income "before the fact" (budget, forecasts, profitability studies), ineffective management, or an inaccurate determination of income "after the fact" (income report). The role of business income as a device to appraise the administrative process should not be minimized. Facing uncertainty and risk, as well as seeing to it that workers perform according to plan, are important responsibilities of management. Success or failure in solving these problems is reflected in the amount or rate of income earned. Accordingly, a most significant role of income determination is to disclose overall efficiency or inefficiency of management.

Accountants are interested in the determination of business income both before and after business activity, though their greater interest has been in past income, possibly because of their inability to make reliable determinations of future income. But new techniques of measurement and greater stability in the overall economy as civilization has advanced indicate that predictions of income may be more possible in the future. Computing future income is necessarily based more on estimates than determining past income, but both are acceptable measures of income.

2.4 THE NEED TO EXPAND THE BUSINESS INCOME CONCEPT

All forces motivating and controlling business actions cannot be attributed, of course, to business income. For example, a personnel director or the person in charge of labor negotiations might endeavor to determine how well an objective was performed without concern for the income determination question. Further, it is not possible to group all forces motivating and controlling individual actions under the basic income concept. There are other motivations which impel man to seek to maximize his welfare outside of the motivation of income. Also we must recognize that income is not an accurate index of the extent to which all wants of man are satisfied. Many non-income motives run counter to the income motive. Pigou confirms this observation in substance, though presenting it in economic terms, by stating, ". . . economic welfare will not serve for a *barometer* or *index* of total welfare." [3]

In addition, as we move into the affluent society, it may be that income will prove even less of an index of total want satisfaction. An anthropologist states, "The outstanding discovery of recent historical and anthropological research is that man's economy, as a rule, is submerged in his social relationships. He does not act so as to safeguard his individual interest in the possession of material goods; he acts so as to safeguard his social standing, his social claims, his social assets.   He values material goods only in so far as they serve this end." [4]

These discoveries suggest that accountants, in the not-too-distant future, may seek to broaden the classical concept of business income and adjust it to the expanded nature of contemporary man's wants.   This step may be necessary because business income should always be defined in such a way as to be an effective representation of the forces motivating economic activity.   If business income should ever lose this characteristic of being the strongest motivation, the loss to society in the form of a loss of a universal purpose might loosen the stability of our society as a democratic organization.   Man needs to be tied to his work, sociologists and psychologists contend, and this is particularly true in a democratic society where man more or less decides for himself what he will do.

The business-income objective does tie man to his work and, within limits, the measured amount of this income may and should be changed to meet the needs of democratic society.   For example, failure to include the services provided by government as being part of the business income of an individual may weaken the significance of individual business income as a motivating force in society.   For the business enterprise, failure to exclude certain gains due to inflation from measured business income may misdirect business activity.   Choosing the proper business income to reflect that which best motivates society is a most difficult accounting problem, because the extent to which measured income does describe the forces motivating and controlling activity depends on the way income is defined.   A broad concept of income would include a great number of the motivating forces, while a narrow concept would omit consideration of many of them.

2.5 THE OPERATING ROLE OF THE INCOME CONCEPT

The widely quoted assertion that "once a business gets too big for one brain to handle, accounting takes over the job" may well account for the expansion of the role of the income concept into an "operating" function. But whatever the reason, the fact is that in addition to its institutional roles as the motivator of activity and the evaluator of business success, measured income plays the role of a lubricant, facilitating the functioning of society in an operational sense.   Specifically, measured income is used as a computed amount to accomplish objectives necessary for the operation of society.   That is, the operations of society require more than motivation and evaluation of performance.   There have to be means and techniques which facilitate the performance of what a business or individual does. These means and techniques may be quite crude.   For example, there may exist great motivation to produce the maximum income, and evaluation of performance may reveal that such an objective has been well attained, but this does not reveal *how* the objective was attained. The motivation may have been fear and the effectiveness may have been attained by physical force. As another example, at the social level, to assess taxes only on persons owning property would represent a means of tax collection not related to the income concept. Further illustrations could be set forth to illustrate the ability of society to use means other than income to "operate" society. But as society has developed man has discovered that such techniques as instilling fear, using physical force, and enforcing property assessments are not the best methods to use to make society operate smoothly. Increasingly, the concept of a computed amount of income has been substituted for fear, physical force, and property assessment as a tool or technique of administration. For example, a measured amount of income has been substituted for property as the basis for tax assessments. For other operational needs, measured income is used as a basis for evaluating programs, for controlling "unfair" actions, for paying dividends, and for many other operating actions. For an individual company, measured income may be used as a technique to determine the amount of bonus to be paid to an employee, the stock options of managers, or the rent to be paid under certain types of contracts. For the nation as a whole, it may be used to facilitate decisions on desirable types of social legislation. The operating role which income plays in society may be as significant as the motivational and evaluating roles discussed earlier. Certainly the use of income as a means for tax assessment or as a restriction on dividend payments facilitates the operations of our total society. Further, it seems reasonable to suggest, in view of the current trend, that it is in the operating role that we may expect to see the greatest development of income measurement in the future.

REFERENCES

1. George O. May, *Financial Accounting* (New York: Macmillan, 1943), page 3

2. Sidney S. Alexander, "Income Measurement in a Dynamic Economy," *Five Monographs on Business Income*, report by Study Group on Business Income (New York, 1950), page 6

3. A. C. Pigou, *The Economics of Welfare* (London: Macmillan, 1938), page 12

4. Karl Polanyi, *The Great Transformation* (New York: Farrar and Rinehart, 1944), page 46

Chapter 3

The Nature of Income

3.1 PSYCHIC, REAL, AND MONEY INCOME

Three basic concepts are evident in the literature and discussions on the nature of income:

(1) *Psychic income*, which refers to the satisfaction of human wants.
(2) *Real income*, which refers to increases in economic wealth.
(3) *Money income*, which refers to increases in the monetary valuation of resources.

As a motivating device, psychic income is the basic force directing human activity. (For a breakdown of psychic income, see [1].) It directs activity in that it results from efforts of individuals to satisfy their lackings, which in turn are the causes of human wants. The extent to which the lackings are satisfied represents, basically, the proper measure of the amount of psychic income. But since man is not sensitive to all his lackings, only those lackings which have been recognized and advanced to the stage of a want really bear on human action. In this sense psychic income is an overall measure of the extent to which all wants of an individual have been met and, at this level of analysis, the distinction between economic and noneconomic wants is not significant. It is only when the economic wants of man press so hard on him that they are the effective wants to be satisfied that a measure of "real" income may be assumed representative of the force which motivates activity.

Since psychic income is the basic motivating force, quantitative measurement methods should be developed to measure and communicate information about it. Conceptually, this might be accomplished by the following three sequential activities:

(1) Breaking psychic income down into its component elements such as power, prestige, and economic, social, and psychological wants or needs.
(2) Developing measurement methods, such as scaling, to provide some kind of information on each component element.
(3) Developing means for communicating the resulting measurements to users of such information.

But obtaining information about psychic income is easier said than done, for there exists at present neither an itemized list of the component elements of psychic income nor mathematical methods to measure them satisfactorily. So, with some reluctance, the income measurers in society, except those engaged in research, have turned to the concept of real income as a reasonable objective.

Because so many psychic wants are satisfied by goods and services (economic values), it may be assumed that the individual who acquires control over the use of goods and services acquires control over means to satisfy most of his psychic wants. In this sense the net inflow of goods and services may be said to represent means for the satisfaction of psychic wants. The inflow of these means is defined as the "real" income accruing to an individual. It must always be remembered, however, that if psychic income changes due to a change in the wants of people, the psychic value of the real income may also change. The result of such a change is that the same flow of goods and services may have different psychic values in different periods of time and for different cultures. This is true whether real income is conceived to be economic value or physical goods and services. The point is that economic goods and services represent only one of several needs which man has, and should other values become more important than economic values, changes in real income, whichever way it is defined, would not be representative of changes in psychic income. Stated from the point of view of psychic income, the idea is that a change in psychic wants may change the relative value of real income and economic goals.

More important, the real-income concept ignores variations in the psychic wants of different people. To one person, a real income of an apple may be a means to satisfy a number of his psychic wants, but to another an apple may have very little consumption or other psychic value. Consequently, a measure of real income, if it is to be related to the psychic-income concept, would be an average representation of the extent to which psychic income has been provided.

Money income represents a means of acquiring goods and services. Being even further removed from psychic income than "real" income, it is therefore less of an approximation of the basic income concept which motivates economic activity. In times of rapidly fluctuating prices, when money income may not be a reasonable approximation of "real" income, the gap between "money" income and "psychic" income may be so wide that the assumption that "money" income is the force motivating activity is inaccurate.

Despite the preceding rational conclusions, the objectives of making money income is so ingrained in habitual patterns of thinking that for business purposes, there is merit to the proposition that money income motivates economic activity in society   To the extent that money income also increases psychic income, there is no social reservation to accepting this concept for decision-making purposes. But insofar as the quest for money income directs the economic activity of business in a direction contrary to that which the business activity would follow if psychic income were used as the motivating force, the measurement of money income may be socially undesirable. In fact, we may realistically ask whether or not the accountant, by confining his measurement to a monetary amount, could be motivating economic activity in a socially undesirable direction. Such would be true if the money-income concept varied significantly from the psychic concept.

Depending on the level of study, income may be considered to involve all three concepts of psychic, real, or money gain or loss. [Fisher blends the three concepts in the following manner: "The income of a person reckoned by these three methods will ordinarily be very similar, though in theory, and sometimes in practice, it may differ widely. As long as we understand the various kinds of income, and the relations between them, we are at liberty to consider any one of them as 'income' in its proper place. But we can scarcely understand any one without having had at least some view of both of the others."] [2]

It seems that the basic study of income would involve the study of human wants or even human lackings, which might well lead to research in the areas of psychology, anthropology, sociology, and possibly biology. Admittedly, research on psychic income is important and should be encouraged. Nevertheless, in terms of the present civilization, real income serves as the motivating force of the business part of world society. This suggests a primary need for research and study in economics and business practices, with due concern for developments in the concept of psychic income. Moreover, many people believe that business income should be confined to real income. This belief is supported by an implied, informal social arrangement in which business has responsibility for providing the economic values or goods and services needed by society, whereas the nonbusiness sector of society, such as governments, churches, social clubs, and other associations, has responsibility for other psychic income items. Finally, income may be studied in terms of money; and the study of money income, aside from the fundamental issue of determining its relation to real income and economic motivation, may be an involved problem in itself. Questions as to the proper time for recognizing when money income exists, determining the appropriate content of it, or measuring the amount involved are typical of the areas of study.

So long as we understand the relationship among the three concepts, we can study business income in terms of all three concepts, and avoid the controversy which arises when people try to define business income as being either a special type of real income, an index of psychic income, or identical with money income.

3.2 BUSINESS INCOME

Business income is a measured income, and is a central concept around which a growing number of measured-income concepts rotate. Although it derives its meaning from its capacity to satisfy individual wants, the business income concept can be less inclusive than the income concept of an individual. For example, psychic income, which is basic to an individual, would have no meaning to a business enterprise. But acquiring or producing economic resources to meet the psychic-income needs of individuals would be within the scope of business income activities. In fact, the social justification for the existence of a business entity is that it produces something desired by individuals who collectively represent society, and this is true whether the thing desired is psychic or real. In return for the effort made by the business entity, society rewards and supports its existence by paying for its production. If the entity puts forth a highly desirable product, in the sense that the product provides a means to satisfy a great number of human wants, people will pay a high price for it. But if a business entity puts forth a product which does not provide a means of satisfying individual psychic wants, society eliminates that entity by not buying its product and returning no income to it. Thus business income represents the price paid by consumers for the products of business in excess of the expenses of the business. And, aside from monopoly situations and other special cases, business income reflects the extent to which business has created values which consumers believe will satisfy individual wants.

It is, however, the reward paid by individuals to business entities for their productivity which represents business income; and therefore, it is the reward and not productivity which acts as the motivating force in a free market economy. From the point of view of society as a whole, it is sometimes considered undesirable for business to be motivated by the reward concept of income. That is, business entities exist to satisfy individual psychic wants, and this should be the sole objective of an economic entity. But what form of motivation would cause economic entities to produce solely for the satisfaction of individual psychic wants? Would force and punishment be a desirable motivation? To most, it would not. Could some other reward besides consumer payment be used to motivate economic activity? Possibly, but the nature of such a reward is not clear. Could the altruistic reward of doing something for others serve as the motivating force? Perhaps, but it is doubtful if human nature has evolved to the stage where individuals will truly act according to the precept that "it is better to give than to receive."

Thus, there exists in most business minds the practical view that the reward, in the form of a payment, is the force which motivates business activity. Although society may provide rules and restraints which ensure that the reward payment is made only for production which satisfies consumer psychic wants, and in this way equate the reward payment with the value created, the reward payment is more easily measured and more accurately reflects the motivation of managers.

When the desire for business income motivates economic activity, it is the expectation of the income, rather than the realization of it, which causes the activity. In everyday terms, this means that a company with $10,000 will use the funds on those projects where the company hopes or expects to gain the greatest reward. Assuming everything else equal, if there are two opportunities (X and Y) where the $10,000 could be used, with opportunity X providing an expected return of $12,000 (a $2000 reward) and opportunity Y providing an expected return of $11,000 (a $1000 reward), the company will be motivated to pursue opportunity X. The fact that expectations were wrong and that X realized an income of only $500 while Y, followed by another company, realized a $1500 income has no bearing on the initial decision of the company. Of course, that which is expected in the future depends to a significant degree on past results, which partially explains the interest accountants have in past income. But the motivation of business activity is expected future income. Unfortunately, this notion is not so clear as it sounds, for we are then faced with the question of the type of income which the manager must expect before he is motivated to carry out economic activity. Broadly, there are three related, yet separate, types of business income which a businessman may be motivated to acquire: subjective income, realizable or market income, and realized or transaction income.

3.3 SUBJECTIVE INCOME

The subjective value of an asset or group of assets is the present value of the expected receipts which the resource(s) will yield. More precisely, subjective value is the receipts expected by a person discounted at a rate of interest which that person expects to be the appropriate rate. To different individuals, having different expectations, an asset or group of assets would have different subjective values. The expectations of a business firm are those of the top management or the planning group to whom the valuation task is assigned. Thus the subjective value of the assets of Company A would be the present value of the future receipts expected by the top management of the company discounted at the rate of interest which the top management expects to be appropriate.

Subjective income is the change in subjective value between two dates. It may be computed either *before the fact* or *after the fact*. When computed as a before-the-fact income, it is a measure of the anticipated or expected increase in subjective value over a period of time. When computed as an after-the-fact income, it is a measure of the change in the subjective value of resources between two dates, whether expected or unexpected. In this sense, after-the-fact subjective income is equal to before-the-fact subjective income (expected), plus unexpected gains and losses.

Example

Assume that Company A acquires resources which the management expects on Jan. 1, 1965, will bring in revenue as follows:

YEAR	AMOUNT
1965	$10,000
1966	10,000
1967	10,000

If the management believes it can invest its funds elsewhere at a rate of interest such that it would not buy any resources unless the purchase would yield a rate of return of 6% a year (the target rate of interest required for this three-year period), the maximum price which the management would pay for the resources would be the present value of the future receipts discounted at 6%, computed in Table 3–1 on the following page.

The $26,730.11 is the management's subjective value of the resources and, since management will not pay more for the resources than they are worth, it is also the maximum price the management will pay.

It is possible to compute also on Jan. 1, 1965, the expected value of these resources one year later on Jan. 1, 1966, as in Table 3–2. Since the change in the subjective value is the change expected on January 1, 1965,

TABLE 3–1

Year	Expected receipts at end of year	Present value on Jan. 1, 1965
1965	$10,000	$10,000/1.06 $\quad$ = $ 9,433.96
1966	10,000	$10,000/(1.06)^2$ = $\quad$ 8,899.96
1967	10,000	$10,000/(1.06)^3$ = $\quad$ 8,396.19

Present value of estimated receipts
on Jan. 1, 1965, estimated on 1/1/65 $\qquad$ $26,730.11

TABLE 3–2

PRESENT VALUE OF RESOURCES ON
JAN. 1, 1966, AS ESTIMATED ON JAN. 1, 1965

Year	Receipts at end of year	Present value, Jan. 1, 1966
1965	$10,000	$10,000.00 (on hand on 1/1/66)
1966	10,000	9,433.96 ($10,000/1.06)
1967	10,000	8,899.96 [$10,000/(1.06)^2$]

Present value of estimated receipts
on Jan. 1, 1966, estimated on 1/1/65 $\quad$ $28,333.92

the expected subjective income for 1965 would be:

Expected subjective value on Jan. 1, 1966	$28,333.92
Expected subjective value on Jan. 1, 1965	26,730.11
Expected subjective income for 1965	$ 1,603.81

The expected subjective income for 1965 may also be computed by taking 6% (the expected rate of asset growth) of the subjective value on Jan. 1, 1965 ($26,730.11 × 0.06) to yield a before-the-fact subjective income of $1603.81.

The computation of past subjective income requires another estimation of the present value of the anticipated receipts on Jan. 1, 1966. At that time management will be better informed than it was on Jan. 1, 1965, and can make a better estimate of receipts. The revised estimate made on Jan. 1, 1966, of receipts and their present value are presented in Table 3–3.

TABLE 3–3

Year	Jan. 1, 1966, expected receipts at end of year	Present value of expected receipts on Jan. 1, 1966
1965	$10,000	$10,000.00 (on hand)
1966	8,000	7,547.17 (8000/1.06)
1967	9,000	8,009.96 [9000/(1.06)^2]

Present value of estimated receipts on Jan. 1, 1966, estimated on 1/1/66 $25,557.13

The after-the-fact subjective income would be measured in the following manner.

Subjective value estimated on Jan. 1, 1966	$25,557.13
Subjective value estimated on Jan. 1, 1965	26,730.11
Subjective income (a loss) for 1965	($ 1,172.98)

Since the difference between after-the-fact and before-the-fact subjective income is unexpected subjective income, the after-the-fact subjective income may be analyzed as follows:

Expected subjective income	$ 1,603.81
Unexpected subjective income (loss)	(2,776.79)
Past (after-the-fact) subjective income (loss)	($ 1,172.98)

The unexpected subjective income may be computed by comparing subjective value on Jan. 1, 1966, with what subjective value was expected to be when it was estimated on Jan. 1, 1965:

Subjective value, Jan. 1, 1966, as expected 1/1/65	$28,333.92
Subjective value, Jan. 1, 1966, as expected 1/1/66	25,557.13
Unexpected change in 1/1/66 subjective value	($ 2,776.79)

3.3.1 Limitations to subjective income

Although subjective income is the basic nature of business income in the sense that it represents what businessmen will strive to maximize, measuring the concept is so difficult that it is questionable whether an effective measure could be developed. The measurement difficulty lies in management's inability to separate its realistic true estimation of future receipts from its emotional opinion regarding future receipts. By an appropriate selection of interest rates for discounting purposes and by inaccurate estimates of future receipts, management could cause subjective income to be almost any amount. Despite this limitation, however, if a management wishes to know how efficient it is in projecting future economic events and its own operations, the subjective income concept, even crudely measured, could provide useful information.

3.4 REALIZABLE INCOME

Realizable income, like subjective income, is the change in value of individual resources between two dates. Normally, it is measured in terms of changes in the sales market price. Realizable income indicates the income which *could be realized* by selling resources which have increased in market value. It remains realizable, therefore, until the sale takes place and realization occurs.

While realizable income may be computed before-the-fact by deducting present sales value from estimated future sales value, it is normally computed after-the-fact in order to evaluate objectively the overall effectiveness of management. Before-the-fact realizable income is, of course, expected, while after-the-fact realizable income includes both expected and unexpected items.

3.4.1 Relationship of realizable to subjective income

Subjective value is a personal evaluation, and different managements will have different subjective values for the same resource. The interplay of these subjective values in the marketplace results in *market value*. In a somewhat vague sense, market value is an average of these subjective values of a particular resource or resources.

Example

Assume that on Jan. 1, 1965, the market price of the resources which Company A subjectively values at \$26,730.11 (present value of \$10,000 a year for three consecutive years discounted at 6%) was \$24,160.87. This sales price would be the result of bargaining among buyers and sellers of the resources. But it would also be related to the discounting process because of its dependence on subjective values. In effect, it is the result of discounting the "average" expected future receipts at the "average" required rate of return. Thus the \$24,160.87 of market value could be related to subjective value as in Table 3–4. The relationship of the two before-the-fact incomes is that subjective income is equal to expected realizable income plus any expected increase in the difference

TABLE 3–4

COMPARISON OF MARKET VALUE WITH SUBJECTIVE VALUE

Year	Discount rate (average and subjective)	Expected receipts at end of year		Present value, Jan. 1, 1965	
		Average	Subjective	Average	Subjective
1965	6%	$10,000	$10,000	$ 9,433.96 $\left[\dfrac{10,000}{1.06}\right]$	$ 9,433.96 $\left[\dfrac{10,000}{1.06}\right]$
1966	6%	9,000	10,000	8,009.96 $\left[\dfrac{9.000}{(1.06)^2}\right]$	8,899.96 $\left[\dfrac{10,000}{(1.06)^2}\right]$
1967	6%	8,000	10,000	6,716.95 $\left[\dfrac{8,000}{(1.06)^3}\right]$	8,396.19 $\left[\dfrac{10,000}{(1.06)^3}\right]$

	Average	Subjective
Present value (1/1/1965)	$24,160.87	$26,730.11
Based on this information, the present value expected for 1/1/1966 would be	25,610.52	28,333.92
From these comparative estimates, expected realizable income would be	$ 1,449.65	
And expected subjective income would be		$ 1,603.81

between market value and subjective value, as illustrated below:

Excess of subjective value over market value on 1/1/1965 ($26,730.11 — $24,160.87)	$2,569.24
Expected excess of subjective value over market value on 1/1/1966 ($28,333.92 — $25,610.52)	2,723.40
Expected increase in excess of subjective value over market value	$ 154.16
Plus expected realizable income	1,449.65
Equals expected subjective income	$1,603.81

Up to this point, there is no evidence to indicate whether or not Company A's subjective estimate of income is more accurate than that anticipated by the market. If A is correct, subsequent events will result in the realization of the $10,000 of annual receipts in cash and market value will adjust to it. On the other hand, if market expectations prove to be correct and A's estimates are inaccurate, the inability to convert subjective value into market value will indicate an unexpected decline in subjective income. To illustrate this relationship between the two income concepts, assume that actual receipts were $10,000 in 1965; $10,000 in 1966; and $8,000 in 1967. Since expectations of both Company A and the market were identical for 1965, and since expectations were realized, the after-the-fact 1965 income would coincide with before-the-fact 1965 income. Assuming those expectations existing on Jan. 1, 1965, were still held on Jan. 1, 1966, the before-the-fact 1966 incomes could be computed as follows:

	SUBJECTIVE	MARKET
Expected value 1/1/1967	$29,433.96*	$26,547.17*
Value, 1/1/1966	28,333.92	25,610.52
Expected income, 1966	1,100.04*	936.65*

If actual results in 1966 corresponded with the subjective value of Company A, after-the-fact income would be computed as follows:

	SUBJECTIVE	MARKET
Value, 1/1/1967, 1965 receipts	$10,000.00	$10,000.00
1966 receipts	10,000.00	10,000.00
1967 P.V. of future receipts	9,433.96	7,547.17
Total value, 1/1/1967	$29,433.96	$27,547.17
Value, 1/1/1966	28,333.92	25,610.52
After-the-fact income, 1966	$ 1,100.04	$ 1,936.65

The relationship of the two after-the-fact incomes is that subjective income is equal to realizable income less unexpected realizable income, plus any expected increase (decrease) in the difference between market value and subjective value, as illustrated.

Expected change in the amount by which subjective value exceeds market value:

(1) Excess of subjective value over market value on
1/1/1966 ($28,333.92 − $25,610.52) $ 2,723.40
(2) Expected excess of subjective value over market value
on 1/1/1967 ($29,433.96 − $26,547.17)   2,886.79

      Expected increase in excess of subjective value over
      market value $ 163.39

Plus after-the-fact realizable income $1,936.65
Less unexpected realizable income   1,000.00   936.65
Equals after-the-fact subjective income $ 1,100.04

---

* This assumes that realized receipts are held and not used to produce further receipts. This assumption of nonproductivity of receipts is a simplification for illustrative purposes only.

Alternatively, if the market correctly anticipates future receipts, as is the situation in 1967, after-the-fact subjective income must also be adjusted to reconcile subjective and realizable incomes, as shown below.

Before-the-fact income	SUBJECTIVE	MARKET
Expected value, 1/1/1968	$30,000.00	$28,000.00
Value, 1/1/1967	29,433.96	27,547.17
Expected income, 1967	$ 566.04	$ 452.83
After-the-fact income		
Value, 1/1/1967	$28,000.00	$28,000.00
Value, 1/1/1967	29,433.96	27,547.17
Expected and unexpected income	$(1,433.96)	$ 452.83

The relationship of the two after-the-fact incomes may be revealed in the following manner:

After-the-fact subjective income		$(1,433.96)
Plus decrease in excess of subjective value over market value during 1967:		
Excess on 1/1/67 ($29,433.96 − $27,547.17)	$1,886.79	
Excess on 1/1/68 ($28,000 − $28,000)	0	1,886.79
After-the-fact realizable income		$ 452.83

Over the life of the resources, after-the-fact subjective and realizable income, although differing each year, may be equated as shown below:

	INCOME	
YEAR	Subjective	Realizable
1965	$1,603.81	$1,449.65
1966	1,100.04	1,936.65
1967	(1,433.96)	452.83
Excess of subjective value over market value on 1/1/1965 ($26,730.11 − $24,160.87)	2,569.24	
Total	$3,839.13	$3,839.13

3.5 REALIZED INCOME

Realized income does not come into existence until a sale has been made or some other objective recognition point has been reached. The fact that goods and services could be sold does not, according to this concept of income, represent income. From this it follows that realized income will normally lag behind realizable income since the sales date normally follows the salable date. Like other concepts of income, realized income may be computed before or after operations.

3.5.1   Relationship of realized to realizable income

Realized income differs from *realizable* income in that realized income is computed by valuing unsold resources at cost, whereas, in computing realizable income, these same resources would be valued at the sales-market value.

The distinction between the two concepts in after-the-fact measurement may be illustrated by assuming that resources acquired in bulk for $24,160.87 and used over a three-year period were sold for $10,000, $10,000, and $8,000 in each of the three years, respectively. Realized income may be computed and compared with realizable income as in Table 3–5.

TABLE 3–5

Year	Acquisition cost	Expense*	Realized revenue	Realized income	Realizable income
1965	$24,160.87	$ 8,628.88	$10,000	$1,371.12	$1,449.65
1966	24,160.87	8,628.88	10,000	1,371.12	1,936.65
1967	24,160.87	6,903.11	8,000	1,096,89	452.83
Total	$24,160.87	$24,160.87	$28,000	$3,839.13	$3,839.13

* Expense was computed by allocating acquisition cost to expense in proportion to realized revenue. Any appropriate allocation could be used.

3.5.2   Limitation to subjective, realizable, and realized income

Subjective, realizable, and realized income are distinct concepts, but in themselves they include no explanation as to their source. All three kinds of income, for example, could result from activities such as holding assets to make a gain over time, or using assets to make a gain by a variety of operations. Also, price level changes could explain part of each type of income, if income were measured in terms of an unadjusted monetary unit. And it may be just as important to know the cause, source, or origin of the income as to know its nature. While there are no inherent benefits in a multitudinous subclassification of income concepts, nevertheless there is no reason not to provide subclassifications of income, either by source or other characteristic, if the results provide data which will facilitate the operations of society. That is to say, it may be possible to overcome the limitations of the three broad types of business income by breaking them down into a variety of component parts. And since these component parts may be classified according to different characteristics, it would be possible to formulate a multitude of classified income concepts from any one of the three broad business income concepts.

In general, most classified concepts of income are formulated from one of the following two sets of classification characteristics:

(1) *Use characteristics:* Classified income concepts are formulated by considering the use to be made of the measured income.
(2) *Source characteristics:* Classified income concepts are formulated by considering the source of the measured income.

These satellite concepts of income differ from each other and from the basic concept of business income either in terms of items included or excluded from the measured-income concept, or in terms of the manner in which the items of income are grouped or classified for disclosure purposes. For example, an income of $10,000 might be classified or described as being composed of different concepts, as follows:

	CLASSIFIED AS TO USE	CLASSIFIED AS TO SOURCE
Income available for dividends	$ 8,000	
Income for other uses	2,000	
Income from holding assets		$ 4,000
Income from using assets		6,000
Total realized income	$10,000	$10,000

3.6 USE CLASSIFICATION OF MEASURED INCOME CONCEPTS

In accordance with the dictate of usefulness, which has the support of a great deal of business thinking, business income has been classified as follows:

(1) *Current income,* which influences business decisions on activities to be undertaken in the near future.
(2) *Long-range income,* which influences business decisions on activities to be undertaken which will have a long-run influence on the type of work which the firm will perform.
(3) *All-inclusive income,* which has a bearing on survival and expansion opportunities of the firm.

These three concepts may best be explained by an illustration in terms of realized income. Assume that a firm, having on hand at the start of a year $80,000 of noncash assets, acquires $100,000 of assets from other companies during the year, pays $30,000 for other current cost factors (rent, wages, etc.), makes sales of $150,000 during the year and ends the year with $70,000 of noncash assets. From this information, an all-inclusive income report could be prepared, as follows:

INCOME REPORT

Sales		$150,000
Resources on hand at start of year	$ 80,000	
Resources purchased from other companies	100,000	
Resources available	$180,000	
Resources on hand at end of year	70,000	
Resources used during the year	$110,000	
Current operating expenses	30,000	
Total expenses		140,000
All-inclusive realized income		$ 10,000

Assume, however, that an examination of the $110,000 of resources used during the year reveals one item of $20,000 which measures obsolescence of an old machine due to an unexpected new invention. This discovery was completely fortuitous. Clearly this "expense" had nothing to do with current operations. Further, because of its nonrecurrent nature, there is no reason to think that a similar situation will take place in the future, nor is it safe to assume that unexpected events result in gains as often as they result in losses. It is evident, therefore, that the $20,000 loss would not influence long-term decisions, unless we could predict its recurrence with some degree of assurance.

Assume additionally that further examination of the $110,000 of resources used during the year reveals that $40,000 of them would have been lost due to expected depreciation and general deterioration with the passage of time. These expected and anticipated expenses, even though involuntary, would not be considered in a company's decision whether or not to produce in the current year. They do not bear on the management's decision-making process as regards current operations, though they would be considered in such long-term decisions as replacing the building. In deciding on activity in the current period, management would consider only the otherwise avoidable expenses to be purposely used up to produce the sales, for only they would be sacrificed by making sales in the current period. From this additional information, an income report could be prepared to cover all three types of business income. An example of such a report is shown in Table 3–6.

TABLE 3–6

INCOME REPORT

Sales			$150,000
Resources on hand at start of year		$ 80,000	
Resources purchased from other companies		100,000	
Resources available during year		$180,000	
Less expected but unavoidable costs	$40,000		
Less unexpected losses	20,000	60,000	
Resources which would be on hand if not used		$120,000	
Resources on hand at end of year		70,000	
Resources purposefully used to produce sales		$ 50,000	
Current operating expenses		30,000	80,000
Current income			$ 70,000
Supplementary expected but unavoidable expenses			40,000
Long-range income			$ 30,000
Unexpected extraordinary loss			20,000
All-inclusive realized income			$ 10,000

If expressed in terms of realizable rather than realized business income, these concepts are similar to certain economic concepts of income. Current income may be identified with Keynes' concept of *producers' income*, which he contends ". . . is the concept relevant to decisions concerning current production . . ." [3]   Long-range income is similar to Keynes' concept of *consumers' income*, and to Alexander's definition when he states, "A year's income is, fundamentally, the amount of wealth that a person, real or corporate, can dispose of over the course of the year and remain as well off at the end of the year as at the beginning." [4] The all-inclusive income includes windfall gains and losses which are often charged directly to capital. Keynes, for example, indicates that although the windfall loss (or gain) enters into a business man's decisions when he is considering income available for spending, it does not enter into them on the same scale as long-term operating income. (For further study of the nature of income, see [5].)

An examination of the nature of classified measurements of business income, in the light of these use concepts, raises questions as to which expenses are expected and which not, which are involuntary and which voluntary, and why expectations enter into the measurement of business income at all. Let us, therefore, digress for a few pages, reexamine the notion of subjective income from a slightly different point of view, and endeavor to clarify these questions.

3.7 ROLE OF EXPECTATIONS IN MEASURED INCOME CONCEPTS

In the light of the preceding discussion, it is evident that resources are purchased by a business entity for the *expected receipts* they will yield. Since these receipts are unknown at the time of purchase, it is clear that the price a businessman will pay for resources depends on his expectations of the receipts from the resources. As noted previously, under similar conditions of risk and uncertainty a businessman would clearly pay a higher price for an asset which would bring in $12,000 of receipts in one year than for one which would bring in $11,000 in the same period of time. And it is his own subjective expectations as to the amount of receipts from specific resources which determine the maximum price he will pay.

The *time factor* also influences the maximum price a businessman will pay for the expected receipts from resources. Normally, the sooner the receipts are to be realized, the higher the maximum price the businessman will pay. This is due to the fact that money not tied up in resources is productive. To illustrate, if a businessman ties up $10,000 in resources which will provide $12,000 of receipts five years from now, he has lost the interest or income which the money would have otherwise produced in the five-year period. Another investment which would bring in $11,500 of receipts in one year might be more attractive because of the shorter time factor.

Finally, the *risk factor* must be considered in determining the maximum price to be paid for resources. If, as is the normal situation, the businessman is not certain that his expectation of future receipts will be realized, he will want to cover, as an additional cost, the insurance needed to compensate for the risk. Insurance may be either self-insurance or formal insurance with an outside insurance company. Normally, this uncertainty type of risk is covered by self-insurance, and we shall so treat it here. [If the insurance is provided by an outside company, the present worth of the cost of the insurance premium should be deducted from the otherwise maximum price to be paid to determine the ceiling price which the businessman should pay for the resources.]

Both the time factor and the risk factor involved in determining the maximum price a businessman should pay may be accounted for by the discounting process. That is, the expected future receipts may be adjusted back to the present by eliminating both the time and risk factors. To illustrate, assume that the productivity of money in a riskless investment is 4% per year (the approximate rate on Federal government bonds). This rate could be used to discount the future $12,000 of receipts to $9,863.12 [$12,000 discounted at 4% annually for five years, computed by dividing $12,000 by $(1.04)^5$]. As a result, if the resources that will bring in $12,000 in five years should cost more than $9,863.12, the businessman would be better off purchasing Federal bonds.

The risk factor may also be reduced to an annual rate by having the businessman estimate the chances of realizing the $12,000. (For an explanation of this technique, see [6].) Assume that, on the basis of his past experience, study, and intuition, the businessman expects that once in every $16\frac{2}{3}$ years the opportunity for the $12,000 of receipts will be lost. Thus the annual insurance charge to cover the possible loss due to risk is approximately 6%. That is, if this possible loss were to be avoided, it would be necessary to deposit with an insurance company slightly more than the 6% approximation of the value of the future receipts, to cover administrative expenses and provide a return to the insurance company, to ensure against the possible loss. Under self-insurance, the equivalent of these annual insurance premiums could be deducted from the otherwise anticipated $12,000 to determine expected receipts. More conveniently, however, the otherwise anticipated receipts of $12,000 could be discounted at an annual rate of 6% to cover the risk element. Assuming that the businessman decides that his expectation of risk is 6% per year, and adding the 4% to cover the time factor, the $12,000 would be discounted at 9.76% [0.06 + 0.04 − 0.06(0.04)], which rounded to 10% a year yields a maximum price of $7,451.05 [$12,000 ÷ $(1.10)^5$] for the resources which will bring in the expected $12,000 of receipts in five years.

The $7,451.05 is the subjective value on one specific date which the businessman, on the basis of his expectation of future receipts and discount rates, assigns to the future receipts. It was pointed out earlier that at another date he may have other expectations which would give another maximum price to be paid for the resources. To compute the windfall gain or loss type of business income in terms of subjective value, it would be necessary only to measure the change in the maximum prices which should be paid for resources at different dates. (For a more complete discussion of the nature of subjective value, see [7].) Since maximum price would be the result of expectations, a different maximum price could exist only if expectations were to change; and if expectations were to change, it would mean that an unexpected development had taken place since the first expectations were used to determine maximum price.

Example

To illustrate the measurement of windfall gains or losses in terms of subjective value, and to reiterate in slightly different terms the previous discussion on subjective income, assume that the subjective valuation of $7,451.05 was computed on the basis of expectations existing on March 15. Assume that the same businessman is asked on March 31 to give (a) his expectations of receipts which he now believes would have resulted from acquisition of the resources on March 15 and (b) what he now thinks was the correct expected risk factor. Let us assume that, after he discounts these expectations back to what would have been the subjective value of the resources on March 15 if he had felt then as he does on March 31, a subjective value of $8,421.62 results. The subjective windfall gain would be computed as follows:

Subjective value on March 15, computed on the basis of expectations prevailing on March 31	$8,421.62
Subjective value on March 15, computed on the basis of expectations prevailing on March 15	7,451.05
Subjective value of unexpected change in expectations between March 15 and March 31 (windfall gain)	$ 970.57

The concept of *windfall gain* differs from the previously discussed concept of unexpected subjective income, in that it is computed in terms of the unexpected change in the subjective value of the resources at the *beginning* of the period (March 15), whereas previously unexpected subjective income was computed in terms of the unexpected change in the subjective value of the resources at the *end* of the period (March 31). Unexpected subjective income would have been computed, according to the earlier description, as follows:

	SUBJECTIVE VALUE, MARCH 15	EXPECTED INCREASE, MARCH 15–31	SUBJECTIVE VALUE, MARCH 31
Estimated March 15	$7,451.05	$ 31.04(10%)	$7,482.09
Estimated March 31	8,421.62	35.09(10%)	8,456.71
Windfall gain	$ 970.57		
Unexpected interest gain		$ 4.05	
Unexpected subjective income			$ 974.62

The issue involved is whether or not the $4.05 is unexpected. Since the expected discount rate of 10% per year has not changed, it may be contended that the $4.05 was not unexpected.

This process of computing the extraordinary gains and losses for the income report might be used by an individual businessman to determine his ability to predict future events, and might help him improve his prediction process. In fact, this computation, if it could be made, would disclose ability in one important area of management responsibility: predicting future results.

A related characteristic of this type of managerial talent is a businessman's ability to determine where the gap is greatest between the market value of a resource and his own subjective value of it. By this process the businessman can make a further income, if income is measured in terms of increases in subjective value.

To illustrate with a highly oversimplified example of capital budgeting analysis, a businessman having cash with both a subjective value and a market value of $8,000 could increase the subjective value of his property if he could buy, at a market value of $5,000, resources having a subjective value of $7,451.05. His income could be computed as follows:

Subjective value after resource acquisition		
Cash ($8,000 — $5,000)	$3,000.00	
Subjective value of resources	7,451.05	$10,451.05
Subjective value before resource acquisition		
Cash		8,000.00
Subjective income (income due to ability to use		
resources effectively)		$ 2,451.05

Since subjective income differs from realizable income, windfall gains or losses are different under each concept. Subjective windfall gain is related to objective windfall gain in the same sense that subjective value is related to market value. And, to review an earlier discussion in more detail, the relationship of subjective value to market value is similar to the relationship of one specific man's income to that of the average income of all men in the area.

Example

Three men, A, B, and C, each own resource X, and together with three other men, D, E, and F, they are all the businessmen in the community. Let us assume that each man computes his subjective value of resource X by discounting the future receipts he expects the resource to bring in at a rate he believes appropriate, with the following results:

BUSINESSMAN	SUBJECTIVE VALUE	BUSINESSMAN	SUBJECTIVE VALUE
A	$2,000	D	$4,000
B	3,000	E	2,500
C	2,500	F	1,500

Since A, B, and C each own resource X, A would sell if the market value were above his subjective value of $2,000, while B would require more than $3,000 before he would sell, and C would not sell for anything less than $2,501. D, E, and F would buy resource X if the market price were to be below $4,000, $2,500 and $1,500, respectively. The outcome of the bargaining which results as each seeks to make the most advantageous exchange (assuming that each has perfect knowledge of the situation) is a common market price of approximately $2,500, and A will probably sell to either B or D.

Thus market price is the result of the expectations of all businessmen in the market. It eliminates extreme views on the value of resources and is more nearly accurate, on the average, than subjective values.

Market value changes, of course, as expectations of businessmen change. In the sense that the market value of a resource at one particular time is the result of expectations prevailing at that time, a change in market value could only be an unexpected development in the average value. [This would not include those changes in market value due to the shortening of the time future receipts are discounted. Such change in market value would be expected and would be part of operating income.] Conceptually, *objective windfall gain or loss* may be defined as unexpected changes in the sales value of resources, regardless of the cause of the unexpected change: a fire, a new invention, or any factor which causes expectations on the average, to change unexpectedly. A businessman might criticize this conception of the nature of windfall gains and losses as not accurately reflecting his own personal subjective windfall gains and losses. The farsighted businessman, whose own expectations accurately precede expectations reflected in market-value changes, may contend that waiting for changes in market values results in an undesirable delay in recognizing windfall gains and losses. But this conception has the advantage of being objectively determinable. For cases in which the gap between subjective windfall gains and losses and their estimate by the market is substantial, it may be appropriate to prepare both subjective and objective reports for any business manager who can use them.

The measurement of realizable windfall gains and losses is actually more difficult than the measurement of subjective windfall gains. That is, realizable gains and losses must be computed by comparing sales prices at two dates, and there is no way of knowing precisely the extent to which any change in sales price was expected on the average. This same measurement issue arises when recognized windfall gains and losses, which differ from realizable windfall gains in the same manner that realizable income differs from realized income, are computed. Because of the difficulty in distinguishing the expected from the unexpected, realized windfall gains and losses are typically counted as "extraordinary gains and losses," which allows expected elements to be included as part of the gain or loss. As measurement methods improve, it may become possible to break extraordinary gains and losses down into expected and unexpected items. For the present, the distinction between expected and unexpected realized income may best be examined from the vantage point of current and long-range operations income.

3.8 OPERATIONS INCOME AND EXPECTATIONS

The role of expectations in the set of classified or measured income concepts (current income, long-range income, and all-inclusive income) is twofold. A consideration of expectations is necessary to distinguish operating income from windfall gain; and, as the following analysis will show, it is necessary in order to distinguish between two operating income concepts.

Resources on hand must be used if they are to generate the expected receipts which give them value. But, as we have been reminded many times, it is in the nature of things that all resources are on an irreversible journey to the junk heap due to the wear and tear of the elements. If we add to this changing wants, new discoveries, and inventions, it becomes evident that many resources will lose value merely because of the passage of time. These losses differ from true windfall losses in that they are expected. The services in these resources may be used and, in fact, normally are used in producing sales; but their signal characteristic is that they will disappear in a given period of time whether or not they are used to produce sales. In the long run, of course, sales price must be high enough to cover these expected losses, or the company will go out of business.

As previously noted, the distinction between the expected (even though involuntary) gains and losses and the unexpected windfall gains and losses is difficult to measure in an objective manner. In the sense of what is possible, everything is expected to some degree. A large earthquake might or might not be expected by the business community. In general, the distinction between the expected and unexpected may be determined only by an examination of those losses against which businessmen normally insure themselves. Normally insurable losses, whether or not formally insured with an outside insurance company, would be classified as expected loss, while losses so unforeseen as not to be insurable would be windfall losses. The tendency, however, to make no distinction between windfall and expected losses and to treat both as operating expenses may not provide meaningful income concepts to users of income reports.

To clarify the distinction between expected and unexpected losses, let us examine in more detail the nature of expected losses. Conceptually, the expected but involuntary losses of a period of time may be broken down into the following two categories:

(1) Expected losses of values which were used to produce sales
(2) Expected losses of values which were not used to produce sales

The relationship of the second category of expenses to the first may be used as a general measure to reveal the excess capacity cost of the period. If we think of full capacity as the full use of resources on hand, there would be no case where expected losses would not be used to produce sales, for all resources would be fully used. Idle or excess capacity would exist when all resources were not used to produce sales, and the resulting loss of values, expected in the form of depreciation and fixed overhead, would reflect the unused capacity. The relationship of the unused to the used expected fixed expenses (losses) would measure excess capacity above necessary capacity.

For example, assume that a company anticipates fixed expenses of $180,000 during 1969, but traces only $120,000 of these to production or distribution effort. The $60,000 or unused expected losses, when expressed as a percentage of used expected losses, would reveal excess capacity of 50% ($60,000/$120,000). Income measured before deducting both windfall items and unused expected losses would reflect the efficiency with which used resources provided income to the company, and could be used as an index of current operating efficiency.

In addition to the involuntary but expected expenses, which are used to produce revenue, a business manager must voluntarily incur a number of expenses to produce the sales of a period. Such costs as commissions and similar items which are used to produce sales illustrate this type of expense. Current income, which results when only these necessary, voluntary, and expected expenses are deducted from sales, is a measure of the wisdom of operating in the current period. When both the used and the unused involuntary but expected losses are deducted from current income, the resulting long-range income is a general indication of the success of the long-run operations of the business.

The distinction between involuntary and voluntary expected expenses is at times difficult to make. For example, raw material on hand which would perish if not used to produce a finished product for sale might be treated as an expected but involuntary expense. However, if the raw material has a current sales price, so that the material can be sold if it is not used to produce the regular sales of the company, the current sales price is a measure of the short-run voluntary and expected expenses of the period.

Since current income and long-range income motivate different types of business decisions, let us consider both. For example, it is obviously the expectation of a long-run future income that motivates an economic entity to specialize in the production of a particular product or service. Thus a particular entity elects to manufacture and sell shoes on an indefinite basis because of an expectation that this activity will realize an income in the long run. On the other hand, it may be observed that economic activity will be undertaken in the short run, and direct costing will reveal why, even when it is expected that results in the short run will result in a loss in the long-run sense. This is true when the current income reduces the amount of the long-run loss which would otherwise be realized.

It would be possible to define measured business income for a specific set of decisions as the excess of expected payment to be received over expected future cost to be incurred, and treat the result as the force which motivates these specific decisions. This could represent a concept of business income which would be valid for both long-run and short-term decisions on specific future activities. But in order to evaluate the effectiveness of all managerial activities over a period of time, it is necessary to adopt a concept of business income which may be used to hold management responsible for all decisions made during this time period. This is the function performed by long-range income.

Example

A company spends $25,000 on equipment to manufacture a particular type of shoe. Later the management decides that this was a bad decision, and decides to use the equipment to make another type of shoe for which only 50% of the equipment will be used. That is, it needs only $12,500 of equipment to produce the new shoe. Assuming that there are no other expenses and that the equipment has no resale value, should the sale of the new kind of shoes for $15,000 yield an income of $2,500 or a loss of $10,000?

In terms of the specific shoes, clearly only $12,500 of effort was applied to produce the $15,000 of revenue and the short-run income is indeed $2,500. But in terms of the effectiveness of management, $25,000 was applied to produce some type of revenue. Thus it may be concluded that management was ineffective to the amount of a long-range loss of $10,000. Of course, if the management would have lost the entire $25,000 investment had they not produced the new shoes, it may be contended that management lost $25,000 on one decision and made $15,000 on the next decision (to make the new type of shoe). The issue may be stated in question form, as follows: Is measured business income to be considered the result of past decisions which are realized in one period of time, or is income to be the result of decisions made in that period of time? The question can never be answered except by specifying purpose. Each concept reveals different things, and both reflect the effectiveness of different management decisions. Both concepts should be available to evaluate all management's actions.

The notion that income cannot be used to measure managerial effectiveness because any one managerial group necessarily inherits resources from former managerial groups is a measurement problem. Effort should be made to measure and disclose separately income or loss caused by a predecessor group.

Because it is possible to break down all three of the basic concepts of business income (subjective, realizable, and realized) into the three uses (current, long-range, and survival), nine classified concepts of income exist, as shown in Table 3–7. Now, if one allows certain items within any one of these nine to be excluded in computing income, a host of somewhat arbitrary concepts of income would be formulated. When this is done, however, one should disclose the variation from any one of the nine use-classified income concepts. This suggestion is, of course, valid only if the use-classification system is to be used in identifying income concepts.

TABLE 3–7

INCOME CONCEPTS

Nature of business income	Income classified as to use		
	Current decisions	Long-range decisions	Survival decisions
Subjective income	Concept No. 1	Concept No. 2	Concept No. 3
Realizable income	Concept No. 4	Concept No. 5	Concept No. 6
Realized income	Concept No. 7	Concept No. 8	Concept No. 9

3.9 SOURCE CLASSIFICATION OF MEASURED INCOME CONCEPTS

The preceding study of classified business income reveals that no one concept is appropriate for all purposes. The question now is whether or not the accounting discipline should be expanded, both in bookkeeping procedures and accounting reports, to reveal more than one concept of measured income. It is possible, of course, to develop an almost unlimited number of measured-income concepts which could be presented to users of income data. The idea of classifying income concepts according to the use to which the income is to be put is but one income-classification scheme. To illustrate further the process of developing measured-income concepts, assume that income concepts are to be classified according to the nature of the *source* of the income. There is another three-way classification of the amounts included in the three concepts of business income, which may be stated as follows.

(1) *Operating income*, which is the gain resulting from the matching of operating revenues with the current replacement cost of the resources used to produce the revenue. This concept reveals the operating efficiency of management in combining resources into goods or services for society. Operating income measures the value added or value destroyed by the company in combining resources into a product worth more than the separate resources used to make and sell it. It would measure the net addition by the company to the wealth of society. Society as a whole is better off by the amount of income so created. Operating income differs from current income, with which it is sometimes confused and sometimes combined, in that it covers both current and long-range operating activities. It reveals income derived from the so-called "normal" economic operations of a business.

(2) *Investment income*, which is the gain resulting from holding resources. Investment income includes rents, interest, and appreciation in the value of all assets over time. For resources held and then used to produce operating income, investment gain would be measured by deducting acquisition costs from current replacement cost of the used resources. Only the realized portion of this type of income would be included if realized income were reported.

(3) *Venture income*, which is the gain arising from innovation and from speculative endeavors. More often than not the gains and losses from this type of undertaking cannot be predicted with any degree of confidence. It may be composed of both operating and holding elements, but is essentially an income or loss from new and untried activities. Included in it is a high risk element, for innovations are often unsuccessful. A study by the National Industrial Conference Board in 1964 found that over 30% of the new products launched by 87 corporations in a five-year period (1958–1963) failed and were withdrawn.

These three classified-income concepts developed from the set of sources of business income may be stated in terms of realized, unrealized, or subjective gains and losses, which would define nine income concepts. In addition, there are price-level changes, aside from appreciation in values, due to changes in the purchasing power of money. Leaving subjective income out of consideration, since most of the interest in source classifications of income seem to be directed to realized and realizable income, each of the remaining six concepts may be stated in "real" (adjusted for changes in the value of money) or "money" terms, bringing to twelve the number of classified-income concepts which could exist.

TABLE 3-8

COMPONENTS OF SELECTED INCOME CONCEPTS*

Income concepts	Operating income				Investment income				Venture income			
	Realized		Unrealized		Realized		Unrealized		Realized		Unrealized	
	Real	Money	Real	Money	Real	Money	Real	Money	Real	Money	Real	Money
Realized income		X				X				X		
Taxable income		X				X						
Managerial income		X		X		X		X		X		X
Economic income	X		X				X				?	
Social income	X		X								X	
Stockholder income	?X	?X			?X	?X			?X	?X		

* These components are submitted as being in some way related to the needs of modern society. Other lists could be developed. For example, Alfred Marshall [8] suggested three component elements of profits: (a) net interest, which is the reward for waiting, (b) reward for risk bearing, which depends on the degree of uncertainty surrounding a business, and (c) earnings of management, which rise in proportion to the troublesomeness of managing a business.

Each of the twelve concepts could be measured in a number of ways. For example, the amount of realized income would be different each time the point for recognizing realized income is changed. Similarly, the measurement of realizable income depends on a decision as to when realizable income exists. To some people, realizable income comes into existence as soon as plans are made, which ties realizable income closely to subjective income. To accountants, however, income does not arrive at the stage of being realizable income until market price recognizes the gain. If different measures of the same income concept were included in any compilation of measured-income concepts, the list of classified measured-income concepts which could be developed, and the possible extent of the variations in amounts, would lengthen to the point of being disturbing.

Furthermore, analysis of the income concept proper allows an almost unlimited list of the components of source classifications of income. For example, the element of income which arises from good bargaining conceivably might be separated, as might the gain due to favorable contracts, or the gain due to superior knowledge of the market, or the gain attributable to a favorable location, and so on indefinitely. A few of the more significant possibilities which might be derived from the list of twelve possible elements of an income concept are suggested in Table 3–8 on page 46.

In addition to the limitation that each of these income concepts may not be precisely appropriate for specific purposes and thus suffer, though to a lesser degree, from the criticism now directed at the one general concept of income, there is the possibility that multiple income reports may be more confusing than helpful. An income report may be used for a purpose for which it was not intended, because of unfamiliarity with the variety of income reports available. The solution is to expand the income report and include a number of measured income concepts in one report.

Conclusions

Income is a complex concept, but it plays a significant role in the effective operation of our society. Seemingly, the more complex society becomes, the more complex the income concept becomes, although it is in the measured-income concepts rather than the basic concepts that most issues arise. It may well be that the determination of measured business-income concepts should be preceded by a study of measurement methods. Before undertaking such a task, however, it is beneficial to review schematically the interrelationships among the constitutive concepts set forth in this chapter. We have done so in Diagram 1, which is to be found on the following page.

Diagram 1 | THE NATURE OF INCOME

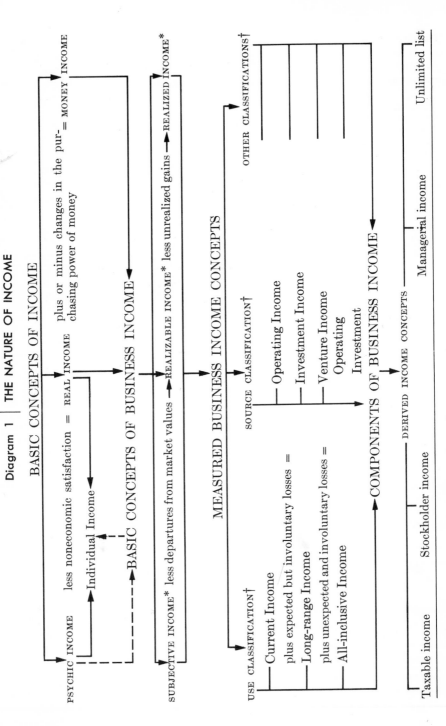

BASIC CONCEPTS OF INCOME

MEASURED BUSINESS INCOME CONCEPTS

* Each of these could be expressed in psychic, real, or money terms.
† Each of these could be expressed in terms of psychic, real, money, subjective, realizable, or realized concepts.

REFERENCES

1. ABRAHAM H. MASLOW, *Motivation and Personality* (New York: Harper, 1954), Chapter 5

2. IRVING FISHER, *The Nature of Capital and Income* (London: Macmillan, 1906), pages 177–8

3. JOHN M. KEYNES, *General Theory of Employment, Interest, and Money* (New York: Harcourt Brace, 1936), pages 52–61

4. SIDNEY S. ALEXANDER, "Income Measurement in a Dynamic Economy," in *Five Monographs on Business Income*, by the Study Group on Business Income (New York: American Institute of CPA's, 1950), page 1

5. PALLE HANSEN, *The Accounting Concept of Profit* (Amsterdam: North-Holland Publishing Co., 1962)

6. ROBERT SCHLAIFER, *Introduction to Statistics for Business Decisions* (New York: McGraw-Hill, 1961), pages 3–48

7. EDGAR O. EDWARDS and PHILLIP W. BELL, *The Theory of Business Income* (Berkeley: University of California Press, 1961), Chapter 4

8. ALFRED MARSHALL, *Principles of Economics*, 8th edition (New York: Macmillan, 1948), Book VI, Chapter 6, page 588

The Measurement of Income

4.1 INTRODUCTION

The constitutive nature of income was described in the preceding chapter, and it is normally assumed that the measurement of income should be distinguished from the concept of income. The determination of income, in accounting, however, is assumed to include both the concept and its measurement. Nevertheless, the commonsense notion that we ought to know what we are trying to measure before we attempt to do so suggests that, in any discussion of constitutive income, the two issues should be treated separately.

In Chapter 3, after we discussed the underlying concepts, we specified some general characteristics of income. The following attributes illustrate additional properties which may be considered in developing measured concepts of income.

(1) Income is composed of gains and losses due to:
    (a) Holding resources
    (b) Advantageous buying, due to market imperfection
    (c) Effective bargaining
    (d) Producing a product or service to satisfy an existing demand for the product or service
    (e) Changing wants of individuals through advertising which increases the demand for the product

(f) Fortuitous and unexpected external events which change the demand for the product or the supply of the resources used to produce it

(g) Price-level changes

(2) Income results from the performance of such business activities as:

  (a) Acquiring services from others

  (b) Recombining the services into a new form

  (c) Disposition of services acquired and created

For those desiring to study income characteristics, Walter Froehlich [1] has formulated a rather comprehensive list of characteristics of an income concept and proposed that a number of distinctions in income concepts could be developed from it.

The characteristics given in Chapter 3 were considered in terms of the uses of the income measurement and the source of the income. On the basis of these characteristics, we further identified the general nature of business income, which we had previously described as the objective which motivates business activity, as a general concept covering a variety of measured-income concepts. We also noted that the various measured-income concepts differ from one another by the way they are classified and by the components of income included in or excluded from the measurement. From this it follows that if business income is to exist as a single-valued measurement of constitutive income, the many distinct income measurements will have to be welded together in some way in order to reflect a single overall concept. (For an analysis of the inadequacy of the notion that a single distinct concept of constitutive business income exists apart from the various satellite income concepts, see [2].)

4.2 METHODS OF MEASURING BUSINESS INCOME

If the concept of constitutive business income is to represent the central core of the galaxy of measured-income concepts now used in economic society, it will have to be drawn from all the properties or characteristics of all the measured-income concepts. That is, it will have to be drawn from a collectively exhaustive and mutually exclusive list of all properties of income. In a statistical sense, this is a problem of measurement. More specifically, the problem of drawing together a mass of measured-income concepts into one representative concept is analogous to drawing together a mass of numbers into one representative average number.

There appear to be two methods by which the overall concept of constitutive business income may be formulated to meet the requirement of being representative of all satellite concepts. First, business income could be an *arithmetic average* of the measured amounts of the satellite incomes. In this sense business income would have no precise constitutive meaning, but it would represent a point in a solar system around which the planets might orbit. However, this arithmetic average business income would be difficult to determine, for the problem would remain of determining the relative weights to be assigned to each concept of measured income included in the average. The advantage of this method is that it lends itself to statistical analysis. In an actual measurement of this concept, it would be possible to compute and report not only the "average" income but also the range of the incomes from which it derives, as well as the probability and extent that any one income measurement would deviate from this average.

The second method for developing a constitutive concept of business income consists of selecting *one concept which is "best"* for society and simply defining it as business income. This approach is, of course, the one now followed in most of the attempts to enunciate the concept of business income. It has resulted in extended discussions, similar to the discussions in Chapter 3, on the nature of income. But the method suffers by reason of the fact that no one *knows* what is best for society. The indefinite constitutive makeup of the concept has thus resulted in controversy over the elements constituting income (current operating income versus all-inclusive income) and over the proper unit by which to measure income (adjusted versus unadjusted monetary unit). There is, however, an underlying general constitutive concept which seems to hold the controversy over the nature of the "best" concept of income within certain bounds. It is the notion of value as a "generalized means to satisfy individual wants." Value is, of course, a commonsense concept which lacks precise meaning and which we cannot measure directly, but it does serve an effective function in limiting the discussion of the best constitutive concept of business income.

Neither of the two possible methods of formulating a measurable constitutive concept of business income is particularly satisfactory. It might even be impossible to develop a single constitutive concept of business income, except by conventional agreement on a concept which is then authoritatively enforced. But for purposes of further analysis, let us assume that an overall constitutive concept of business income exists, or can be formulated, and let us then turn to the problems involved in measuring such a concept.

4.3 THE NATURE OF MEASUREMENT

As a means for examining, in the most basic sense, the problem of business income measurement, let us first discuss the nature of measurement. The role of measurement in society is a significant one. Walter Eucken [3] observes, "Historians have shown . . . how the constant refinement of economic calculation altered the character of business management, which, in turn, influenced economic development. The knowledge of double-entry bookkeeping was a precondition for the south German expansion of the beginning of the sixteenth century. Where this knowledge was lacking or slow to penetrate, as in the Hansa towns, economic development was delayed. It would seem that the conclusion must be that, as the methods of economic calculation improved, a complete transformation occurred in men's attitude to economic life."

There are many definitions of measurement. Possibly the most representative is that of Bertrand Russell [4], who said: "Measurement of magnitudes is, in its most general sense, any method by which a unique and reciprocal correspondence is established between all or some of the magnitude of a kind and all or some of the numbers, integral, rational, or real as the case may be." [By magnitude, Russell means the amount of a property or an object.]

There are at least three levels at which measurement may be discussed:

(1) *The counting level*, or the process of assigning a measurement to something, such as counting the amount of inventory, which involves comparing the quantity to be measured with the standard measurement language (numbers) and the expression of the quantity in terms of numbers.

(2) *The measuring unit level*, or the process of developing a suitable yardstick or measuring device, such as the selection of the monetary unit rather than the physical unit as the device by which the amount of inventory is to be expressed. This involves consideration of the use to be made of the measurement, the acceptability of the measuring unit to the user of the measurement, and the extent to which the unit lends itself to disclosing useful information.

(3) *The measurement process level*, or the process of developing different kinds of measurements, which involves consideration of the characteristics of numbers themselves and of their use.

4.4 KINDS OF MEASUREMENT PROCESSES

Measurement in the social sciences employs a much broader point of view than measurement in the physical sciences. To social scientists any process which either distinguishes one thing from another (classification and symbolization of items), or merely indicates that one thing is greater than or less than another, or indicates how much greater or less one item is than another represents a type of measurement. This is significant to accounting research, for it may be that accounting will have to assume responsibility for reporting new types of data in the future. If so, this may mean that these types of measurements will have to be used if income is to be measured in a meaningful constitutive sense. But these new measurement techniques are still in the process of development. Consequently, it is not yet possible to indicate how they may be used to measure any type of constitutive income, even though preliminary developments are somewhat encouraging. In any event, the new types of measurement should be part of the kit of tools of the accounting researcher.

For the present and near future, however, measurement in accounting is restricted to the assignment of numbers to a property. Unfortunately, accounting measurements fail to indicate the kind of information the numbers represent. This is significant, since there are at least two different meanings which could be attributed to any number measurement.

First, there is the fundamental kind of measurement which is a means by which *numbers are assigned to the property being measured.* The numbers are assumed to be a symbolic reflection of the constitutive amount of the thing measured. [There are a number of reasons why the symbols (the set of real numbers) used in accounting measurements represent a good measurement language. They are *ordered*, have the same *distance* between each successive number, and start with a desirable *origin* (zero). Also this language is widely used and understood by a great number of people.] Measuring the physical units of inventory on hand is a kind of fundamental measurement. This type of measurement, which tells how many of a certain type of thing exist, is the laymen's conception of a measurement.

The second kind of measurement is an indirect one. It has been described as *measurement by fiat,* because we measure some variable other than the basic thing for which a measurement is wanted. Measurement by fiat is based on the assumption that the variable measured is related to the basic concept. For example, we may count the number of times the wheels of an automobile turn as a means of measuring distance. This kind of measurement is best used when it is impossible to measure the basic concept directly. Whereas the fundamental measurement has both constitutive and operational meaning, in that we know both what we measured and how we measured it, measurement by fiat has only operational meaning. It could have constitutive meaning only as an index of the amount of the basic concept; but because this would be valid only if the assumed relationship between the variable measured and the basic concept were proved, we think of measurement by fiat as having only operational meaning. This does not mean that there is something wrong or logically incorrect about the procedure. It has been used extensively in both practical and theoretical areas. In fact, where measurement by fiat produces desirable results, it really does not matter whether it has a constitutive meaning.

Most students of business do not need rigorous proof to convince them that the accounting measurement of income does not and could not measure the constitutive amount of psychic, real, or money income of a business firm. That is, the measurement does not reflect the incoming of dollars of money, real economic goods and services, or psychic satisfaction of a business firm in a period of time. Intuitively it seems obvious that the accounting measurement of overall business income has no one precise constitutive meaning and, unless measurement techniques advance substantially, there is no realistic expectation that such constitutive measurements will ever be made.

On the other hand, it is by using the fiat kind of measurement that it becomes possible to develop a measured single-valued concept of business income. The development of such an operational measurement of business income will be the subject of the remaining chapters of this book. Acceptance of this objective on the part of accountants will mean then that the accounting measurement of income will not have to be an accurate reflection of any of the constitutive elements of income discussed in Chapter 3. This measurement may be assumed to be a reasonable approximation of any one of the constitutive concepts, although this assumption should be tested before it is accepted. But even if the operational measurement is a reasonable approximation of some type of constitutive income, this measure of business income does not solve all the measurement problems. The question of a measuring unit and the problem of effective counting still remain, and these must be considered before drawing the conclusion that constitutive income may be approximately measured.

4.5 THE MEASUREMENT UNIT

In one sense we can contend that constitutive business income is not a homogeneous concept. Such would be the case, for example, if income were measured in terms of physical units of resources, for then income would have to be defined in terms of the increase or decrease in each physical asset of the company. In this precise technical sense, it would be impossible to say that a company had an overall net income unless there were an increase in every one of the physical assets of the company. An increase in two machines and a decrease in one item of inventory could or could not represent an overall net income to the company.

If a suitable measurement unit could be developed, however, it would be possible to provide a measure of overall constitutive income. All that would be necessary would be to measure the common characteristic of all assets. Income would then be the increase in the amount of this common characteristic. The common characteristic which seems to have evolved over several centuries is the notion of "value." Although the value concept has been rejected as a precise meaning of a constitutive overall business-income concept, an operational concept of income, if it is to be an approximation of a constitutive concept of income, apparently has to be an approximation of an increase in value. In any event, for want of a more precise enunciation of the constitutive element which is approximated by the operational measurement of income, let us assume that value is the constitutive element to be measured. This assumption will permit us to examine the problems of the measurement unit and the counting process.

If value is the constitutive element of income, in the same sense that land is the constitutive element of natural resources or that any substantive element is the constitutive element of any phenomenon, the quantification of the amount of the particular element known as value requires the selection of a measuring unit in which to express the quantity of value. Just as the quantity of land may be expressed in terms of acres or square miles, or cloth may be measured in terms of yards or inches, or weight may be stated in terms of pounds or kilograms or stones, value will have to be quantified in terms of a measuring unit. While it has been suggested that value should be measured in terms of "utils," the generally accepted measurement unit is the monetary unit of the country in which the measurement will be used. Thus income may be measured in terms of dollars, pounds, francs, pesos, or rupees. All such measurements, however, are means for quantifying value as the constitutive element of income. In fact, there appears to be no reasonable substitute for the monetary unit as the unit for measuring income as the increase in the constitutive element of value. [Let us avoid confusing value and money as the constitutive element of income when value is measured in terms of the monetary unit. Actually, it is not the inflow or outflow of money which is the substance of accounting income. It is the inflow or outflow of *value*, and this may occur with or without a flow of money, even though the value flow is measured in terms of the monetary unit.]

Selecting the monetary unit as the means for quantifying a constitutive concept of income restricts somewhat the scope of the income concept which may be considered in a study of income determination. This is so because any element of income which cannot be measured in terms of the monetary unit is automatically dropped. For this reason, the accounting discipline should never abandon theoretical discussion of alternative measurement units in determining either constitutive or operational business income. At the applied level, we should try to clarify the nature of the monetary measurement unit that accountants should use, which brings us to the problem of price-level variations and changes in the purchasing power of money. (For a technical discussion of this issue, see [5].)

Conceptually, there are two bases for suggesting that the monetary measuring unit should be adjusted for price-level variations. First, an adjustment may be proposed on the grounds that the monetary unit is not suitable for the measurement of value, but that it can be made so by adjusting the monetary unit. This proposal apparently is founded on a belief that income should be measured in terms other than the monetary unit. It is, of course, true that the value of a product will vary subjectively from person to person even though the monetary valuation remains unchanged, and this suggests that an improved measuring unit is undoubtedly needed. Some type of adjustment would be needed if each person were to be able to adjust the monetary unit to meet his particular subjective values. But it is not clear how the monetary unit could be adjusted to meet such a problem. Since all this is rather nebulous, it seems appropriate to suggest that if the proposal has merit, it needs considerable research and clarification. For this reason, let us discard this proposal.

The second proposal for the adjustment is supported on the grounds that the monetary unit is not a stable measuring unit, but a rubber yardstick which should be adjusted or corrected for variations in the unit when it is used as a measuring device. This view cannot be dismissed. It must be considered whether income is defined operationally or constitutively.

4.6 PRICE-LEVEL VARIATIONS

Prices vary from time to time, from place to place, and from one occupation to another, and these price variations confuse the measurement of business income. An income of $150 which will purchase one machine at one time or one place cannot be compared with another income of $150 which will purchase two identical machines at another time or another place. Any representation that they are comparable is not in accord with the general notion of income. The two $150 amounts are not identical, it is contended, because the measurement unit is not a uniform unit. To correct for this nonuniformity in the measuring unit, it has been suggested that price-level changes over time should be eliminated by an appropriate adjustment.

This same proposal is seldom suggested for price variations in different locations, even though it may be shown that in some instances price variations in different geographic areas vary more than price variations over time. For example, the cost of a machine may vary more between New York and Bogalusa, Louisiana, than it will over a three-year period of time, as illustrated in Table 4–1.

The realization that prices may vary over time less than they vary in different geographic locations, or in the way different occupational groups spend their money, indicates that if there is a conceptual base for adjustment due to price variation over time, it should also exist for adjustments due to price variations for other reasons.

TABLE 4-1

PRICES OF IDENTICAL MACHINES AT DIFFERENT TIMES AND PLACES

	New York	Bogalusa	New York variation
1965	$115	$100	15%
1966	$120	$104	15%
1967	$129	$110	17%
Variation from 1965:			
1966	4%	4%	
1967	12%	10%	

At the practical as contrasted with the theoretical level, we can endorse adjustment for price-level changes over time and not do so for other price variations. This position is supportable if we assume that the monetary unit should be adjusted only for major price variations and that only over time can price variations be material. This is reasonable since, for all other dispersions, arbitrage will prevent any significant price variations. Although this position is defensible, it is also impractical, since no criterion exists to indicate when a price-level change is significant enough to call for an adjustment. Until such a criterion is developed, the most reasonable thing to do is to adjust the measuring unit for all price-level changes over time, even though other price-level variations are inconsistently ignored.

The problem of adjusting for price-level changes involves a number of procedural problems of some magnitude. (For a brief analysis of the basic procedural problems, see [6].) Possibly the most discussed of these is the selection of the "right" index number to be used for the adjustment, and this requires an examination of the nature of a price-level index. A price-level index is computed by comparing prices of identical goods and services between two points of time. The distinction between general and specific indexes depends on the number of products or services used in computing the index. The Consumer's Price Index, for example, may be computed by determining on the average, the extent to which prices have changed for those products on which consumers spend their money. A representative list of about 300 products, covering most consumer expenditures and price changes of these products, weighted according to the relative amount purchased, may be used to compute a general index of price changes. A more specific index of price changes might be computed by considering only products of a certain type. For example, an index of price-level changes for construction materials might be computed by determining the average price change of representative materials, properly weighted, which are used in the construction industry.

A very precise, accurate, and specific index for one product could be computed by expressing the acquisition cost of the product as an index number and the current-replacement cost as another index number. The two index numbers could then be used to adjust acquisition cost to current-replacement cost. This method of determining current-replacement cost is seldom used; but the more specific an index number becomes, the closer it approaches a method for replacing acquisition cost with current-replacement cost. This relationship of index numbers to current costing is seldom discussed, and there have been instances in which specific index-number adjustments have been supported and current-replacement costing rejected, on the grounds that they were in no way related.

Thus price-level adjustments by specific indexes and by general indexes are two separate things; for the former are similar to current-replacement costing, as is evident by the method of their construction, whereas the latter provide an adjustment for changes in the value of the measuring unit. The relationship between the two types of price-level changes may be clarified by means of an analogy whereby specific price changes are likened to the separate waves of the ocean and general price changes are compared with the movement of the tide. The separate price changes are superimposed on general price changes, though both fluctuate up and down. Both types of adjustments may well be needed to adequately measure operational income, as we shall see later. For the present, however, our only conclusion is that an adjustment for changes in the purchasing power of money, as reflected in changes in the general price level, is necessary if we desire a homogeneous measuring unit to apply in the measurement of either constitutive or operational income.

4.7 THE COUNTING PROCESS

The selection of the numbers of arithmetic as the measurement language and the adoption of the monetary unit as the measurement unit are the more fundamental problems in measuring income. But this should not be construed to imply that the counting process is a simple one. In fact, the counting process in determining constitutive income is often so difficult that an accurate count is not considered possible. Consequently, the endeavor becomes one of developing a reasonably accurate standardized counting process. This is particularly true when income is measured as the net result of an inflow and outflow of resources (revenue less expense), because the outflow is difficult to count. The annual depreciation computation is an illustration of this problem, since it is an attempt to measure the amount of a fixed asset which has been used in a year.

The accounting solution to the problem of counting has been to develop a number of measurement formulas. Thus the problem of counting the amount of depreciation is solved by formulas such as the straight-line over time method,

$$\frac{C \text{ (cost)} - S \text{ (scrap)}}{L \text{ (life in years)}},$$

or one of the declining-balance methods. Other formulas have also been developed to count merchandise used: FIFO, LIFO, NIFO, and even HIFO (highest in, first out) have been proposed. The accounting assumption that the cost of resources used may be counted by the application of a limited set of formulas apparently rests on some type of unarticulated theory of an ordered universe. Such a world would be necessary for straight-line depreciation to reflect accurately in every instance the extraction of usefulness from acquired resources. Only by the assumption of uniformity would two or more firms ever use identical resources in such a way that straight-line depreciation would reflect accurately the cost of the services used. And only by an assumption of uniformity, appropriately adjusted for the time value of money, would straight-line depreciation ever measure accurately the annual cost of the resources used by one company year after year. Any assumption that a company either plans to use or does use fixed assets equally each period of time or that different companies use fixed assets an identical amount each period of time is so contrary to common sense that any counting procedure based on that assumption must be questioned. It is often contended that this assumption is not needed, because different formulas would be used for different situations. This contention, however, would require a body of knowledge, not now available, to indicate when each formula should be used. Moreover, it is also naïve to assume that the limited number of simple formulas now part of the accounting kit of tools could reflect the actual amount of fixed assets used year after year for all companies using the formulas. Consequently, counting procedures based on this assumption should also be examined in more detail, and this we shall do later.

Defenses for the formula approach are many. Probably the most widely cited defense is that for the depreciation formulas. The defense is that depreciation is not a valuation process at all, but merely an allocation procedure which assigns acquisition costs to periods of time on a systematic basis. (For an impressive analysis of the inadequacy of this concept, see [7].) While this is obviously true, it is equally true that constitutive income, after a deduction for "allocated" depreciation, is supposed to be a significant determination for the effective operation of economic society, and different depreciation allocation formulas result in different measures of constitutive income.

Another defense for depreciation formulas is that different formulas are needed for different purposes. This, incidentally, is not the same as the contention that different formulas are needed to reflect what did happen in different situations, which we maintain is not possible with the limited number of depreciation formulas available to the accounting discipline. The idea of different formulas for different purposes is best illustrated by the incentive depreciation formula allowed a business entity for income-tax purposes when the entity is performing work in areas of economic activity desired by the Federal Government. Other formulas have been proposed for other purposes, and there now exists the notion of depreciation systems with different depreciation formulas for each system. Thus, in addition to incentive depreciation systems, reference has been made to pricing depreciation systems, time depreciation systems, activity depreciation systems, and marginal depreciation systems. An examination of the formulas devised to meet the needs of the different depreciation systems reveals that they may in some instances not serve the purpose intended. For example, assume that the Government, wanting to encourage the production and distribution of "Wygats," allowed for tax purposes incentive depreciation at the rate of $33\frac{1}{3}\%$ a year on all equipment used in making "Wygats." If the normal use of this type of equipment covers a 10-year period, the incentive depreciation formula of $33\frac{1}{3}\%$ per year might well do as an incentive technique; but if some of the equipment had a normal life of two years, the incentive depreciation formula would not accomplish its purpose. The point is that no depreciation formula yet proposed can anticipate every situation of real life, no matter what the objective of the formula may be.

Probably the most realistic defense for the formula approach is the practicability of its application. For most purposes, and on the average, it is a reasonably accurate count of the cost of the resources used. The implication is that the formula approach provides a count which generally serves the purpose for which it is intended.

The discussion of the problem of counting depreciation merely illustrates the many problems involved in counting the amount of income. The entire counting process is now and will be for some time an area in need of considerable accounting research. Specifically, there is a need to develop counts in terms of probabilities and variations. That is, it is high time the accounting discipline formally included, as part of its technology, statistical techniques useful in indicating the reliability of any count. The range of possible error should be disclosed, and the tendency of variations to deviate from any one count should be reported in the form of the standard deviation of the count. These measures should be common to all accounting measurements of income. The probability of the accuracy of a count, as well as its possible variation from the true count, should be required for any measurement. For too long accountants have implied that their counts have an accuracy which cannot exist, as the preceding discussion of depreciation indicates.

Including probability calculations as part of its counting process would place the accounting discipline in the company of most areas of science. Nagel [8] explains the situation and the need for probability measurements in the following terms. "The doctrine that knowledge of matters of fact is only probable is one of the central themes of contemporary analysis of the scientific method. The implementation of this doctrine with modern logical and mathematical techniques is relatively recent." He also reassures us regarding the validity of these measurements when he states: "Contemporary empiricists who maintain that our knowledge of matters of fact is 'probable' do not thereby maintain that such knowledge is inferior to knowledge of some other kind . . . On the contrary, they maintain that 'probable knowledge' is the only kind of knowledge we can find or exhibit, and that the methods and techniques of science are efficacious and dependable precisely because they make available knowledge of that character." [8]

Underlying probability and all other measurements is the need for consistent and uniform counting procedures. In general, the need to count the amount of income requires that some standard be established so that uniform counting will result. If different accountants can get different counts for the same income-generating activities, because the counting process is not sufficiently standardized, there is a tendency to reject the results as well as the income concept on which it rests. Indeed, there is a tendency to reject any concept of income which does not lend itself to a uniform counting process.

The term *objectivity* has been used to designate certain characteristics which will provide for a standard count of money income by different accountants. The idea is that only things which can be objectively observed by everyone should be counted. This approach seems to have promise, but the use of "objective" may be unfortunate. Unprofitable discussions on whether or not something is objective or subjective have been carried on without regard to the problem objectivity was intended to solve. If an acceptable count is defined as the count that would result if different accountants were to do the counting, it could well be that counting the amount of income would not be such an unsettled issue as it now is.

It is our conclusion that the problem of counting the amount of constitutive income, which is the nature of the income concepts discussed in Chapter 3, is at present so unsatisfactorily solved that only by adopting an operational concept of business income can we handle the counting problem in a realistic manner.

4.8 EFFORTS TO MEASURE CONSTITUTIVE INCOME

It seems appropriate to suggest that the accounting profession abandon efforts to measure one overall constitutive concept of business income. In the first place it appears to be almost impossible to develop one overall measurable concept of constitutive income; and in the second place, the assumption that operational income is a reasonable approximation of a constitutive concept engenders difficult measurement problems. Specifically, considerable research is needed to develop new measurement techniques. Also, the fluctuating value of the monetary unit will have to be adjusted. Finally, the counting process will have to be further developed before we can measure any overall constitutive concept of business income in any precise sense.

Aside from these problems of measuring the one overall constitutive concept, the measurement of business income should provide for the disclosure of a variety of constitutive satellite incomes within the overall concept. Essentially, this is a problem of classifying various components of overall income in such a way that various satellite concepts of income will be measured. Thus it is a problem of classification.

4.9 CLASSIFICATION OF INCOME

Classification of income is a type of measurement in that it distinguishes items. This is true even though it merely indicates that things are different without disclosing the extent of the difference, which the usual measurement process does. In any event classification, like any conventional measurement, is a means of disclosing information. It is used in measuring income, for business income has been described as the central core of a group of satellite concepts all interrelated in some way. It is the function of classification to disclose this interrelationship. In this sense classification is part of the problem of measuring constitutive business income. Specifically, the classification process should provide a means for disclosing several satellite concepts of income within the framework of one single-valued measurement of business income. This does not mean that all satellite concepts of income should be disclosed by the classification process. In fact, the satellite concepts are legion and beyond the scope of the classification problem. But it is possible, by classification, to disclose the main

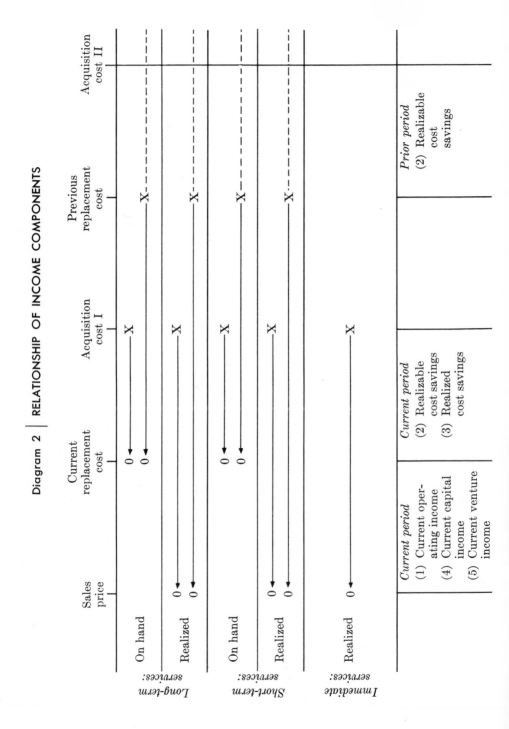

Diagram 2 | RELATIONSHIP OF INCOME COMPONENTS

components of income so that a number of different satellite concepts of income can be developed. Edwards and Bell [9] have suggested, in somewhat different terms, four basic components of business income, and we have added one more. From these we could formulate satellite concepts of income, assuming that the components were separately classified in the income-disclosure statement. The five component elements are:

(1) *Current operating income,* which is the difference between the regularly recurring operating revenues during a period and the current replacement cost of the services used up to provide the revenues. It may be either realized or unrealized by a sale, depending on the point selected for revenue recognition.

(2) *Realizable cost savings,* which is the difference between the current replacement cost of the services in the assets on hand and their booked valuation. It is a measure of the gain or loss arising from holding resources in a period of time.

(3) *Realized cost savings,* which represents the difference between the current replacement cost and the historic acquisition cost of resources used to produce revenue during the period. It is a measure of the gain or loss arising from acquiring resources prior to their use.

(4) *Current capital income,* which is the difference between the sales price of nonoperational assets and the current replacement cost of such assets. It is normally recognized when realized by sale or other disposition.

(5) *Current venture income,* which is the difference between the sales price of nonrecurring products representing innovations and speculative endeavors and the acquisition cost of the services used up to provide such revenue. It may be subdivided into holding gains and activity gains.

The relationships of the five components are shown in Diagram 2.

The list of five elements is not, of course, comprehensive. Let us suggest, however, that the measurement of income is best accomplished by classifying the components of income, rather than by disclosing all satellite concepts of income, within the framework of one basic single-valued measurable business income. Since this disclosure is possible under either a constitutive or an operational concept of overall business income, let us now examine the operational concept.

REFERENCES

1. WALTER FROEHLICH, "The Role of Income Determination in Reinvestment and Investment," *American Economic Review* (March 1948), pages 78–91

2. C. WEST CHURCHMAN, *Prediction and Optimal Decision* (Englewood Cliffs, N.J.: Prentice-Hall, 1961), Chapter 3

3. WALTER EUCKEN, *The Foundations of Economics: History and Theory in the Analysis of Economic Reality* (Edinburgh, Scotland: William Hodge & Co., 1950), page 283

4. BERTRAND RUSSELL, *Principles of Mathematics*, 2nd edition (New York: Norton, 1938), page 176

5. *Reporting the Financial Effects of Price-Level Changes*, Accounting Research Study No. 6 (New York: Accounting Research Division, AICPA, 1963)

6. PERRY MASON, *Price-Level Changes and Financial Statements* (Columbus: American Accounting Association, 1956)

7. GEORGE TERBORGH, *Realistic Depreciation Policy* (Washington, D.C.: Machinery and Allied Products Institute, 1954), Chapters 3–5

8. ERNEST NAGEL, *Principles of the Theory of Probability* (Chicago: University of Chicago Press, 1939), pages 4–5

9. E. O. EDWARDS and P. W. BELL, *The Theory and Measurement of Business Income* (Berkeley: University of California Press, 1961), Chapter 4

Chapter 5

An Operational Concept of Income

5.1 INTRODUCTION

Whatever one's faith in the customary ways of doing things and the customary ways of approaching the problem of determining income, there can be little doubt that substantial progress may be achieved if the problem is approached from new and broader paths. And there can be no doubt that, of all the new routes which have been followed by other disciplines, the *operational approach* has been the most successful. It has proved particularly helpful in such disciplines as physics and psychology, and appears to offer the greatest promise for accounting.

Operationalism is successful because man's view of the nature of things changes over time, due either to the discovery of new knowledge about nature or to the changing nature of man, and this changeableness precludes any permanent unchanging conception of almost anything. In the study of income determination, an operational approach would start with the proposition that the nature of income changes over time, place, and situation, as the needs and wants of man fluctuate, or as man comes to understand his wants and needs more precisely. What is income in one situation may not be income in another time or in another environment.

Thus we may consider the nature of income to be constantly changing in an unpredictable way, even though a consistent set of measurement procedures are followed over time, space, and cultures. This suggests that if there is any constancy, measurement procedures are the constant element, and the substance which constitutes income the inconstant element. If this conjecture is valid and the existence of a variety of income notions suggests that it is then accounting can have precise meanings for us over time, space, and cultures only if we understand the operations involved in measuring income. If we do understand these operations, we can comprehend the meaning of measured income at any time or in any culture and adjust the measurement to fit the needs of the time or culture. Alternatively, we can avoid using the measured amount to represent an inappropriate income notion.

The operational approach implies that it is primarily the measurement rather than the substance of income which should be the subject matter of income-determination theory. Before we analyze income-determination theory in terms of operationalism, however, let us look at certain characteristics that outline the general nature of operationalism.

5.2   THE NATURE OF OPERATIONAL CONCEPTS

"In general, we mean by any concept nothing more than a set of operations; *the concept is synonymous with the corresponding set of operations.*" [1] "We must demand that the set of operations equivalent to any concept be a unique set, for otherwise there are possibilities of ambiguity in practical applications . . . The proper definition of a concept is not in terms of its properties but in terms of actual operations . . ." [2]

Essentially, operationalism is an attempt to clarify the meaning of a concept by insisting that the proper definition of a concept is not to be found in what men say or even think it to be. Rather, the meaning of a concept lies in the operations performed by its measurements, including a specification of the areas in which it is useful.

It is generally assumed that operationalism is a result of the impact of the theory of relativity on conventional concepts in physics. [While some authorities reject the notion that the impact of the theory of relativity caused operationalism to come into being, they offer no better explanation.] In any event, the theories of relativity could not be explained by old concepts. A new way of looking at concepts was needed to prevent physics from being hemmed in by conventional concepts, and to control the use of conventional concepts in areas where they were not appropriate. The operational approach, by providing a detailed description of a concept and a means for designating the environment or area in which the concept applies, eliminated a great deal of ambiguity and vagueness regarding the meaning of the concept. The idea spread, and a number of disciplines adapted the operational point of view to their needs.

Hence operationalism now has a number of definitions. Underlying them all, however, is the general idea that a concept can have a precise meaning only when we completely understand the operations it involves.

From the standpoint of accounting, operationalism may be explained in terms of the income concept. If we say that income is a change in our capacity to satisfy wants, we have assigned a verbal definition to it. If, in measuring income, we elect to exclude capital gains and losses from income, we have a concept of income which is different from the concept we would have if we included capital gains and losses as income. Only by knowing how income is measured can we obtain a precise definition of it. Since there are many varying methods which can be applied to the measurement of income, only by knowing the operations by which income is measured can we understand the precise meaning of the income reported.

The view that income can only be defined in terms of the operations performed to create it is another, somewhat more loosely conceived, view of operational income. Thus if we exclude the operation of making capital gains and losses from the income-generating operation, we have a concept of income which is different from the concept we would have if we included the capital gain and loss making operation. Since the operations by which a business firm makes income are numerous, income can be defined precisely only by stating the operations performed to make the income.

Deferring for the moment further discussion of the nature of operational income until we clarify the nature of operational concepts, we may note that, in an extreme sense, operationalism suggests that nothing exists unless it is measured. This view implies that attempts to describe a concept first and then measure it are not particularly effective, because a verbal description is merely a crude measurement process of classification. That is, a verbal description only provides a loose general notion of the nature of the concept. This is partly because of the fact that words cannot convey precisely the idea intended, but also because a verbal description does not require a precise conception of the nature of a concept. A verbal description at best merely distinguishes, in a crude way, one concept from another. About all a verbal description of a concept does is to offer a general view of its nature. Of course, verbal descriptions represent a process of distinguishing and classifying different concepts. Thus verbal description is merely a crude measurement process known as classification.

As we mentioned in Chapter 4, classification is considered a measurement process because it distinguishes one thing from another, and this is essentially what any measurement does. According to this view, three apples differ from two apples in that the batches are distinguished from each other, just as we classify an orange as one thing and an apple as another. A verbal description of a concept may be so crude, however, that only by a more precise measurement can the concept be refined and adequately defined. [George O. May, at a meeting of the Study Group on Business Income on May 13, 1950, called attention to the close relationship between measurement and classification with the observation, "A difference in degree is ultimately a difference in kind. Thomas Adams used to say that the difference between a fifty percent tax and a five percent tax was more than a matter of degree."]

The trouble with this extreme view of the nature of a concept is that the preciseness it provides is not needed for a great number of useful concepts. In addition, it violates our commonsense intuitive feeling that there is something real about a concept, as opposed to just a set of measurements. Income is very real, and intuitively we feel that it has a distinctive constitution of its own whether or not it is measured. Further, there is much literature, including Chapter 3 of this study, devoted to the constitutive nature of income, literature which supports the notion that income is a constitutive concept. Therefore, if we are to apply the operational approach to income-determination theory, we shall have to modify and adapt the approach to the needs of the accounting discipline. We need an approach that will provide a basic concept of income to which a variety of satellite income concepts can be related.

5.3 TRANSITION TO THE OPERATIONAL INCOME CONCEPT

The transition from a constitutive point of view began some 30 years ago, when it was recognized that different concepts of income existed, and modifying words were added to the word "income" to distinguish different concepts. Taxable income, marginal income, capital gain, and accounting income are typical modified concepts which are widely used. More recently, even this breakdown has proved inadequate, and the feeling has emerged that different incomes are needed for different purposes. It is this feeling which led to the idea that only an operational concept of income is appropriate for modern society. Practically speaking, the operational concept applies to the operations of the business entity rather than the measurement operations of the accountant in determining income. That is, the notion exists that operational income excludes certain gains and losses, such as those arising from treasury stock transactions, not because they are not measured but because they are not part of business income-generating operations.

The change in thinking from a constitutive to an operational concept of income was that income was no longer conceived in constitutive terms as the total increase in economic wealth of a business entity. Rather, income came to be thought of as only the increase arising from those activities X of business which were business operations. A gain, to be considered income, had to be created by business operation. Thus it became possible to evaluate the effectiveness of business operations by computing operational income. In general, this approach to income theory may have been anticipated for several years, but it was definitely recognized as we shall see later, by the time the matching procedure to measure income evolved.

Further examination indicates that operational income is also distinct from constitutive income as a "generalized means to satisfy human wants." This difference may be explained in part by noting certain elements of constitutive income which may be omitted from operational income. If income were to be considered as the increase in "generalized means to satisfy human wants," it would have to include gifts, stolen goods, findings, gains from illegal activities, contributions, and similar items, because all these would fall within a constitutive concept of income. Normally, most of the above items are not considered part of business income. This indicates that business income is more operational than constitutive. Although most people think of business income as the gain due to business operations, the nature of the business operation which creates the gain is a general notion which has never been precisely specified, and this needs to be done.

To draw an analogy from physics, where it was found that certain concepts lose their meaning in new environments, it may be that certain ideas of income are just not meaningful when applied in differing environments for different purposes. For example, income from gifts may be an effective measure of the success of a church, but is of negligible use in evaluating the success of a business corporation. Further, the fact that gains on treasury stock transactions are not business income suggests that all the constitutive "generalized means to satisfy human wants" accruing to the stockholders are not business income.

Thus, because a business operates in a constantly changing economic and social environment, notions of income must change over time. Such a development could also explain the emerging theoretical support for the proposal that bond interest payments, like stock dividends, should not be deducted when one is measuring income. The nature of the business objective may have changed from that of maximizing income for stockholders to that of maximizing the income generated by the assets of the business.

The notion of operational income, therefore, has been developing for some time, although its form has been but dimly seen. For example, Canning [3] critically concluded that ". . . what is set out as a measure of net income can never be supposed to be a (constitutive) fact in any sense at all, except that it is the figure that results when the accountant has finished applying the procedure which he adopts." Since we now perceive that measured business income can have no uniform constitutive meaning, except in the context of a particular environment, we may admire Mr. Canning for his insight but question his foresight in being critical of the accounting measurement.

Out of the mist and fog surrounding the issue there have slowly emerged two criteria which help to clarify and define the nature of an operational concept of business income. First, operational income must be more than merely those measurement procedures which are applied to business operations. Second, operational income must be related in some way to the extant intuitive notion that income is a constitutive concept. We may gain further insight into the nature of operational income by studying the set of operations to be used to determine business income.

5.4 TWO CONCEPTS OF OPERATIONAL INCOME

As noted previously, when used in an accounting application for the determination of income, operationalism may be conceived of as one of two sets of operations.

(1) Operational income may be defined as the result of a set of operations performed by a business entity. These specified business activities or operations would set the boundaries of income activities, and the gain or loss from them would be business income. The accounting process of measuring business income would be distinct from the operationally defined concept of income. But since classification is a measurement process, the listing of the income-generating operations would be a nonaccounting measurement activity. The point is that this concept of operational income, like all operational concepts, may be considered a measurement process.

(2) Operational income may be defined as a set of operations performed by the accountant in measuring business income. According to this view, business income does not exist apart from the accounting measurement process. In fact, it is the measurement which gives meaning to the concept.

While the second definition conforms more closely to the classical view of operationalism, it may be deficient as a guide to methods for continually improving the accounting measurement of business income. This is so because once a set of measurement operations has been established, it may be hard to change them. The first definition, on the other hand, by separating business operations from accounting measurement, provides a basis for critical examination of the measurement processes used at any one time, and thus leaves room for any needed changes to be made in the measurement process. Further, a classification (measurement) of business operations utilizes an intuitive approach in the measurement of business income. Finally, this definition conforms to the accountant's matching procedure. Thus it is more pragmatically meaningful. For those who support the operational concept fully, the first definition remains consistent because it treats classification as part of operationalism.

Herbert Feigl [4] has presented a criticism of the operational point of view:

> Operationism is not a system of philosophy. It is not a technique for the formation of concepts or theories. It will not by itself produce scientific results. These are brought about by the labor and ingenuity of the researchers. Operationism is, rather, a set of regulative or critical standards. In the light of these critical standards the meaningfulness and fruitfulness of scientific concepts may be appraised. It seems that the outstanding requirements which operationism has quite justifiably stressed may be formulated as follows: Concepts that are to be of value to the factual sciences must be definable by operations which are (1) logically consistent; (2) sufficiently definite (if possible, quantitatively precise); (3) empirically rooted, i.e., by procedural and, finally, ostensive links with the observable; (4) naturally and, preferably, technically possible; (5) intersubjective and repeatable; (6) aimed at the creation of concepts which will function in laws or theories of greater predictiveness.

According to the general view of the nature of a concept, the proper conception of business income is in terms of the classified operations performed by the business entity from which income emerges. Thus accountants are concerned with business income, and the term "accountant's income" appears to lack operational content. It is the operations of the business entity which create the income, and the accounting operations are confined to the measurement of the business operations by which the income is created.

This view of the proper nature of "accountant's income" is contrary to that which some authorities visualize. Carl Devine [5] says:

> The usual concept of income is related to values that may be withdrawn without changing the prospects of an organization. Attempts have been made to make this concept operational by specifying rules for comparing discounted expectations at the beginning and end of each period, but accountants have been disturbed by the amplified effect of changes in optimism or pessimism in such a subjective measurement system.
>
> Professional measurement conventions for income determination are more modest and consist of rules for recognizing and measuring new asset values (revenues), corresponding rules for recognizing and measuring declines in value (sacrifice), and further rules for matching (correlating) the results in periodic reports.

Compare this with the view of Palle Hansen [6], who has remarked that ". . . the contents of the profit calculation are dictated more by certain conventional rules (including legislation) of realization of income than by a proper economic point of view."

When we accept the operational concept of business income, this does not mean that we completely abandon the notion that income is an increase in economic or financial worth. But it does mean that we restrict income to those increases arising from business operations. Assuming that the objective of a business firm is to increase its economic or financial worth, the content of business income then depends on which business operations are to be *included* as income-generating operations.

Unfortunately, the theoretical approach to income determination has instead been to cite operations to be *excluded* in measuring income. The positive approach—citing operations to be included—has not been used, in spite of the fact that there needs to be an itemization of the operations included rather than a partial list of the operations excluded. Only by knowing precisely which operations are included is it possible to understand the meaning of measured income.

Admittedly, any itemization of the set of business operations which create income would be an arbitrary listing, since different observers would have different ideas as to the activities involved in creating business income. This implies that the accountant is not a "trained observer" capable of making true observations of fact. In this context, we must concede that the "trained observer," like the "economic man," does not exist in any precise sense of the words. Nevertheless, it does not follow that the observations regarding income-generating activities will be widely diverse. Therefore, although accounting income does represent the accountant's view of the proper set of business operations, we need not assume that accounting income is distinct from business income.

Precise listing of all the operations of a business entity may be most involved if we seek a great deal of detail, since the detailed operations of each business entity differ somewhat from those of every other business entity. This means that the income of each specific operation of one entity is not comparable with the income of each specific operation of other firms. One of the objectives of the accountant's measure of business income, however, is to make possible comparisons of income among different companies. If we are to describe business-income activities in general terms, we must, therefore, enumerate in a broad manner those operations which produce income.

Generalized statements suffer from the inadequacy of not revealing details, and consequently the significant operations of any one particular entity may not be disclosed. Furthermore, excessive generalization does not provide for adequate disclosure of operations. Nevertheless, there is a middle ground which we may utilize when we formulate the set of business operations which create income, and this middle ground will permit comparisons among companies. This set would be a generalized description of business operations, providing, in the first place, the possibility of combining elements within the set to provide for an even more general list of business operations. Alternatively, the intermediate list of business operations should be described in such a way that each operation in the list could be broken down to provide for a more detailed subset of business operations. The advantage of this type of an operational set of business operations is that it lets us utilize varying concepts of income for different purposes.

[The letters of the alphabet may be used symbolically to represent the general set of business operations involved in creating income. Numerical subscripts may be used to represent detailed aspects of each general operation, and bracketed letters of the alphabet may be used to denote a more generalized description of business operations. Thus A might be the symbol for the operation "acquiring funds for a business unit by borrowing on credit"; B could be the symbol for the operation "acquisition of economic resources by spending funds." In more general terms, the symbol $(A + B)$ could refer to the operation "acquiring economic resources on credit." A less general classification of operations might have the symbol B_1 for the operation "ordering economic resources." B_2 might refer to "receiving ordered economic resources." B_3 might refer to "inspecting economic resources." The main advantage of such symbolization of business operations is to provide clarity and preciseness, as the concept has just been used to indicate the nature of business operation. While symbolization will not be used in this study, it seems appropriate to introduce it as a subject for further investigation, because the future development of operational income may depend on its use.]

5.5 BUSINESS OPERATIONS

To meet the practical needs of contemporary society, an ideal concept of income should include the following three characteristics:

(1) It should be useful for the varying purposes to which people put the concept of income.
(2) It should be measurable, in the normal sense of measurement.
(3) It should provide some conformity with a variety of satellite concepts of income, so that the relationship of one concept to another will be understood.

These characteristics serve as a guide for the development of a list of the business operations which best describe operational income.

5.5.1 Acquisition of money resources

We may view the measurement of business income from a general frame-work of the operating steps of a typical business entity. Let us assume that the first operation of a new business entity is to acquire money resources from investors through the sale of stock, and from creditors by the issuance of bonds or notes or by borrowing on an open account. This operation may be referred to as the *acquisition of money resources*. By money resources is meant cash and other direct claims to cash, such as a commercial bank balance, which may be used to purchase service resources. Money resources derive their value from their purchasing power rather than their productive capacity. That is, money derives its value from the fact that it can be used to buy economic resources. It is the economic resources which represent income-creating capacity.

5.5.2 Acquisition of services

In general, the second operation of a business entity is to acquire service resources in exchange for its money resources. Service resources come in a variety of forms: machines, buildings, labor, utilities, materials, and a multitude of others. Their common characteristic is that they are means for the creation of economic goods and services for consumers. This common characteristic is the service capacity of the resources, hereinafter referred to as *service resources*, and it is apparent that the amount of money resources to be given in exchange for specific service resources will be related to the service capacity of the asset. In fact, it is also evident that what is being acquired is not the physical resource itself but the anticipated services in the resource. In this fundamental sense, the essential ingredient in assets, other than money resources, is the services which will be extracted from them. [Money resources represent a means of acquiring service resources, and because money may be used to acquire many types of useful services, money resources might be classified as *general services*, as contrasted with the *specific services* contained in service resources. That is, money resources may represent general services, whereas service resources contain specific services.]

By services is meant the capacity of assets to render useful activities which will provide revenue for the business entity. [A terminological distinction should be made between "services" and "service potential" and between "service potential" and "potential services." Current litera-ture tends to differentiate "services" and "service potential," but "service potential" is essentially "services" at rest. Just as mass is energy at rest, so "service potential" is merely "services" in an inactive state. Similarly, the tendency not to distinguish "service potential" and "potential services" is a cause of confusion. "Potential services" are the maximum services possible assuming ideal conditions, while "service potential" refers to the expected services which will in fact be used. To avoid this confusion, we shall use the word "services" to refer to services at rest, services as performance, and maximum services, hoping that the context of the sentence will indicate the meaning intended. As regards conventional references to "goods and services," since we have defined goods as bundles of services, we shall use just "services" and eliminate the redundancy involved in the term "goods and services."]

For example, identical machines have different useful services if one is located in the bottom of the Atlantic Ocean and the other is in the plant ready for operation. Thus, as between two different machines, the price to be paid for the machines would be identical only if identical services could be extracted from each machine.

Irving Fisher's [7] classic view of the service nature of assets is still valid:

> The services of an instrument of wealth are the desirable changes effected by means of that instrument. For instance, the services of a loom consist in changing yarn into cloth, or what is called weaving. Similarly, a plow performs the service of changing the soil in a particular manner; a bricklayer, of changing the position of bricks. A dam or dike performs the service of preventing the water from overflowing the land; a fence, of preventing cattle from roaming; . . .

It should be noted that it is not the *potential* service capacity of an asset with which we are concerned. It is the *expected* service capacity. Unless a buyer or owner can extract services for his own use, an asset has no value to him. Consequently, the price a buyer is willing to pay for an asset depends on the number of services he expects to get out of it.

Services in the form of assets may be classified in a variety of ways, but for purposes of this framework, a three-way classification will be used: (1) *immediate services*, (2) *short-term services*, and (3) *long-term services*. According to this view of the nature of assets, all cash expenditures represent either payments to acquire services or disbursements to creditors and investors. Any assumption that a credit to "cash" and a debit to an "expense" are appropriate bookkeeping entries must be justified on the ground that they are short-cut procedures. In terms of business operations, two activities would have occurred. The acquisition of services, which entails the expenditure of cash, is one activity, which operationally would call for one bookkeeping entry. The subsequent use of the services, and the concurrent reduction in the services acquired, should require a second entry.

An example of an *immediate service*, in which services are not stored but are used as acquired, is labor. For such services the short-cut booking procedure is appropriate. [The theory that wages paid to labor represent a distribution of income, that labor is not a commodity but is a participant in the collective enterprise of big business just as stockholders are, and that the cost of labor should not be deducted in computing income may well be an emerging concept to which accounting theorists should direct attention. But for the present it is foreign to the accounting notion of business income.]

Typical of *long-term services* would be services acquired in the form of buildings, machinery, and other fixed assets, a substantial portion of which are stored in the fixed assets for a long period of time before being used.

The expectation which gives "value" to fixed assets is that services in these assets will be used in future periods of time. While immediate service acquisitions represent services to be used in current operations, long-term services represent commitments to future operations. A business entity motivated solely by the income concept acquires services in the most economical form possible. It is indifferent to the form in which the services are packaged. Thus the accounting convention of classifying services according to the form in which they are contained does not reflect precisely the business operation involved. Although there is no need to reject this convention, there is also no compelling reason to be bound by it. The important distinction is between the acquisition of services for immediate use and the acquisition of those to be used later, for the latter require an examination of future plans before the acquisition is made. In fact, not all services acquired for future use are homogeneous, since they will be used in different ways. It is desirable, therefore, to distinguish between future services which are used concurrently with the physical use of the form containing the services (materials and supplies), and those services which are extracted from the form without any noticeable change in the physical object (buildings and machines). For convenience, these future services will be classified according to the length of the normal storage period before the bulk of the services are used as *long-term* and *short-term* services.

Thus the second step of our framework of business operations, which we have referred to as the investment of money resources, basically involves the *acquisition of services*. Let us note, however, that this activity and the measurement of it, or of any activity, are discrete issues involving different problems. For example, the questions of measurement which arise when we analyze the acquisition activity might include the following: (1) When shall services be assumed to have been acquired? (2) At what amount shall the acquired services be valued? (3) How shall the acquired services be classified? These problems, which we encounter when we try to measure and communicate information on the acquisition activity, will be examined later.

5.5.3 Utilization of services

Step three in the business operations framework is the use of the services in a given period of time. In terms of business activity it is called the *utilization of services*. It is a separate and distinct activity, and does not involve the question of where or how the services are used. The utilization operation exists because services are stored in assets and in any given period of time a company may draw the services to be used from different assets. The operation requires the company to decide which service resources, if any, should be used and which held in a period of time. Economically speaking, it is possible that, holding previously acquired services may result in more income than would be generated by using them, and the company must consider this fact when it determines the services to be used. Operationally the utilization operation might be described in terms of the culmination of the operation of holding services. However, since the operation of either not-holding or using the services seems in the main to better describe the change in the services from their acquired state, the term *utilization of services* has been used to denote both the activity involved in the extraction of services from resources previously acquired and the activity of holding resources. The sense of the term will be evident from the context in which it is used.

5.5.4 Recombination of acquired services

The fourth step in the accounting cycle relates to the *recombination of acquired services*. This refers to the operation by which services previously acquired in different form are recombined into a new product or service. For example, the process of using previously acquired services in the form of leather, labor, electricity, and supplies to produce a pair of shoes would represent the recombination activity. For proper perspective, let us draw an analogy between the business activity of recombining services into a new form and the housewife's activity of baking a cake. Both processes involve the gathering together of different services in different forms and mixing them to produce a new form into which the services are grouped. In addition, if the mixing process is well performed, the resulting product will have a created value in excess of the combined value of the individual services which went into it. That is, the recombination process adds services to those previously on hand. The finished product is worth more than the sum of the individual parts or services used to produce it. This value added, if it is such, is a constitutive type of business income; but it is not all of the value-added concept of business income, since it represents only that which results from one of several business activities.

5.5.5 Disposition of services

The fifth step in the framework of itemized business operations is the *disposition of services*. Normally this refers to the disposition of the services recombined in the new product and includes the services added or destroyed by the production and distribution process. In addition, it includes all other dispositions of services. To draw a distinction for a moment between acquired services and created services (value added or value destroyed), let us say that acquired services may be disposed of either to provide revenue, in which case they are termed expense; or they may disappear without providing revenue, in which case they may be referred to as losses. Expense cannot exist without providing revenue, for by definition expense is the cost of acquired services used to provide revenue. Losses, representing the disappearance of services without any contribution to the revenue of the period, may exist at any time. The fifth operational step completes the process by which firms make business income.

To summarize: Business operations have been described as the process of acquiring services from others, using them and recombining them in order to produce and distribute goods, which are services in bundle form, and services, in direct form, to customers. In this process services are added; and it is the services added, as reflected in the difference between revenue and expenses and losses, which is the substance of business income. The process may be described diagrammatically, as in Diagram 3, which indicates that the following operations and results took place during 1964 (February to October).

> Acquisition of money resources: prior to date of diagram
> Acquisition of services: $70,000 ($10,000 + $30,000 + $30,000)
> Utilization of services: $58,000 ($27,000 + $31,000)
> Recombination of services: June 30 through September 30
> Disposition of services: September 15 through September 30

By this process, the firm has realized an income of $22,000 ($80,000 − $58,000). Although the straight line AC indicates that this was earned regularly, in fact, line AC could have curved up and down in the interval between A and C, due to changes in the market value of the product. Losses were not considered in the diagram, but could be a deduction of services at any time in the operational process. Although the diagram indicates that income and services are added primarily by the recombina-

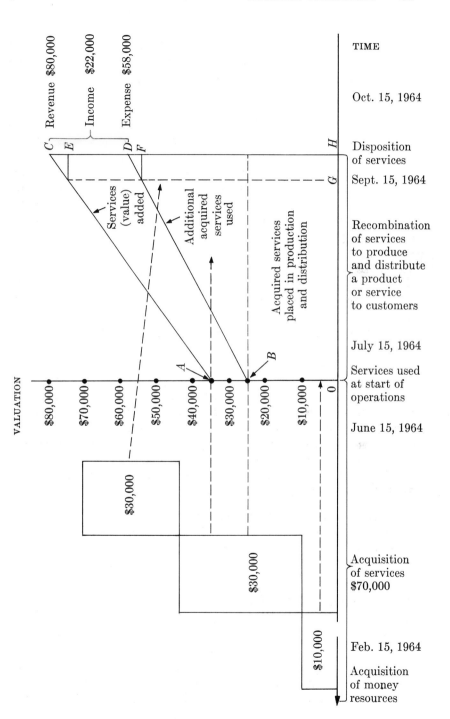

Diagram 3 | BUSINESS OPERATIONS AND BUSINESS INCOME

tion process, which includes both production and distribution efforts, a great deal of business income is created in the other operational activities as well. In fact, the $10,000 of value added prior to the time the services were used $(A - B)$ and the $1,000 of value added after the product was delivered to the customer (Point G) $[(C - E) - (D - F)]$ indicates that 50% of business income was created by the other operational activities.

5.5.6 Distribution of income

Business operations do not end with the creation of operational income but extend to the problem of distributing the income. For the time being we shall set aside the question of how income should be distributed, and deal only with the distribution operation itself, since business consumption of income consists of income distribution and use. In this area there are a host of problems relating to the amount of a distribution, especially a dividend in kind, the time when a distribution is to be recorded as having been made, and the description of the distribution. *Distribution of income*, the sixth and last operational step, normally takes place when there is a severance of assets for the benefit of the equity holders. This is a measurement question which we shall examine in succeeding chapters.

5.6 SUPPORT FOR THE OPERATIONAL INCOME CONCEPT

The advantage of an operational concept of income is that we need not define it in a formal constitutive sense, although we can do so if we wish. In fact, in a broad sense there is no need to know the nature of the goal or object pursued by business operations. The only requirement is to determine the results of the operations, and this may be accomplished without knowing precisely why they were carried out. In fact, the operational income concept assumes that there are multiple motivating objectives. But note the underlying fact that the results of the operations normally are operationally defined in terms of the observed objectives or operations.

We can, however, obtain many benefits from defining income operationally. First, such a definition most accurately describes what is being done in practice at the present time. In view of the heterogeneous collection of formulas used in accounting measurements and the fluctuating value of the monetary unit, accounting measurements of income can hardly represent a constitutive concept of it.

More important, an operational definition of income reveals to accountants not only a host of satellite incomes which are now measured, but others which should and will be measured for society in the foreseeable future. Accountants should not restrict themselves to a single concept of income which economists and others may effectively criticize. The strange thing is that accountants have never measured income as a constitutive concept at all. Nevertheless, they have talked and written as though they did. They have contended that something is or is not income on the grounds of its constitutive ingredients.

Implementation of the operational concept of income will place new reporting requirements on accounting, for accountants will have to disclose, in some detail, what they measured and how they measured it. Hopefully, there will be few variations in measurement methods, an aspect which we shall discuss in subsequent chapters. But with or without uniformity, measurement methods and operations performed should be disclosed in the income report.

Finally, the operational point of view will substantially increase opportunities for the use of accounting data by society, since a number of needed constitutive satellite concepts will then be developed to facilitate the operation of organized society.

The operational income concept of accounting will probably acquire a constitutive meaning as well. Since it is the nature of man to attach meaning to things, we may expect a constitutive conception of operational income to emerge. This, in turn, will lead to an analysis of the income report in such terms as "holding gains," "acquisition gains and losses," "measuring unit gains and losses," and "production income." Operational income will involve disclosure of all types of income of a firm; to measure it, accountants will have to employ many satellite constitutive income concepts. Before examining the problem of measuring such an operational income, which turns out to be the greatest current problem of income determination, let us consider an alternative set of business operations for determining operational income.

5.7 ALTERNATIVE SETS OF BUSINESS OPERATIONS

Income-generating operations may be described in more or less detail, but it is likely that in the future accountants may have to provide more detailed and precise information to enable management to act more efficiently. [There is at present a great need in our society for a detailed description of business operations. As business becomes more and more complex, there is a tendency to lose control of the manner in which certain basic operations are performed. Duplication often results, operating costs rise, and workers become dissatisfied.]

Churchman and Ackoff [8] contend that operational accounting, of which operational income measurement is only part, should perform the following functions:

(1) Provide data in sufficient detail so operations research techniques can be applied to select optimum policies.
(2) Use statistical probabilities in the control function.
(3) Generate data which will be needed in future research.

In all cases, however, there should be a means for relating different sets of business operations to one another. Unless this is done, income measurements resulting from different sets of income-generating operations may be misunderstood. However, a really detailed list would represent a set of operations of such magnitude that measuring the income-generating aspects of each operation would be of limited significance, and would be possible only at considerable cost. Further, each company would have different lists, and over time each company would change the details of its operational procedures. Nevertheless, such a detailed set would allow systematic combinations of elements in the detailed set, and the combined elements would represent a more general set of income-generating operations. Different combinations of the basic elements in the detailed set would enable accountants to measure a variety of alternative sets of income-generating activities. And because each alternative set would be related to the basic set, it would be possible to explain different operational income concepts in terms of basic elements omitted from one measurement or the other, and to reconcile all satellite income concepts.

We might say that only such a systematic conception of business income-generating activities would reconcile the various constitutive income concepts which today's society apparently needs. But because such a comprehensive empirical list is not a reasonable undertaking at present, even though essential if business operations are ever to get on a completely scientific basis, we must start from our intuitively derived list of six operations and break them down into subelements, and thus make possible a more detailed description of income-generating activities. Table 5–1 on pages 86 and 87 is the result of one such breakdown, developed on an intuitive or commonsense basis.

From the set of detailed elements, different sets of income-generating activities could be developed. For example, the following set of business operations might be formulated:

     I: Acquisition of services (S_1, S_2, S_3)
    II: Holding services (S_4, U_5)
   III: Risk bearing $(U_1, U_2, U_4, D_1, D_3)$
    IV: Production (U_3, R_3)
     V: Demand creation (R_2)
    VI: Delivery (R_1, D_{21}, D_{22})
   VII: Financing (M, S_5, D_4, I)

From such alternative sets of income-generating activities, assuming each activity in each set can be quantified in a suitable manner, we could disclose other aspects of operational income. There is no limit, of course, to the number of alternative sets of business operations which could be formulated. We might begin the scientific development of the income concept with a listing of the basic elements and then study possible alternative sets so that we might quantify them in terms of their usefulness to society.

To illustrate how possible alternative sets could be formulated, let us assume that the concept of current income includes three concepts: operating income, investment income, and venture income. We might use the following sets of income-generating activities to describe each of these in a general way:

(a) Current operating income (appropriate items of S_{11}, U_3, R_1, R_2, R_{31}, D_2, D_{41})

(b) Current investment income (appropriate items of S_{11}, S_4, U_5, D_4)

(c) Current venture income (appropriate items of S_{12}, R_{32}, D_3, D_{42})

That is, the quantification of current operating income, for example, could be accomplished by performing the following operations:

(1) S_{11}: Measuring receipt of regularly acquired services

(2) U_3: Measuring services used in regular operations

(3) R_1, R_2, R_{31}: Measuring services used in regular operations to distribute services to customers, to advertise and create a demand for the company's products, and to produce the products

(4) D_2: Measuring regular services disposed of to produce revenue

(5) Matching D_2 against appropriate measurements of D_{41} to disclose current operating income

To further illustrate the use of alternative sets of income-generating activities, let us look at the five components of business income listed below. These components could be variously grouped to disclose a variety of satellite concepts of income. To be useful, these components must be measured. Thus we have below a set of operations, in symbolic form, to which is appended a representative measurement by which one could, by comparing measurements, quantify each component.

(1) *Current operating income* $(D_{41} - D_2)$, assuming that revenue is measured in terms of cash or cash equivalent on the revenue recognition data and that the services used up are measured in terms of current replacement cost. Although the set of operations by which this income is generated include S_{11}, U_3, R_1, R_2, R_{31}, and D_2, it may be measured by comparing the measured amounts of D_{41} and D_2.

TABLE 5–1

INCOME-GENERATING OPERATIONS

Symbol	General element	Detailed element
M	ACQUISITION	
M_1	OF MONEY RESOURCES	Acquired from common stockholders
M_{11}		Cash acquired from common stockholders
M_{12}		Subscriptions acquired from common stockholders
M_2		Acquired from preferred stockholders
M_3		Acquired from creditors
S	ACQUISITION	
S_1	OF SERVICES	Ordering the resources
S_{11}		Regularly acquired services ordered
S_{12}		New product services ordered
S_2		Receipt of services
S_3		Inspection of services received
S_4		Storing the services received
S_5		Paying for the services received
U	UTILIZATION	
U_1	OF SERVICES	Time deterioration of services
U_2		Obsolescence of services
U_3		Operating use of services
U_4		Sudden loss due to act of nature
U_5		Holding of services
R	RECOMBINATION	
R_1	OF SERVICES	In performing distribution function
R_2		In demand creation
R_3		In product creation
R_{31}		Regular products produced
R_{32}		New products produced
D	DISPOSITION	
D_1	OF SERVICES	Expected loss of services
D_2		Services used to provide revenue
D_{21}		Delivery of services to customers
D_{22}		Acceptance of services by customers
D_3		Unexpected loss of services
D_4		Revenue received from disposition of services
D_{41}		Regular product sales
D_{42}		Venture product sales
D_{43}		Other asset sales

TABLE 5–1

(*continued*)

Symbol	General element	Detailed element
I	DISTRIBUTION	
I_1	OF MONEY RESOURCES	To stockholders
I_{11}		Dividends
I_{111}		Cash dividend
I_{112}		Dividend in kind
I_{12}		Capital distribution to stockholders
I_2		To creditors
I_{21}		To pay liabilities
I_{211}		To pay current liabilities
I_{212}		To pay long-term liabilities
I_{22}		To pay interest to creditors
I_3		As gifts

(2) *Realizable cost savings* (U_5 valued at current replacement price $- S_2$ valued at acquisition cost and less U_5 of the previous period, valued at the previous period's current market price, which are still on hand), assuming that resources on hand are valued on the reporting date and that acquired services are valued at acquisition cost on the acquisition date.

(3) *Realized cost savings* ($D_1 + D_2 + D_3$, all valued at current replacement cost, $- S$ valued at acquisition cost), assuming that services acquired from outsiders and disposed of are valued on the date of disposition.

(4) *Current capital income* (D_{43} valued at sales price $- D_3$, valued at current replacement cost), assuming that services disposed of are valued on the disposition date.

(5) *Current venture income* [D_{42} valued at sales price $- R_{32} + (R_{32} - S_{12})$], assuming that the difference between R_{32} valued at current replacement cost on the disposition date and S_{12} valued at acquisition cost measures the holding gain or loss on ventures, while the difference between D_{42} and R_{32} measures the operating element. Practically speaking, it may not be possible to break ventures down into holding and operating elements because of the indefinite nature of any market valuation used to evaluate the services used in the R_{32} operation.

The development of means for quantifying each of these in such a way as to allow the matching procedure to be used would bring about a significant advancement in operational income determination. But this appears to be beyond the level to which accountants now aspire; hence our examination will be confined to the general set of business operations previously set forth. We can always hope, of course, that there will be further refinement and development of the alternative sets of business operations.

Before we examine the accounting problems arising in each of the elements of the general set of business operations, however, we shall consider the overall problem of income determination in terms of the matching procedure as it is now widely applied.

REFERENCES

1. P. W. BRIDGMAN, *The Logic of Modern Physics* (New York: Macmillan, 1927), page 5

2. *Ibid*, page 6

3. JOHN B. CANNING, *The Economics of Accountancy* (New York: Ronald Press, 1929), page 99

4. HERBERT FEIGL, "Operationism and Scientific Method," *Psychological Review* **52**: 250–259 (September 1945), 258

5. CARL T. DEVINE, "Accounting," *Encyclopedia Britannica* (1963 edition), **I**, 78–80

6. PALLE HANSEN, *The Accounting Concept of Profit* (Amsterdam: North-Holland Publishing Company, 1962), page 76

7. IRVING FISHER, *The Nature of Capital and Income* (London: Macmillan, 1912), page 15

8. C. WEST CHURCHMAN and RUSSELL L. ACKOFF, "Operational Accounting and Operations Research," *Journal of Accountancy*, **IC** (February 1955), page 33

Chapter 6

Measurement of Overall Operational Income

6.1 THE USEFULNESS OF OPERATIONAL INCOME

As we discussed in Chapter 5, business operational income is, in effect, a summation of a series of incomes derived from the acquisition, utilization, recombination, and disposition operations. Nevertheless, we should not assume that overall operational income is not a useful measure. On the contrary, business operational income is an index of the effectiveness of the entire business entity, and it should be examined as a distinct concept.

Certain characteristics of the overall measurement should be noted. First, operational income determination is concerned with actions, not objects; and the property to be measured is the effectiveness of the actions and not the worth of the objects. That is, operational income is concerned primarily with those things which an organization *does*, and only incidentally with the nature of the objects which the organization *has*. This simple distinction between actions and objects is far reaching, for underlying the operational point of view is the realization that words or concepts have different meanings, depending on how they are used. We can now begin to realize that, in addition to the fact that different income concepts are needed for different purposes, different income concepts, with varying shades of meaning, inevitably emerge when any income concept is put to different uses. Thus we perceive that the call for "different income measurements for different purposes" is in reality a call for "more definitive income concepts for different purposes."

As an illustration, let us consider the operational definition in terms of modern data-processing concepts. Suppose we have a "word" in the storage unit of an electronic data-processing computer. The word, in a constitutive sense, may be either an *order* or an *operand*, or both. There is nothing in the word itself which distinguishes one meaning from the other, but the computer does distinguish the two meanings and defines the word as an *order* when its cell address enters the instruction counter, but treats the word as an *operand* when it is brought into the arithmetic unit of the computer. The constitutive meaning of the word depends on the operation involved.

The same circumstances apply to operational income, for the constitutive meaning of overall operational income depends on the operation or use made of the measurement. Operational income, as a measured amount, exists as a statistic whether or not it is used. It is appropriate for accounting to distinguish constitutive and operational concepts such as this; the two types of definitions are well established in the social sciences.

Torgerson [1] distinguishes the operational definition from the object definition as follows: "The formal connection between constructs on the one hand and the rules of correspondence on the other establish two different kinds of definitions which are used in science. The former were called *constitutive* definitions and the latter *operational* or epistemic definitions."

The fact that overall operational income has no one precise constitutive meaning does not mean that it can be measured according to an arbitrary set of uniform measurement rules. In no way is it possible to define income by such a process, for one of the requirements of measured operational income is that it must include data which will allow a variety of satellite constitutive concepts of income to be drawn from it. As we have noted, operational income has this capacity when it becomes a measured reflection of the operations of business.

6.2 THE MATCHING TECHNIQUE OF MEASURING INCOME

In an earlier chapter it was suggested that the matching technique of measuring income represented an approximation of the operational income concept. From the vantage point of this familiar income-measurement technique, we can develop a means for measuring the overall operational income. In fact, we can use the matching process as a technique to measure all types of operational income.

The matching technique of measuring income, as it is now used, permits one to gauge overall managerial efficiency, in that it matches efforts applied (productive resources used) against the accomplishments (money resources acquired) of such efforts. According to this method of measuring, income is not a measure of the increase in economic resources or "values" accruing to a company over a period of time. Rather, income reflects the ability of the company to use in an effective manner resources acquired from others. Normally, the effective use of such resources results in an increase in the "worth" of the business, but the measurement of this increase by the matching process does not presume to reflect all increases in value accruing to the business entity. Income, as computed by the matching process, therefore, is more of an index of managerial effectiveness than it is a measure of "value" increases; and it is so recognized by most students of accounting. Since revenue represents accomplishment, in that revenue is assumed to be a measure of the worth of products delivered to customers, and expense represents effort applied to acquire the revenue, the net result of matching the two is an index of the effectiveness with which the company has used resources. This measurement need not be, and probably never is, a measure of the amount a company could distribute and be as well off at the end of the time period as it was at the beginning.

Despite the seeming unrelatedness of operational income and the constitutive concept of income, it may be possible to define revenue and expense under the matching procedure in such a way that somewhat similar results may be obtained under both concepts. [Practically speaking, if we ever expect to see the operational concept widely adopted as the accounting concept of income, we may have to tie the operational concept to the general constitutive notion of accounting income. This is necessary to comply with the requirement of "continuity and change" which seems to be essential for progress in our society. Subsequently, we would suppose that the constitutive requirement would be abandoned and that the operational concept would stand alone as the nature of the accountant's concept of income.] To the extent that similar results are accomplished, operational income will be reconciled with a type of constitutive income. That is, if the same measured amount results whether income is conceived as an operation or a constitutive concept, the one measured amount will measure both concepts of income. At the moment, however, it seems unlikely that accountants will achieve this ideal measurement, since our previous analysis of the constitutive nature of income suggests that it exists as a multiple-valued concept. For this reason we shall proceed to develop a measurement of operational income using the matching technique as a measurement method, though our results might be viewed as a reasonable approximation of a constitutive concept.

We can best present the issues and problems of measuring operational income by analyzing the current use of the matching technique for measuring income. In effect, the current concept telescopes a selected number of the operations of a business into two operations: (1) applying effort, and (2) realizing accomplishment in the form of revenue. The separate operational steps cited in the preceding chapter are not recognized as such, and no attempt is made to evaluate effectiveness in each operation. Only total, undifferentiated operations are matched against final accomplishment in the form of revenue. Income measured by this matching process does not reveal separately, for evaluation purposes, information on the acquisition, utilization, recombination, and disposition activities. The difference between the operational point of view, as described in the preceding chapter, and the current use of the matching technique is primarily one of degree of detail disclosed. Thus an examination of contemporary matching procedures from an operational point of view will contribute both to current accounting practice and to the conceptual framework of accounting thought.

Measurement of business income by the matching process involves recognizing the revenues of a period and determining the cost of the services used up to provide the revenue. Consequently, until revenue is recognized, it is not possible for expense to be recognized. Therefore, the present methods of measuring business income require selecting a point in the operational process when revenue can be recognized, and developing means by which the cost of the resources used up to produce the recognized revenue can be determined.

6.3 THE NATURE OF REVENUE

Revenue may be defined in a basic sense as the "value" of the services rendered to customers. That is, it is a measure of the extent to which a company has accomplished the objective of providing for the economic needs of society. The customary procedure of measuring services rendered to customers in terms of the inflow of money received in exchange for them tends to obscure the social conception of the basic nature of revenue. Basically, from the viewpoint of society as a whole, revenue is an outflow of services rendered to customers and not an inflow. It is not possible now, however, to evaluate those services without the yardstick of the inflow of money given in exchange for the services. This situation merely reflects the inadequacy of our measurement technology. Of course, this view of the nature of revenue is not new, for Adam Smith [2] recognized it almost 200 years ago:

> As every individual . . . endeavors as much as he can both to employ his capital in support of domestic industry, and so to direct that industry that its produce may be of the greatest value; every individual necessarily labors to render the annual revenue of the society as great as he can. He generally, indeed, neither intends to promote the public interest, nor knows how much

he is promoting it ... by directing that industry in such a manner as it produces may be of the greatest value, he intends only his own gain, and he is in this, as in many other cases, led by an invisible hand to promote an end which was no part of his intention ...

Society needs measures of accomplishment for all types of organizations. Revenue as an inflow is one means for measuring accomplishment in that it reflects the sales value of the goods and services which a company delivers to customers. But the lack of a means for measuring accomplishment for other types of organizations is an inadequacy which prevents the measurement, in terms of an inflow of revenue, of the effectiveness of a government, a church, or other nonprofit organizations. Whoever discovers a means for measuring objectively the accomplishments of such organizations will contribute greatly to the accounting discipline.

Recognizing that the basic nature of revenue is an outflow of services to customers is only the beginning of the accounting problem of measuring revenue. Conceptually, there are three broad questions which have to be answered before revenue can be measured:

(1) When should revenue be *recognized*? This is the problem of revenue recognition. We need some standard or criterion which can be used to decide when revenue has come into being.

(2) How should revenue be *classified*? Since there are different types of revenue, we need some type of scheme to indicate how various revenue items should be grouped or classified.

(3) What is the proper *valuation* of revenue? We need to be able to determine the quantity or amount of revenue which should be recognized. The arrangements by which goods and services are rendered to customers are often somewhat vague so far as specifying the value involved, and this is what causes the problem of valuation.

6.4 THE RECOGNITION OF REVENUE

Revenue may be recognized either preceding or following actual delivery of the goods and services. Basically the entire effort of a company's production operations is geared toward getting a desired product into the hands of customers. The process is a continuous one, starting from the time raw services are acquired for use by the business and continuing up through the delivery of the production to customers. Revenue creation is thus a process which is strung out over a period of time and can be recognized at any time in the process. For certain purposes it may be recognized as soon as it is created. At other times it may not be recognized until cash is received from customers in payment for the product. The *time* when revenue should be recognized is a decision which the accountant must make.   There are two general theories regarding this: (1) *realization recognition*, and (2) *point recognition*.

According to the first of these, revenue should be recognized as soon as it is realized.   The trouble with this concept is that there is no clear constant notion of what is meaznt by "realized." To some people it means the date they personally realie that the cash will be collected.   To others, it is the date a normal person would realize that the goods and services will be delivered to customers.   Even the notion that revenue should be recognized at the time of a transaction is not unambiguous, for the concept of a transaction is a crude one at best and does not cover all activities in which revenue arises.   For example, interest revenue accrues and is recognized in measuring income before any normal kind of transaction occurs. Even when a transaction is defined as the transfer of rights, which justifies the recognition of interest on an accrual basis, one may refer to allocated depreciation since, as a recorded activity, it fits no known concept of a transaction.

The conclusion is that the transaction concept, while useful for crude measurements of income, is not the answer to the basic question of when revenue is realized.   As a result, the concept of realization is actually lacking on two counts.   First, there is no principle of what has to be realized, whether it is knowledge that cash will be received or knowledge that a resourse is worth more than it previously was.   Second, there is no statement as to whose realization—that of the accountant, the manager, or the public—is the proper realization to be used.

Point recognition of revenue is quite arbitrary.   It requires only that some point in the revenue-creation process be selected as the time to recognize revenue.   Any point could be selected, ranging from the time production is started to the time the customer pays cash for the goods and services.   Bowers [3] has explained the possibilities in the following terms.

> Accounting income must be identified with discrete events.   The possible events with which the recognition of income may be identified vary usually in time from the initial activity of acquiring agents of production to the final act of closing the productive process in its broadest sense.   That is, it begins with the purchase or commitment for productive agents; it ends with the collection of cash without liability or contingency attached.   This series of events may be itemized as follows:
>
> (1) Purchase of material agents or services
> (2) Receipt of orders for a good or service
> (3) Physical production
> (4) Delivery of goods or service to the buyer
> (5) Transfer of legal title
> (6) Receipt of cash or the equivalent
> (7) Termination of guarantee or similar contingency

For all practical purposes, however, the three points or times which are generally discussed in accounting literature are:

(1) Cash receipts date
(2) Delivery (sales) date
(3) Creation (production) date

In terms of conditions to be met before revenue is recognized, these three points may be stated as follows:

(1) *Availability:* the inflow from a revenue transaction must be available for use before revenue should be considered realized. In effect this means that revenue will be recognized at the cash receipts date.
(2) *Validation:* a "tangible" incident must take place to establish the validity of the revenue and remove doubts about its existence. Since the *"tangible"* incident is normally the sales event, this condition supports the delivery or sales date as the revenue recognition point.
(3) *Conversion:* the services must be converted into a final product or service. If this is interpreted to include conversion into work-in-process as well as the finished product, it corresponds to the creation or production revenue recognition point.

While realization recognition is now widely acclaimed, its indefinite nature and the opportunity it affords a company to manipulate the time for recognizing revenue, by merely stating that revenue is realized earlier or later than previously, suggest it is the less desirable of the two possible guides for measuring revenue. For example, a company formerly recognizing income on a consignment basis increased revenue in one year by moving the realization date up to the time the merchandise was issued to the retailer, calling the shipment a sale but granting the retailer "full return" privileges.

The strong features of point recognition are its objectivity and its consistency, assuming that management is not permitted to change the recognition point haphazardly, and the fact that point recognition makes it possible to compare different companies. From an operational standpoint, a recognition point as close to the creation date as possible would be preferred, in order to tie revenue closely to operations. But the lag between the creation of revenue and its recognition at any other point is not so great in a time period as long as a year as to preclude any of the possible recognition points from consideration. This lag becomes significant if shorter time periods are involved. Consequently, if operational reports in which revenue is included are prepared for a period of less than one month, there should be footnoted explanations of the extent of the lag involved.

It appears, therefore, that the accounting profession could spend its time more profitably in debating the proper point to recognize revenue than in engaging in endless controversy over the nature of realization. The latter is an accounting invention and can be inventionally defined for purposes of argument.

6.5 THE CLASSIFICATION OF REVENUE

Normally classification of revenue is governed by the criterion of disclosing useful information to managers, creditors, and stockholders. Such a criterion permits flexibility in the classification process. Conceptually, revenue might be classified according to any one of several schemes:

(1) *The time within which the acquired resource will be converted into cash.* This would give us such categories as "immediate cash," "zero-to-thirty-day cash," "thirty-to-ninety-day cash," and so forth.

(2) *The types of persons from whom the revenue is derived.* This would result in such categories as "sales to government," "sales to chemical industry," "sales to large companies," and a host of others.

(3) *The types of products or services, or groups of them, given up in the exchange.* Such accounts as "product A revenue," "financial revenue," "nonrecurring revenue," and others would result. For example, should a customer fail to take the discount on a $10,000 sale under terms 2/10, n/30, the revenue would be classified as:

Normal sales revenue	$9800
Financial discount revenue	200

A host of additional classification schemes might be developed, and there is no reason why one classification scheme should be used throughout. For example, some revenue might be classified as "sales to government" and other revenue of the same company in the same period of time might be grouped under the "product A revenue" account. Variation from a consistent classification scheme should be justified by showing that the resulting information is more useful.

The entire problem of the proper classification or description of revenue is an issue which should be of greater concern to accountants. As a business entity grows, its normal operations may come to include a diverse group of activities, which did not hold true when the entity was small. As a result, the sales of a large entity may not be a homogeneous classification, and grouping all sales of a large company under one "sales" account would not reveal the detail which would be available if the one large entity were replaced by a number of small companies. So diverse have the operations of large businesses become that the notion of normal sales, meaning the normal products which the company sells, has little significance. For a small company making and selling shoes, "sales" would represent the dollar amount of shoes sold. For a large company selling hundreds of different products, "sales" carries no such connotation. In fact, the term "sales" as the one revenue account is not now of much use, and might well be abandoned by the accounting profession. Several sales accounts may be appropriate.

In the last 120 years, the impressive rate of increase in the gross national product per capita has caused another classification problem. As Table 6–1 indicates, the United States has enjoyed a continuous increase in absolute production at a continuous per capita rate of increase. This suggests that specific natural resources will increase in importance relative to specific items of labor, because of the scarcity of the former and the abundance of the latter. In response to this long-run development, business operations have changed substantially in the last thirty years. The population expansion, the increased productivity of the economy, and the stability of natural resources have caused the gain from holding resources to become relatively much more significant than it formerly was, and business objectives have changed accordingly. Dramatic evidence of the profitability of the holding operation is provided, as shown in Table 6–2, by the increase in the average value of the land sites of new houses appraised for FHA mortgage insurance.

TABLE 6–1

RATE OF GROWTH PER YEAR IN GROSS NATIONAL
PRODUCT AND POPULATION*

Period	Gross national product	Population	GNP per capita
1840–1880	4.03%	2.73%	1.26%
1880–1920	3.52%	1.88%	1.61%
1920–1960	3.15%	1.31%	1.81%

* From Simon Kuznets, "Notes on the Pattern of U. S. Economic Growth," in Edgar O. Edwards (editor), *The Nation's Economic Objectives* (Chicago: University of Chicago Press, 1964), page 16

Of course, the gain derived from the use of resources still remains by far the more significant objective of business and, if our economy is to continue to grow, it must always be so. The point is that a company making business decisions on future actions must now, when it acquires resources, consider the holding-gain opportunity as well as the gain from using the resources.

TABLE 6–2

AVERAGE PRICES OF FINISHED HOME-SITE LAND*

Year	Price	Increase over previous year
1950	$1,035	—
1951	1,092	5.5%
1952	1,104	1.1%
1953	1,291	16.9%
1954	1,456	12.8%
⋮	⋮	⋮
1960	2,470	4.6%
1961	2,594	5.0%
1962	2,715	4.7%
1963	2,972	9.5%
1950–1963 (average)	—	8.6%

* From *The Wall Street Journal*, May 19, 1964

So long as the holding-gain portion of business income remained an incidental gain relative to the operating gain, the need to disclose revenues from the holding operation was not pressing. Consequently accounting procedures were restricted to disclosing only the gain or loss on disposition of investments and fixed assets, though the need to disclose the full revenue arising from operations was noted, and appropriate accounting procedures suggested. As the holding-gain portion of business income increases, governments, creditors, employees, and the public generally need to know the rate of return from holding resources. This requires a more complete disclosure of holding operations. Separate classification and disclosure of holding-gain and operating income is necessary because these two distinct activities both represent business operations in modern society.

6.6 THE VALUATION OF REVENUE

Normally revenue is measured in terms of the amount of cash or cash equivalent received from customers on the date revenue is recognized. "Cash equivalent" refers to the amount of cash into which the item received, a receivable or another resource, could be converted on the date the revenue is recognized. That is, it is not cash to be received in the future from any noncash item which sets the value of the revenue resulting from the delivery of services to customers. It is the cash equivalent, on the revenue recognition date, of the item received. A $10,000 sale on account under terms of 2/10, n/30 would represent revenue of $9,800. Similarly, a \$10,000 noninterest-bearing note due in 60 days, received in exchange for services delivered to customers, would represent revenue of only \$9900 if the bank discount rate were 6%.

In addition, in a revenue transaction, estimated uncollectibles and similar revenue adjustments are required in order to determine the cash or cash equivalent received when noncash items are accepted in exchange. This valuation method does not require all noncash items received to be valued at their current immediate cash sales value, though such a valuation may be appropriate if a competitive market exists for the noncash item on the date it is received. Normally it is possible that the noncash item may have a cash equivalent slightly higher than its immediate forced cash sales price. For this reason revenue items having a known probable future cash value, such as receivables, may be valued at the present value of the probable future cash value. Procedurally, this involves deducting from the probable future cash receipts charges for waiting and risk (interest), possible nonrealizable cash amounts (cash discounts, returns, uncollectibles), and cash outlays required to receive the future cash (accounts-receivable bookkeeping and paper-handling charges).

It is more difficult to measure the cash equivalent of noncash items which have an indefinite future cash value, since future cash value may include an amount for additional services added to the resource. Hence the determination of cash equivalent for these types of revenue items is more direct. Current sales price of the resource is the only reasonable valuation. The tendency to accept current purchase price of the resource as the cash equivalent should be discouraged. Purchase price has nothing to do with the amount of a revenue transaction, because for most businessmen and for most products there is both a sales market price and a purchase market price, and the proper valuation of the noncash item received is its value in the sales market.

In noncash transactions, revenue is presumed to be the cash equivalent of the resource received in exchange for the services given up. Actually the distinction between a revenue or sale transaction and an acquisition or purchase transaction is sometimes difficult to make, and the transaction is often valued in terms of the cash equivalent of the services given up or those acquired, whichever is more accurately determinable. This expediency is theoretically unsound; but until the distinction between a sale and a purchase in a barter exchange is clarified, there seems no way to avoid alternative valuations of the resources received.

Logically, one would think that "cash equivalent" referred to the cash sales price of the resource on the date received. But who is to say, when we exchange merchandise A for merchandise B, whether A is sold or B is purchased? If the transaction is a revenue transaction because it represents the sale of A, the proper valuation of the activity would be the sales value of item B received in exchange. On the other hand, if the primary purpose of the exchange were to acquire B, the transaction is a purchase transaction and should be measured in terms of the sacrifice or cost involved in the acquisition. Presumably, this would be the current sales price of the item A given up.

The rule for valuing transactions may be stated, in effect, as follows. Value sales transactions in terms of the resources received in the exchange, and value purchase or acquisition transactions in terms of the resources given up in exchange. Seemingly, the distinction between sales and purchase transactions may be made as follows:

(1) If a flow of money resources is involved, the more liquid money resource governs. If a company acquired a note receivable for cash, the cash flow would govern, and the outflow of cash would indicate that the activity was a purchase transaction. It would not be acceptable to contend that the company had sold cash. On the other hand, if the cash were received and the note receivable were given up, the inflow of cash would indicate a sales transaction and revenue would be measured in terms of the cash received.

(2) In an exchange involving a flow of money resources *and* services, the flow of money resources governs. An outflow of money resources would represent a purchase transaction and an inflow of money resources in the exchange would represent a sales transaction. There may be exceptions to this general rule if a contrary intent on the part of the management is unequivocally evident. For example, an exchange of a machine for a note receivable could represent a purchase transaction if the primary business of the company acquiring the note was dealing in receivables and the management had expressed the intent of buying the note.

(3) In a transaction involving an exchange of service resources, the use to which the resources are put influences the decision. If the acquired resources are similar to other resources regularly used by the company in its productive process and are in fact so used, a purchase transaction is indicated. On the other hand, if the acquired resources are not used in the productive process of the company and efforts are made to dispose of them, a sales transaction is indicated, and revenue would be recognized in the amount of the cash equivalent value of the resource received. This rule is also subject to the reservation that where there is objective evidence that managerial intent is contrary to the rule, objective managerial intent governs.

It is sometimes suggested that every barter transaction is a sale of one product and a purchase of another. This is not necessarily valid and would require all exchanges to be valued at the sales price of the product given up. In general, this proposal does not have much support.

6.7 THE RECOGNITION OF EXPENSE AND LOSS

Expense is the cost of the services used up to provide the recognized revenue. It should be distinguished from *loss*, which is the disappearance of services without bringing in revenue, and it should be distinguished from payments for the use of money, which is *interest*. The latter distinction is necessary if the effectiveness with which services are used is to be separated from the effectiveness with which a business entity is financed. And it has been widely proclaimed in the literature of both accounting and finance that, in the determination of business income, the financing process should be distinguished from the business operation process. To a large business organization the distinction between interest charges and preferred dividends, or even common dividends in most instances, is not a significant distinction for income determination purposes. To the modern corporation, both interest and dividends represent payments for the use of money, and there is no reason why they should be distinct concepts for income-determination purposes. The suggestion applies to all three types of interest:

(1) *Explicit interest*, which is the stated rate of interest, described as such, on a business paper such as a written note or bond.

(2) *Implicit interest*, which refers to a payment for the use of money even though it is not explicitly designated as interest. For example, the payment of $100 for a $94 loan would represent a $6 interest payment whether or not it was so designated.

(3) *Imputed interest*, which is the interest that could have been earned had the funds been invested in interest-bearing paper instead of being used to acquire service resources. This is a special type of alternative cost and should be treated as such and not be confused with a payment for the use of money. [Opportunity cost represents the best of all available alternative uses to which the resources could be put. As a result imputed interest seldom represents opportunity cost.] Of all the senses in which the word "interest" is used, imputed interest is the term which most nearly describes the cost of services used to provide revenue.

Since expense cannot exist unless revenue exists, it follows that the proper recognition of expense requires that we determine which services have been used to provide revenue, which remain as assets to be used in bringing in future revenue, and which have been lost. Essentially, the task of measuring expenses is one of assigning a cost to the services used to provide revenue recognized in the current period of time. The cost of services to be used in providing future revenue are assets, while the cost of services disappearing during the current period are either expenses or losses.

This relationship between assets, expenses, and losses is important for measurement purposes. If any two of them can be measured directly, the third can normally be derived. For example, if a company has $10,000 of services and acquires $60,000 more during the year, the problem becomes one of accounting for the $70,000 of resources. If an investigation reveals that $40,000 are to be used in bringing in future revenue and if $20,000 are identified as expenses of the present revenue, the loss during the period would be $10,000. The concept that service assets are merely future expenses and not future receipts is essential to a satisfactory understanding of asset valuation. Valuation of service assets in terms of future expenses, rather than in terms of the present value of future receipts, is justified on the grounds that the process of creating the future receipts or revenue has not proceeded to the point where revenue is recognized. It means that the proper valuation of services should be made in the buying market and not in the selling market, and this requirement holds until revenue is recognized. When revenue is recognized, measurement shifts to the selling market, and this causes income to be recognized.

Some confusion arises as to which buying market or which selling market is appropriate, but there should be no confusion. According to a certain line of reasoning, partially completed products, which can be purchased in a semifinished state, may have two buying markets. One market would represent the cost of the individual service components of the product in the original form acquired, whereas the second one would represent the cost of the product in its semifinished state. Alternatively, if revenue has been recognized, the valuation of the product could be in terms of the sales market for the semifinished product or the sales market for the finished product adjusted for cost of completion (net realizable value). There should be no confusion of what business operations might have been with what business operations were or are planned. If the company starts operations with a semifinished product, the market where these products are purchased represents the appropriate buying market. If the company concludes operations by selling the semifinished product, this selling market is the appropriate one to use to value revenue. Essentially, the proper buying market and the proper selling market are those markets in which the company operates.

A clear distinction should be made between expense and adjustments of revenue. For example, products sold and then returned by customers are not an expense of the revenue recognized, but an adjustment needed to measure the correct revenue. Similarly sales discounts are revenue adjustments rather than expenses. Revenue adjustments are corrections made in the valuation of recognized revenue to bring revenue to the cash or cash-equivalent valuation. Let us bear in mind this distinction: Expenses are the cost of services used to provide revenue, while revenue adjustment measures the amount of revenue that will *not* be collected. From this we can see that, contrary to current practice, estimated bad debts are uncollectible revenues, and are thus a type of revenue adjustment and not an expense. Merchandise loss, which is normally buried in the cost of goods sold, is the only bad-debt expense which could exist. To further clarify the nature of expense, let us note that a cash expenditure normally represents the cost of services, and that charging such services to expense at the time the cash is paid out is merely a convenience, to save the time of first recording the acquisition of services for cash and later recording the use of the services to bring in revenue. Technically speaking, one should not think in terms of "paying expenses"; but if the acquired services are immediately used to bring in revenue, no harm results from such thinking.

6.8 AFTER-COSTS

We have defined expense as the cost of services used to acquire revenue, and expense is measured as the cost of revenue. If revenue is recognized prior to the delivery of the services to customers, there will be services to be delivered after the revenue recognition date. Thus the concept of expense must be broadened to include the cost of these services to be used. Such after costs are expenses of the revenue recognized, of course, but they do raise the interesting possibility that an expense may exist prior to the acquisition and physical use of the services.

For example, if Company A sold a television set which had cost \$175 for \$300 and guaranteed the set for one year, the cost of making good on the guarantee would represent an after-cost expense of the revenue. If the cost of services normally used to back up the guarantee averages \$25 per set, the expenses of the recognized revenue would be \$200 instead of \$175. A liability of \$25 should, of course, be set up for the estimated cost of the services to be used to comply with the product guarantee.

There are a host of after-costs which, conceptually, could be assigned to expense prior to the time the services are delivered to customers. Another illustration may suggest the extent of this concept. Assume that a machine having an acquisition cost of \$10,000 and a 10-year life is estimated to have a \$2,000 removal cost. Clearly the cost of all the services in the machine is \$12,000, so that the annual straight-line depreciation charge should be \$1,200 (\$1,000 of used services and \$200 of after costs). Actually, there is a need for a considerable study of the after-cost concept, for it should not be extended to include mere possibilities. In other words, a line needs to be drawn between after-cost and normal risk of the business.

At times it is suggested, and with considerable logic, that instead of recognizing after-costs as an expense, revenue should be deferred to any services to be rendered to customers at a future date. The amount of the deferred revenue is normally measured in the proportion to total revenue that after-cost bears to total expenses. That is, the same rate of profit is assumed to be earned on all services rendered to customers. In the case of the television set sale, the deferred revenue would be computed as follows:

Prior-cost expense of revenue	$175.00
After-cost expense of revenue	25.00
Total expense	$200.00
Ratio of after-cost to total expense	25/200 = 12½%
Total revenue	$300.00
Deferred revenue: 12½% of $300	37.50
Current revenue earned	$262.50

The distinction between after-cost and deferred-revenue treatment of undelivered services is illustrated below.

	AFTER-COST TREATMENT		DEFERRED REVENUE TREATMENT
Sales		$300.00	$300.00
Deferred revenue		—	37.50
Current revenue		$300.00	$262.50
Prior-cost expense	$175.00		$175.00
After-cost expense	25.00		—
Total expenses		200.00	175.00
Income		$100.00	$ 87.50

In the subsequent period, an additional income of $12.50 ($100 − $87.50) would be recognized when the services rendered in fulfillment of the guàrantee were provided to customers.

The advantage of employing the deferred-revenue treatment rather than after-cost is that income should not be recognized prior to its creation, and creation is assumed not to have taken place until the process of forming and delivering services is underway. A mere contract to render repair services on a TV set for one year does not represent the creation of revenue, and the amount involved is not revenue until the services are rendered, or so this reasoning goes.

6.9 THE MEASUREMENT OF EXPENSE

Expense is normally measured, under the matching procedure, in terms of acquisition cost. That is, expense is a part of acquisition cost. In the sense that acquiring resources involves decision and effort on the part of management, matching acquisition cost with recognized revenue measures management effectiveness. But if plans change and effort is redirected after services are acquired, perhaps another measure of expense would be more appropriate. In a general way, measuring expense in terms of acquisition costs does measure effort applied, in that it reflects a sacrifice of money which, when matched against revenue, provides a measurement to reveal the effectiveness of the management in its decision to use money resources.

There are, however, reasons why an evaluation of managerial effectiveness based on how much better off the company is by operating than by holding money idle may not be the best evaluation of management. For example, an evaluation of the advantage to the company of operating rather than holding services may be more desirable, and would eliminate from income the gain due to mere holding of services, as illustrated in the following example.

Example

Assume that services having an acquisition cost of $8,000 cash are held for a period of time before being used, a normal assumption. At the time they are sold they have a current replacement cost of $9,000. Assume further that resources used in operations are sold for $10,000 cash. The two methods of computing income reveal their difference.

(a) *Conventional matching procedure*

Revenue	$10,000
Expense (money sacrificed on acquisition date)	8,000
Income (the amount by which the company is better off by operating than by holding money)	$ 2,000

(b) *Possible matching procedure*

Revenue		$10,000
Expense (money sacrificed on acquisition date)	$8,000	
Increase in money value by holding resources	1,000	
Replacement cost on sales date of resources used		9,000
Income (the amount by which the company is better off by operating than by holding resources)		$ 1,000

The impact of changing price levels would be minimized by the second type of evaluation. In fact the measurement of expense in terms of the current replacement cost of services at the time the services were used to provide revenue would, when matched with revenue, provide a measurement by which operating efficiency might be judged more directly.

Although accountants give verbal support to both methods of measuring expense, acquisition costing of expense prevails. However, replacement cost of services used is at times employed and unnoticed as such. For example, repairs are normally considered to be the restoration of services previously used, in the sense that repairs restore equipment to its previous condition. When the cost of restoring these services is charged to "repair expense" instead of the acquisition cost of the services used, replacement cost rather than acquisition cost is used to measure expense. If acquisition costing were desired, repair expense would be computed as the acquisition cost of services consumed and the cash outlay required to restore these services would be capitalized to the asset.

Since expenses are not homogeneous, they are customarily classified under a variety of different groupings. Operationally, the actions of the entity would best be disclosed by a classification of expenses according to functions or activities performed. Only thus would the concept of operational income be reflected in the income report. To the extent that expenses are not so classified, operations are not adequately disclosed.

From the measurement standpoint, possibly the greatest lack in the conventional matching procedure is in the recognition and classification of gains and losses. According to the conventional matching procedure, operating income may be either positive or negative; but it represents only a special type of gain or loss. [*Operating income* refers to the income from the production and distribution activities of a company. *Operational income* includes all types of income from all operations of a business.]

In addition to the operating use of services, a business entity will have losses of services which bring in no revenue. To the extent that the losses can be anticipated by the buyer of resources, price is adjusted downward until it represents only the cost of the services expected to be used in operations. That is, acquisition cost would represent the cost of the services expected to be used. Services *not* expected to be used would have no cost attached to them, even if they were acquired. Loss of services having no cost attached to them therefore do not represent a sacrifice, because they are costfree services. In the accounting sense, they are not a loss. In addition, if certain events otherwise classified as losses can be anticipated and accrued as normal operating items, they become one of the normal sacrifices required to bring in revenue. Thus expected losses become expenses because they are anticipated. The same reasoning applies to expected increases in services, because they too may be brought in as part of operating income. The consequence of this reasoning, which conforms to accounting practice, is that expected gains and losses can be treated as operating items.

Unexpected gains and losses have to be fitted into the operational income concept, for they represent discoveries and not production and distribution operations. The conventional matching procedure does not permit this fitting to be well done. Discoveries, either in the form of services purchased for use, which unexpectedly disappear, or in the form of services which are unexpectedly discovered to exist in resources, need to be accounted for separately from operating income. But to account for them separately poses a number of questions.

(1) Whose realization of the existence of the discovery should be accepted for accounting purposes? Management realization may well precede that of the marketplace, and marketplace realization may precede the accounting realization point.

(2) What degree of realization is needed before the discovery should be considered as existing? Is a feeling, or even a fifty-fifty belief, a satisfactory degree of realization?

(3) If marketplace realization is accepted as the most appropriate point for recognizing these unexpected gains and losses, should disclosure also be made of those gains and losses which management believes exist? If so what type of a gain or loss would these represent?

It is unfortunate that no objective criterion now exists for recognizing discovery gains or losses. In general, losses are recognized at the time management decides they exist; but extraordinary gains, except for certain types of oil discoveries and a few other special cases, are not recognized until the resource is sold. If discovery gains are not recognized and the resources to which they are attached are used in production operations, operating income may be over- or under-stated because it will include nonoperating items, in the form of under-depreciation, over-cost of sales, and similar items. The result may be confusion regarding the meaning of operating income.

All income determined by the matching procedure is, of course, operational by definition. The preceding discussion has suggested at least two classifications of operational income. But making a distinction between operating income as being that income resulting from normally recurring activities of a similar nature and other types of operational income means that, before we formulate an operational income concept, we shall have to distinguish different types of income.

Diagram 4 | BUSINESS INCOME GENERATING OPERATIONS

ACQUISITION OF SERVICES		UTILIZATION OF SERVICES		RECOMBINATION OF SERVICES		DISPOSITION OF SERVICES	
Type	Amount	Computation	Amount	Activity	Amount	Function	Amount
Long-term (building and machinery)	$10,000	Formulas $\dfrac{(C-S)}{(L)}$	$ 1,000	Distribution	$7,000	Sales (revenue)	$15,000
				Issued	7,000	Distribution expense $7,000	
Short-term (merchandise and supplies)	8,000	Formulas (FIFO)	5,000	Production	5,000	Cost of goods sold 3,000	10,000
				Issued	3,000	Operating income	$ 5,000
Immediate (labor and power)	6,000	All acquired (not storable)	6,000	Inventory	$2,000		
Total	$24,000	Total	12,000				
Amount used	12,000	Amount used	12,000				
Amount unused	$12,000	Amount on hand	0				
Losses (long-term)	2,000			(Inventory)	500	Total losses	2,500
						Increase in assets	2,500
Assets at end of period	$10,000		0		$1,500		$15,000

Explanation: The company purchased $24,000 of services, used $12,000 and lost $2,000, leaving $10,000 on hand. The $12,000 of services used were used in distributing the product ($7,000) and producing the product ($5,000). Sales were $15,000 (money resources) and the expenses of the sales were $10,000, so the operating income amounted to $5,000, from which the long-term losses of $2,000 and the $500 inventory loss were deducted, to leave a net increase in assets of $2,500. The $2,500 increase could also be computed by adding the end-of-the-period assets ($10,000 + $1,500 + $15,000) and deducting those acquired ($24,000).

6.10 MEASUREMENT OF OPERATIONAL INCOME

Let us recall from Chapter 5 that the operations of business have been generalized into the following six operations:

(1) Acquisition of money resources from creditors and investors
(2) Acquisition of services in the form of building, machinery, labor, and other resources
(3) Utilization of services in a specific period of time
(4) Recombination of services into a new product; production and distribution of it
(5) Disposition of recombined services to customers in exchange for money resources in payment for them, or through loss
(6) Distribution of money resources to creditors and investors

Diagram 4 reveals the middle four income-generating operations as they are measured in terms of the flow of acquisition costs through the operations. Acquisition, utilization, recombination, and disposition of services are discussed in more detail in Chapters 7, 8, 9, and 10. Accounting problems involved in the distribution of money resources are examined in Chapter 11.

6.11 EXTENSION OF THE MATCHING TECHNIQUE

Normally the matching technique is applied when the income-generating process is complete. But there is no reason why it should be so restricted if suitable methods are available to measure effectiveness in less comprehensive terms. Where accomplishment is measurable in terms of a standard cost or a budget allowance, a matching of actual costs (effort) with the predetermined or even postdetermined desired objective (accomplishment) supplies an index of effectiveness. While there is some reluctance to refer to this type of an index as income or loss, the reluctance stems from doubts as to the validity of the standard cost or budget as a measure of accomplishment, and not from doubts as to the concept. If the standard cost or budget is based on sufficiently accurate measurements, one could undoubtedly recognize this gain or loss prior to the completion of the income-generating process. If the standard cost were expressed in terms of average accomplishment coupled with a standard deviation computation to reduce the possibility of a measurement error, it might well be a satisfactory measure of accomplishment. The matching concept could then be applied whenever production was transferred from one department to another. This procedure would mean that departmental efficiency could be measured by means of the index of income.

Another opportunity for expanding the use of matching techniques lies in the comparison of replacement cost with acquisition cost of resources held. Accountants do not generally do this, since they are reluctant to accept replacement cost as a measure of accomplishment. Such a matching would reveal the gain or loss due to holding assets, as opposed to using them. Of course, holding gains and losses may not be sufficiently significant to warrant separate measurement, but the matching procedure for measuring income could be used to measure holding gains when and if they become a significant aspect of business operations.

The matching of the acquisition cost of a partly completed product with the sales value of the partly completed product at the time the product is transferred from one division to another is another extension of the matching process. This process provides a means for allocating income to divisions of the company. Its application, however, is necessarily based on the assumption that there are market prices at these transfer points.

The matching technique for computing operational income has unlimited uses. It may be used in every case where both cost and revenue can be measured with sufficient reliability to justify it to the business world. One area where it should be used more often is in the nonprofit activities. Lacking a measure of accomplishment, nonprofit or loss operations have not been evaluated in terms of the efficiency of their income-generating activities. If measurement techniques could be developed to provide a measure of accomplishment, the matching process could be used in this area, where it is now most difficult to evaluate efficiency. The result would be a report on all operations of an entity summarized into one operational income figure.

REFERENCES

1. W. S. TORGERSON, *Theory and Methods of Scaling* (New York: Wiley, 1958), page 11

2. ADAM SMITH, *The Wealth of Nations*, **IV** (Modern Library; New York: Random House, 1937), page 423

3. RUSSELL BOWERS, "Tests of Income Realization," *Accounting Review*, **XVI** (June 1941), page 139

Chapter 7

The Determination of Acquisition Cost

7.1 THE ACQUISITION COST PROBLEM

The accounting profession does not have a satisfactory method of accounting for the acquisition of services. Among the diverse practices which are used, there is no prevailing theory to guide the practicing accountant in accounting fully for the activities involved in the acquisition operation. George O. May [1] acknowledged this lack in the following terms.

> Economists concerned with the creation and exhaustion of the national stock of capital assets must recognize the limitations of statistics of accounting origin. They might desire statistics relating to the phases of the development of capital assets which include:
> (1) Research and experimentation to develop and improve types of assets
> (2) Creation of demand for products
> (3) Actual construction of the physical assets
> ... Accounting classifications do not lend themselves to such an analysis. In general, accounting does not take cognizance ..., except to a limited extent, of one and two, but is concerned almost exclusively with item(s) three. ...

Lacking a theoretical framework, accounting practitioners have taken a practical approach to the disclosure of acquisition activities. In the process, however, a number of contradictory procedures have emerged. Acquisitions are normally valued at cost, but cost has been defined in a number of contradictory ways. It has been held at one point to include interest charges and at another to exclude them. More specifically, acquisition cost has been defined both as invoice price and as cash equivalent. In addition, costs of resources have been classified in different ways. Some identical resources are classified as buildings at one time and as equipment at another. Finally, there have been extensive discussions about the point at which specific resources should be recognized as having been acquired. The entire issue calls for an examination of the theoretical basis for the determination of acquisition cost.

Expense is normally measured in terms of the acquisition cost of the services used to provide revenue. For that reason alone, an accurate determination of acquisition cost is important in the theory of income determination. Operationally, however, acquisition is an activity; and if effectiveness in the performance of that operation is ever to be disclosed, some method of quantifying both effort (sacrifice) and accomplishment (value acquired) in the acquisition activity will have to be developed. Traditionally, other than the occasional valuation of raw material acquisitions at a standard cost and the treatment of the variance of actual cost from standard cost as a miscellaneous item of overhead, the distinction between effort and accomplishment has not been recognized in quantifying acquisitions. Technically, however, quantification of both is a prerequisite to the description of the precise nature of the activity.

One acquisition cost valuation is not enough for modern accounting. For example, acquisition cost may have different constitutive meanings if it is a mixture of "bargain," "unlucky," "war surplus," and "free market" prices. Further, if effectiveness in the operation is to be revealed, the precise acquisition cost will have to be matched against some type of an "objective" acquisition cost, such as the average price paid by other companies, which may be assumed to represent accomplishment.

In general terms, let us say that we need to be able to quantify both the actual effort applied to acquire specific service resources and the correct effort, in the sense of a "normal" acquisition price, which should have been applied. The difference between the two measures would represent the effectiveness with which the acquisition operation is performed. In a constitutive sense the net result would be a measure of the gain or loss from buying.

Such an undertaking, however, poses many problems of measurement, and in spite of the fact that it is properly part of the general framework of determining income, it may not represent a pressing need of society. That is, there appears to be no great demand for a constitutive measure of the income generated by the acquisition operation. However, for cases in which the amount involved is significant and can be measured, there is reason to disclose this "gain or loss from buying" separately in the overall income measurement. As communication methods develop and all buyers and sellers become better informed, the gains and losses on buying may become even less significant.

7.2 THE NATURE OF ACQUISITION COST

The convention, established by many years of use, is to assume that the acquisition operation should be quantified in terms of the effort or sacrifice involved in carrying out the operation. The quantification in terms of cost has resulted in the listing of any "gain or loss" due to buying in the total income of the entity, without distinction as to its origin. If separate disclosure of this gain or loss is not needed, acquisition cost valuation seems reasonable. But acceptance of this point of view does not mean that acquisition costing is a simple matter. Acquisition cost normally means the monetary valuation placed on services at the time they are acquired by the business entity. The assumption underlying the selection of the most appropriate valuation is that business acts are purposeful and have a rational aspect. Thus acquisition cost should reflect the effort applied to accomplish the rational objectives of the business entity. Specifically, the assumption is that there must have been an objective or planned use for the services, however vague or general it might have been, or the entity would not have acquired the services.

However, as objectives or planned uses of previously acquired services change, consistent use of the notion that acquisition cost should reflect effort applied to attain specific objectives would indicate that a new acquisition cost should be recorded to reflect effort applied toward the new objective. When two objectives are intimately related, such as might be the situation if a company attempted to make an income by holding services and another income at a later date by using the services, accomplishment of the first objective should lead to another acquisition cost being recorded at the time effort is directed to the second objective. That is, an investment in "excess" inventory means that effort applied to make a holding gain could have a cost of $1,000, whereas the same investment after the holding gain is realized could have an acquisition cost of $1,200, as regards effort applied to production. Where such accounting can be done on a reasonable basis, this is a desirable procedure. The proposition has been introduced to the profession and is receiving support in a variety of places [2, 3]. [It is also mentioned in foreign literature. Subsection 2 of Section 35 of the Commercial Act of Norway states, "All properties are put at the amount they are supposed to be worth at the time in question." This has been interpreted to mean that inventories should be valued at market value on the balance-sheet date.]

For the present, however, quantifying acquisition costs means evaluating services at the time they are first acquired by the business entity. Operationally, this evaluation is but one of three problems involved in accounting for service acquisitions, for in addition to valuation, the services must be significantly classified and recognized in the accounting records. Thus we have an ordered three-element set of problems, as follows.

(1) The services must be *recognized* as services that will be used by, or flow into, the particular entity for which the accounting report is to be rendered.

(2) The services must be *described* verbally by separating them into pre-defined classification units understandable to society generally.

(3) The services must be *measured* precisely by placing a valuation on them to indicate the amount of them. By convention, supported by analyses and historical precedent, this measurement is expressed in terms of money.

7.3 THE RECOGNITION OF ACQUISITIONS

The process by which an operating entity acquires, uses, and disposes of services may be explained by reference to Diagram 5. The left side of the diagram shows services flowing into the business entity, the central pipe represents the use of services, and the right side the distribution of the services to customers.

Resources in the form of buildings, merchandise, labor, and other bundles of services are acquired from various suppliers. Some of these services are used as soon as acquired, but the bulk of them are acquired prior to the date they are put to use. The recognition of the time or point when the services have been acquired is an accounting problem of considerable significance, toward which insufficient research effort has been directed. Conceptually, the recognition of the fact that services have been acquired could take place as soon as evidence exists that the services will be used by the entity. Normally, the earlier the services are recognized as flowing into the business entity the more complete is the accounting record.

Services should not be recognized as flowing into business use however, unless they are subsequently to be used. For example, mere discussion of the desirability of acquiring a certain type of machine would not be sufficient evidence to recognize that services in the machine were going to flow into the use of a specific business firm. On the other hand, the placing

Diagram 5 | **THE FLOW OF SERVICES**

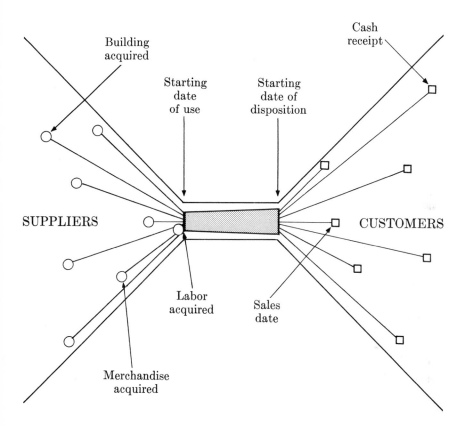

of an order for the machine might be sufficient evidence, for accounting purposes, to warrant treating the services in the machine as having been acquired.

In general, when to recognize the acquisition of services is a question to which different accountants have different answers under different situations and in different periods. Certainly, different recognition points are widely used. There is no reason why the recognition of service acquisition must be restricted to the date that "legal title" to the services passes to the buying entity, although for some purposes this limitation may be desirable. For other purposes different recognition points may be appropriate. For example, if a report to management on resources acquired is to be used as a basis for ordering additional resources, it should include resources ordered whether or not "legal title" to them has passed.

Only in this way would management be advised of the services already available for future use.

For public reporting the recognition date should be early enough to disclose useful information. It should be objective and uniform enough, however, to prevent misunderstanding about any itemization of services acquired by a specific company. But objectivity and uniformity are not enough in themselves. Significant information is also important. For example, a lease arrangement whereby services are to flow to a specific company might be recognized as an asset as readily as those resources for which "legal title" to the physical property containing the services has been acquired. Otherwise, anticipated future actions of the company will not be disclosed as fully as they might be.

For public reporting purposes, the recognition dates customarily used have been: the date "legal title" passes, the date the resources are physically received, and the date cash is paid for the acquired services. These have been supported on the grounds that they represent "convenient" dates. The dates are objective, and any one of them could represent a uniform recognition date. But as the operations of our economy change, as exemplified by the development of lease financing, the consistent, unchanging use of one date exclusively omits significant information on resources effectively acquired. This fact explains much of the current controversy over the nature of assets.

Thus the proper acquisition date to be used for accounting reports could include a variety of dates, such as those given in Table 7–1. The list of possible dates could be infinite. This situation needs to be recognized by accounting theorists. In this changing world, accountants selecting a desirable acquisition date for public reporting purposes should no longer be restricted to the "conventional three."

To show the type of thinking that might result by releasing accountants from such a restriction, let us note that, for income-determination purposes, it would be possible to propose that the proper time to recognize an acquisition depends on the type of income to be measured. Thus, if only realized income were to be reported, one would not have to recognize an acquisition prior to the time the services were used to provide revenue, or were lost. Under the condition that only realized income is to be reported, the reasoning and research involved in selecting the proper point for recognizing the date of service acquisition would presumably depend on nonincome-determination facts. Actually, the proposal that the proper recognition date depends on the type of income measured is not unrealistic, for a number of the satellite concepts of income which society now demands require a measurement of unrealized income. For example, in order for realizable holding gains and losses to be disclosed,

TABLE 7-1

Possible date	Nature of support for the date
(1) Decision is made to acquire services	(1) This would give early recognition of plans of the company and would be more informative than most other dates.
(2) The services are ordered	(2) Practically, the date services are ordered is the date the company has definitely committed itself to the use of the services.
(3) The selling company ships the order	(3) This date confirms not only that the buying entity wants the services but also that the selling entity complies with that want.
(4) The services arrive	(4) This date represents the time the services have been physically received and are available for use.
(5) The seller's invoice for the acquisition is received	(5) Practically, this documentary evidence gives the valuation of the resources and tends to coincide with the delivery date.
(6) Cash is paid	(6) This date is the final commitment of the arrangement whereby the services were acquired.

there must be a determination of income prior to the realization of the income by sale or other validation.

In general, when we look at the full scope of income determination problems, we see that service acquisition should be recorded as soon as the acquisition cost is known. When we have this figure, we can compute realizable savings, a special type of income, for any time period subsequent to the date acquisition cost is known by comparing replacement cost with acquisition cost.

This principle of recognizing acquisition of services as soon as the acquisition cost is known is sound, but before the principle can have operational meaning, we have to be able to determine when acquisition cost is known. One might contend that acquisition cost is known as soon as the contract for the acquisition is accepted by both parties to a purchase and sale of services, and that this date should be used to recognize services acquired. But the fact is that accountants seldom use this date. Too many contracts are canceled. Nevertheless, accountants should agree on one date.

An early recognition of service acquisition is desirable. It permits a determination of several types of operational income. This does not mean that all services so recognized must be disclosed on the balance sheet. There may be reasons why, for balance-sheet purposes, another recognition point may be appropriate for the determination of assets. The two recognition points may be recorded in the conventional manual ledger sheet in the following manner.

MATERIAL

Date	Activity	ACQUISITION COST		REPLACEMENT COST	
		Income determination	Balance sheet	Date	Amount
12/21/65	Ordered material				
12/23/65	Order accepted	$2,000			
12/31/65	Closed the books			12/31/65	$2,300
1/5/66	Material received		$2,000		

In the income statement for 1965, the realizable savings might be separately disclosed and not included as part of income, as follows:

Income		$xxxx
Realizable savings:		
Replacement cost of: materials	$2,300	
Acquisition cost of: materials	2,000	$ 300

Alternatively, one might decide to include realizable savings as part of annual income. In that event, since the $300 of realizable savings would normally be closed to the retained earnings account in the balance sheet, the balance sheet would not balance unless an offsetting debit of $300 were made to some account, possibly to an adjunct account labeled "unrealized income adjustment."

In fact, however, there is no reason why such recording should be done, since the income reported in the income statement does not have to be closed to the retained income account in the balance sheet. The two statements should not be forced into a systematic relationship if the result is to withhold desirable information. To those who view with alarm any tendency to separate the close tie between balance sheet and income statement, let us note that society's demand for information forces the conclusion submitted. [Several advantages might be cited for separation of the balance sheet and income statement, among which would be the tendency to lessen the use of "total assets," as listed in the balance sheet, to compute the rate of return. The point needs to be emphasized that the amount of total assets, as listed in the balance sheet, is only one of several possible valuations of assets.]

A new reporting statement may be needed to reconcile adequately the information given in the balance sheet and that in the income statement. In fact, it may be that the new statement, perhaps entitled "Reconciliation of Balance Sheet and Income Statement Information," will be essential for full disclosure of business operations in a period of time. In any event, it ought to be possible to do research on income determination without the restriction that the income valuations must also be used for balance sheet purposes.

7.4 THE CLASSIFICATION OF ACQUISITIONS

Classification, like all measurements, is a descriptive process; and the classification or grouping of acquired services is the second issue in the set of problems involved in accounting for acquisitions. There are a variety of classification systems that might be used, and there are certain general guidelines which govern their formulation. First, each account in a classification system must be mutually exclusive. There must be no overlapping areas which might properly be assigned to more than one account. Second, the accounts in each system must be clearly defined to assure the correct classification of all items. The third, and most difficult, requirement is that the categories or accounts selected must be those which will prove most useful. Each classification system must comply with all these requirements, and be so complete that under any one system all acquired services could be fitted into one heading or another. Conceptually, services acquired might be classified according to systems which describe resources in a variety of ways. Table 7–2 gives possible classification systems.

In general, it does not seem necessary to limit the number of categories in each classification system into which acquired services must be grouped. Neither does one need a detailed classification. As a rule, there should be enough categories or accounts to reveal meaningful information, but they should not be so detailed as to be confusing or so costly as to be inefficient.

The natural classification of services according to the object containing them is undoubtedly the most widely used classification system. This system groups services under such physical headings as buildings, machinery, merchandise, tools, supplies, and similar objects. To restrict the number of elements in this system, minor items are classified as part of a larger item having a similar use. The rule of thumb which applies is,

TABLE 7-2

Type of classification system	Advantages of the system
(1) *Natural or object classification:* services are grouped under the object containing the services	(1) Simple; does not require a knowledge of future plans
(2) *Functional classification:* services are grouped according to the activity they will perform	(2) Reveals the capacity for action which the entity possesses
(3) *Time classification:* services are grouped according to the time period when it is expected they will be used	(3) Reveals the flexibility of the entity, in that it indicates when services will be consumed
(4) *Responsibility classification:* services are grouped according to persons responsible for their care and use	(4) Provides a means to disclose efficient use of resources
(5) *Product classification:* services are grouped according to the product on which they will be used	(5) Reveals plans of management

"classify together those services to be used together," and this refers to similar use both in periods of time and on activities. For example, the cost of installing an electrical outlet would be classified under "machinery" if the outlet is to be used exclusively by one machine and will have no other use. But if the outlet can be used for all types of electrical equipment and will last as long as the building in which it is installed, it would be classified under "building." By this process the cost of the electrical outlet would be assigned to appropriate periods of time and areas of activity, even though an identical cost might be classified differently because of an anticipated different use.

An advantage of the natural or object classification system is that it is neutral, in that it makes no prediction as to how or where the services will be used. Thus no reclassification of services on hand is necessary when plans change. Furthermore, because it merely describes services according to the form in which they are contained, the object classification system does not reveal why the services were acquired. The characteristic of neutrality is ignored when services are classified according to planned use or responsibility. Both the functional and the time classification systems are more predictive than descriptive of the nature of the services, and the predictive aspects are considered more significant than the descriptive features.

Example

Under a time-classification system, services in a $10,000 machine to be used over a five-year period might be grouped in the following manner:

Cost of services to be used in:

Next 30 days	$ 2,000
Next 30 to 180 days	1,000
Next 180 days to 1 year	1,000
Next 1 to 5 years	2,000
Next 5 to 10 years	4,000
Total	$10,000

Alternatively, the services might be classified functionally as follows:

Cost of services to be used to:

Lift products	$ 3,000
Move products	2,000
Repair other equipment	4,000
Provide scrap value	1,000
Total	$10,000

Because these classifications are predictions of when and how the services are to be used, a reclassification of the services is necessary when plans change. Also both classification systems require revaluation of amounts in each account as plans change. In fact, a reclassification may be necessary even if plans do not change, because the nature of the services acquired may change from time to time. For example, the classification of services of land acquired for oil resources may change when it is discovered that the land contains other services besides oil.

For income-determination purposes, the acquired services should be classified in such a way that measurement of the amount used in a specific period of time or on a particular undertaking is facilitated. But the classification system which would best facilitate measurement of use and revaluation of services has yet to be well defined, and here a considerable amount of research is needed. For the present the natural or object classification system seems to be the most useful.

Possibly the greatest need for the further development of the accounting framework at the theoretical level is the study of the nature of classification. Even though the accounting discipline relies heavily on classification, there has been no theoretical accounting study of the nature of classification. In fact, there has not even been a systematic study of possible classification systems which the accounting discipline could use. The partial studies available have not supported well any one classification system over another. Like Topsy, the accounting classification scheme now used "just growed."

7.5 THE VALUATION OF ACQUISITIONS

There is no reason why acquired services should be valued at their cost, but neither is there any force which compels another valuation. Conceptually, five possible valuations are worthy of consideration in selecting an appropriate base for valuing services recognized and classified. These evaluations and the relationship between them are illustrated below.

Services acquired may be valued at:

(1) *Value to the buyer* (discounted value of subjective future receipts) $1,000
     Less: special value to buyer (user's surplus)   50

(2) *Sales market value* into which the buyer sells $ 950
     Less: variation in wholesale and retail market value   150

(3) *Buying market value* from which the buyer purchases $ 800
     Less: lucky-purchase saving   100

(4) *Invoice amount* $ 700
     Less: adjustment discount   25

(5) *Cost* (cash or cash equivalent at the acquisition date) $ 675

Operationally, however, there is a distinction between accomplishment and effort; and while it may be that a resource will have a subjective value to the buyer or even a realizable market value different from cost, such values represent accomplishment rather than effort or sacrifice. This is not to say that neither subjective value nor sales market value should be used in valuing all service resources on hand at any time. But it does mean that, if such values are used, the resulting valuation is in terms of accomplishment rather than in terms of the effort or sacrifice necessary for the performance of the operation. Only cost represents effort. It is true, of course, that subjective value or immediate sales market value may represent only intermediate accomplishments, for the ultimate accomplishment is the sale of a product to customers. Further, the accomplishment resulting from advantageous buying is a type of accomplishment which must be reported separately from both the accomplishment arising from holding services and that due to effective use of services. This confusion regarding the nature of accomplishment must be corrected before accountants can make any uniform departure from the effort valuation.

Efforts to evaluate "buyers" for department stores in terms of gross margin (sales less acquisition cost of merchandise sold) represent a crude attempt to measure the effectiveness with which the acquisition activity is performed, and indicates that a direct evaluation of the accomplishment of the acquisition activity is needed. By matching the value of acquisition accomplishment against a valuation in terms of effort, one could obtain a measure of activity effectiveness, and acquisitions could then be valued in terms of accomplishment. Certain developments in subjective utility theory indicate that valuation of acquisitions in terms of accomplishment is not entirely a speculative matter.

As of now, however, the only measure of effort is cost applied at the date services are acquired. But what is cost? Basically, *cost is sacrifice*, and this fundamental fact underlies all measurements of services acquired. Furthermore, "cost" implies all sacrifices necessary for the acquisition of services. It does not or should not include unnecessary sacrifices (and here we use the word "unnecessary" in the sense of what a reasonably prudent man would obviously not do). Normally, unless there is evidence to the contrary, the assumption is that in any acquisition a sacrifice is necessary. Thus cost valuation means all sacrifices required to acquire economic services.

Acquisition cost refers to all sacrifice made in order to have the resource available for use at the planned time of use. A distinction should be made, however, between the time services are available for use and the time they are put to use. Services are available for use at the time they are installed and ready to perform the function for which they were acquired. All the sacrifices involved in getting the services in this condition are costs of the services.

Thus acquisition cost includes transportation in, inspection, installation, testing, trial operation, and other cash or cash-equivalent outlays necessary to have the services available for use.

But suppose the services are not put to use as soon as they become available for use. Should any sacrifice involved between the time services are available for use and the time they are put to use be considered part of acquisition cost? The answer seems to depend on the intent of the buyer. If, in planning the acquisition, the buyer anticipates the delay between the time the services will be available for use and the date they will be put to use, he will have considered any cost involved. In this sense he purposefully plans to make these sacrifices in order to have the services at the time they are put to use. Because these sacrifices are expected, they become a part of the acquisition cost of the services to be used.

On the other hand, if the delay in putting the services to use is unexpected and unplanned, any sacrifice due to the delay should not be included as part of the acquisition cost of the services. Where planning is not done well and no information is available to indicate whether or not the delay was anticipated, it is better to include normal sacrifices caused by any delay as part of the acquisition cost. This does not justify capitalizing as acquisition cost those losses due to unnecessary and unplanned developments.

Example

Suppose that a company planned to put a machine in operation on Jan. 1 and paid $10,000 to have it available for use on that date. The $10,000 would represent acquisition cost. But if the company did not put the machine to use until June 30, and paid an additional $200 as property taxes for the six-month period, the $200 would represent a loss, and not acquisition cost. On the other hand, had the company planned at the time of purchase to have the machine idle until June 30 for one reason or another, the $200 of taxes would be considered one of the costs of having the resource available at the time needed, and would be part of acquisition cost.

Thus acquisition cost depends in part on the intent of management, for it represents the cash or cash equivalent purposefully released or sacrificed to have the services available for use at the time needed. Nonpurposeful sacrifices represent losses.

In addition to having these restrictions, the term "acquisition cost" is bounded in another way. As we have said, acquisition cost refers to the cash equivalent which would have to be paid on the acquisition date. Even if the actual cash payment is more than the cash which would have to be paid on the acquisition date, acquisition cost refers to the cash payment required on the acquisition date. Conceptually, all services acquired on open account or under any means of delayed payment should be costed at the present value of the future cash payment. By this process the interest element would be eliminated from acquisition cost. This same conception of acquisition cost requires that apparent cost, as reflected by an actual cash payment on the acquisition date, does not represent acquisition cost unless the transaction is between independent parties dealing with each other at arm's length. Acquisitions from owners, company officials, and others having a close relation to the company are suspect and should be examined closely in order to determine the cash which would have been paid if the transaction had been between independent groups.

The acquisition cost of services is at times confused with the acquisition cost of the object containing the services. Actually, of course, the accounting discipline is concerned with the acquisition cost of the services which the entity expects with some degree of probability that it will use. A $100 payment for a machine represents payment for the services in the machine that the entity expects to use. Should the machine have excess capacity, i.e., should the entity plan not to use all the potential services in the machine, the excess services would have no acquisition cost. They would be free services, and if they were to be lost or destroyed by the elements of nature, this would involve no sacrifice by the entity.

Now the significance of this proposition that acquisition cost refers to the cost of the services acquired and not to the cost of the object containing the services is that income can arise should "free" services become useful or worth something; that the cost of services used, if they are to be related to acquisition cost, should be computed according to formulas which recognize the nature of the acquisition costs (we shall consider this later); and that not all disappearances of services represent losses.

In addition to these general considerations regarding the determination of acquisition cost, there are a number of special issues which we shall refer to here and discuss in more detail elsewhere. Some of these issues must be considered conceptually, even though means for their implementation are not now available.

First, some confusion regarding the amount of acquisition cost may arise when noncash items are exchanged for services. In this situation, as we noted in Chapter 6, the correct cost is the current sales price of the resource given up. Only this price represents the sacrifice of obtaining the new services, and acceptance of any other figure for acquisition cost must be justified on the basis that it represents a reasonable approximation of that price.

Determining acquisition cost is an involved process in still another sense, for any one acquisition of services is, more often than not, merely one of a series of similar acquisitions which will take place. Thus labor services acquired from a new employee may be paid for at a "premium" price in order for the company to be assured that it will obtain future labor services. Looked at this way, the premium paid new employees is not an acquisition cost of the original services but a cost of those subsequently to be acquired. Properly speaking, these premiums should be carried in a "suspense" account until the future services are acquired, at which time they should be removed from suspense and assigned to the services as part of their acquisition cost. The problem is to determine the extent of the premium, which may be caused by the inefficiency of new employees, and to estimate the future labor services to which it applies.

Similar situations exist when the price paid for material depends on the amount of additional material to be purchased in the future, or when the price paid for acquired services is for the purpose of assuring a supply of future services. The reason this jointness of acquisition cost exists is that one individual acquisition cannot be isolated from past and future acquisitions. Whenever the extent of the jointness can be measured, there should be no hesitation about allocating the cost appropriately. On the other hand, when jointness cannot be measured, the better procedure is to treat each acquisition as an isolated transaction and determine acquisition cost accordingly.

Due largely to the necessity of grouping or classifying a variety of different services under one descriptive title, it often happens that the acquisition cost of certain specific physical resources will change as additional services are added to a descriptive title. For example, the acquisition cost of a machine on Jan. 1 may be computed at $10,000, but the subsequent addition of services to the machine at a cost of $1,200 when a new part is added will result in a new acquisition cost of $11,200 for the machine.

A special case of this arises in the case of the so-called "protective costs" (insurance, taxes, etc.) which are payments made to protect the company against a loss of services due to theft, fire, and other anticipated adverse possibilities. Customarily these costs are treated as separate services which are used as they are acquired. Theoretically, however, these payments may be considered as additional acquisition costs of services previously acquired, and might be capitalized as the cost of buildings, machinery, or other assets. This is contrary to the more traditional method of treating these "costs" as separate and distinct from the assets protected.

Summary

The problem of determining acquisition cost is concerned with answers to the following questions.

(1) When should services be recognized as acquired?
(2) How should services acquired be classified?
(3) At what amount should acquired services be valued?

Although accountants now have answers to these questions, there is no reason to assume that the current answers will prevail indefinitely. In fact, a historical review of accounting procedures will reveal that the answers have changed in the past and it may be assumed that they will change in the future. Frequent criticisms of the present answers to these questions suggest that changes may have to be made in the near future. Since the responsibility for developing the changes is the responsibility of accountants, the study of possible future answers to the questions is almost as important as the study of the contemporary answers.

REFERENCES

1. GEORGE O. MAY, "Changes in the Accounting Treatment of Capital Items During the Last Fifty Years." *Problems of Capital Formation*, by National Bureau of Economic Research (Princeton: Princeton University Press, 1957), page 194

2. E. O. EDWARDS and P. W. BELL, *The Theory and Measurement of Business Income* (Berkeley: University of California Press, 1961), Chapter 3

3. ROBERT T. SPROUSE and MAURICE MOONITZ, *A Tentative Set of Broad Accounting Principles for Business Enterprises* (New York: American Institute of Certified Public Accountants, 1962), Chapter 4

Chapter 8

Determination of Utilization Cost

8.1 THE BUSINESS INCOME CREATION PROCESS

William of Ockham, around 1325, proposed the famous formula known as "Ockham's razor," which held that a plurality of entities, causes, or factors is not to be assumed without need [1]. Using this "razor," which pointed out that it is vain to explain by proposing several causes an action which can be explained by a fewer number, Ockham cut through a lot of the grandiose abstractions common in many fields at that time. And throughout subsequent history, this "razor" has been used effectively in many fields to cut through and sort out the continuous plethora of notions which appear as a field develops. At the present time, Ockham's razor might well be used on accounting theory and practices. In particular there is a need to eliminate some of the confusion of concepts and notions regarding the nature of business operations.

The intuitive assumption underlying a great deal of accounting thought has been that the business use of services involves a process of recombining services for the purpose of creating or distributing goods or services to customers. In fact, accounting thought has been dominated by this assumption to such an extent that people have seldom considered the possibility that business activities might include other operations as well. For example, there is the insistence that income arises at the point of sale, and the subtle argument, which supports asset valuation in terms of

128

acquisition cost, that assets are merely expenses of future sales. Both these illustrations imply that the only business activity is to acquire services and recombine them, which represents effort applied, and distribute them to customers, which represents accomplishment. Other business efforts and accomplishments have seldom been considered in accounting theory, though accounting practice has treated the "other activities" as by-products of the basic operation.

Investment, which can be said to be the use of services by holding them rather than by recombining them, has been recognized as a process of using services. But the notion has prevailed that investment operations are not, by and large, a significant feature of business operations. Investments have been considered incidental to the primary objective. They have even been referred to as the use of "excess" cash. Reflecting this point of view, investments, which have provided interest revenue and other gains and losses from holding resources, have not been considered a distinct business operation in the literature of accounting theory. But we live in a time of change, and changes in the environment in which economic activity is carried out are often subtle and far-reaching. It may be that environmental changes of recent years have resulted in changes in economic objectives, as some economists strongly contend [2], and this possibility requires that the tacit assumption of accounting regarding the process by which business income is created be subjected to Ockham's razor.

8.2 INVESTMENT INCOME

Throughout this study, we have referred to the growing phenomenon of holding gains. At the risk of treating this issue excessively, let us examine the notion in more detail.

Business firms have for years invested funds in resources and have held these resources for the income which results from holding them for a period of time. In fact, the word "investment," to many people, implies using money to acquire resources which are to be held, and not consumed in production and distribution. Normally, investments produce an income which comes about because of the passage of time. Interest revenue is a typical example, for it results solely from the passage of time. Accountants refer to "investments" in stocks and bonds and term the gain from such investments "investment income."

But the notion of an investment is broader than merely holding stocks and bonds, for investments include all acquisitions which are held and not used in production and distribution operations. For example, an organization may use excess cash not needed for normal operations to purchase land, with the intent that the land will be held as an investment and not used in production or distribution activities. Clearly such an operation is an investment operation, and any gain from the land, either in the form of rental revenue or gain on sale of the land, would represent investment income.

The concept of investment income, as contrasted with production and distribution operating income, is firmly established in contemporary accounting practice. It may also be quite distinct in an operational sense, for while the dictate of the production and distribution operation is to "avoid tying up idle funds in excessive inventory," effective performance of the investment operation might dictate just the opposite.

What is not so clearly recognized about the investment operation is that this type of holding gain or loss also comes about when services are acquired and held for a period prior to the date they are used. For example, a firm anticipating a rise in inventory prices may increase its investment in inventories. If prices do rise, an investment income will result, although it is seldom recognized as such, due to holding the services. Or a company may purchase excess fixed-asset capacity and justify the extra investment on the grounds that it represents a "good buy," because the resources are expected to increase in price and will be needed at a later date. Thus the phenomenon of investment operations is well established as an important part of business operations. Furthermore, as our economy has developed, investment income has become a relatively more significant part of business income.

The precise meaning of investment operating income, and its distinction from other operating income, is difficult to establish. While there is general recognition that investment income results from holding resources, there is some confusion regarding the time when the holding operation stops and the production and distribution operation begins. Specifically, the question is whether or not price increases which take place during the production interval should be treated as investment income or production income.

Example

A company purchased raw materials on Jan. 10 for $5,000, and held them until Feb. 15, when the raw materials were worth $5,800. They were in the production process until Feb. 28, during which time prices increased so that the raw materials were worth $6,000 on that date. They were then sold as part of a finished product for $9,000. Assume that other production costs were $1,000. If, as is conventional, the company does not separate its investment income from the income from its other operations, it can compute its operating income as follows:

Sales		$9,000
Expenses:		
Raw materials used	$5,000	
Other expenses	1,000	6,000
Operating income		$3,000

If investment operating income is to be disclosed separately, the computation might appear as follows:

Production and distribution operations

Sales		$9,000	
Expenses:			
Raw material used	$6,000		
Other expenses	1,000	7,000	
Operating income			$2,000

Investment operations

Worth of raw materials on date used	$6,000	
Acquisition cost of raw materials	5,000	
Operating income		1,000
Total operating income		$3,000

Some will contend, however, that investment income should be only $800 ($5,800 — $5,000) because the $200 ($6,000 — $5,800) does not represent an investment gain but is incidental to the production process. There is an element of truth to this, but the more compelling thinking is that the $200 is not an income from the production and distribution operation. Furthermore, had a further price increase taken place after the finished product was completed (on Feb. 28) and prior to its sales date, an additional gain due to holding resources would result, and the concept of investment income or loss would be muddled unless the $200 were included to represent the total gain or loss from holding resources. This appears to be the most reasonable solution to this controversial issue.

There remains the possibility that separating investment operating income from other operating income will fail to disclose managerial intent. That is, it may be contended that since management tries to maximize the sum of both production and holding income, there is no reason to separate the two elements. Especially is this so when it is costly to separate them and when it is done without objective evidence. More sophisticated advocates of this proposal allow exceptions for managerial (internal) purposes and for those situations where delay in recognizing holding gains would grossly distort year-to-year income. Intuitively, this proposal has a realistic ring to it. It seems to accord with the facts. It does not involve a pronounced change in current practice. But it overlooks the current needs of investors and others for information not only on the total income of the entity but also on the sources of income.

As a variation of the proposal that separating holding gain from production gain will fail to disclose managerial intent, it may be contended that managers do not intend to make investment income, and that disclosing effectiveness in such an area does not indicate either managerial effectiveness or failure in the investment operation. This may well be true, but the point is that such investment income is now treated as part of normal operating income, and influences judgments regarding the effectiveness of management in the production and distribution operation. Our conclusion is that investment income should be separately reported to disclose managerial effectiveness in the investment operation, or if management does not concern itself with this type of operation, investment income should be separated from other operating income precisely in order to disclose effectiveness in the other operations with which management does concern itself.

If investment income is reported separately, certain consequences follow. One of these is worth mentioning here: Investment acquisitions differ from production and distribution service acquisitions in that many assets normally considered money resources, such as interest-bearing notes receivable, represent investments. The income from holding such resources is investment income. In the sense that money resources are used to provide investment income, they represent investment service resources. Nevertheless, it is not normally desirable to change the concept of service resources to include anything other than the services to be used in the production and distribution of goods and services to customers. But for banks and other financial institutions, it may well be appropriate to treat as service resources items which would be treated as money resources by other companies. The term "monetary service resources" is a fitting description.

A second consequence of inaugurating the separate reporting of investment income is that more involved measurement processes and techniques are needed. Before examining the problem of measuring investment income, however, let us discuss the measurement of utilization cost, for the two measurements are closely related.

Utilization cost means the sacrifice involved in using previously acquired service resources. This cost must be measured whether or not an effort is made to disclose holding (investment) gains, because in any period of time a business entity will consume and use previously acquired services to produce revenue. Determining the utilization cost of these services involves two problems:

(a) Determination of the amount and type of services used in a period of time
(b) Valuation of the services used

8.3 AMOUNT OF SERVICES USED

Contemporary procedures for computing the amount of services used rely heavily on formulas, of which there are a great number. Formulas exist for the following three general types of situation:

(1) *All acquired services are used.* These formulas are applied to immediate services, i.e., those services which are used as acquired and are not stored prior to use. Users of these formulas properly endeavor to charge as utilization cost the acquisition cost of the services, for in this situation acquisition cost is indeed equal to utilization cost. The formulas (if indeed they are formulas and not rules) take no particular form. To make certain that all such acquisition costs are treated as utilization cost, accountants often omit an acquisition-cost entry and charge the acquisition cost of the services to utilization cost at the time acquired.
(2) *There is a physical flow of material objects, and services flow with them.* Merchandise, supplies, tools, and other short-term service resources are normally handled by these formulas, whose objective is to attach a portion of acquisition cost to each physical object, and consider the acquisition cost of the physical object to be the utilization cost of the services in these objects. The formulas used for this purpose include the usual inventory costing procedures of first-in, first-out; last-in, first-out; next-in, first-out; average cost; and a variety of related methods.
(3) *The services are extracted from resources and used without any physical flow of a material object.* Depreciation and amortization of long-term resources are typical cases. These formulas are probably the least reliable as a means for computing an accurate measure of the utilization cost of services used in a period of time. They include such depreciation formulas as the straight-line, declining-balance, and units-of-production methods.

Because so many formulas exist, there should be a standard or criterion to indicate when each should be used. That is, for each situation, there should be one and only one appropriate formula. At present, however, no standard exists, and practice varies widely in deciding which formula should be used for each situation. The notion of consistency over time has been advocated as a solution to this unsatisfactory condition. That is, any utilization formula may be used, provided it is used consistently year after year. Actually, about all this expediency amounts to is that it helps to prevent managerial manipulation of income from year to year, since it prohibits arbitrary changes of utilization formulas. The real need is for a better method of measuring utilization cost.

An ideal method for measuring utilization cost should provide results which reasonably represent the actual amount of services used. Conceptually, the development of such a method involves two distinct problems: determining the number of services used and calculating their cost. These are difficult problems, since evidently any measurement of the number of services used in a period of time would have to be a fiat kind of measurement, for the notion of a service is not sufficiently distinct to permit, even conceptually, a direct count of services. But services used could be measured in such terms as hours of work performed, units of product produced, or amount of time passed. In fact, by using different fiat measurements it would be possible to disclose a variety of aspects of utilization cost.

In terms of a specific current issue, utilization cost could be measured to distinguish services used in production from those consumed with the passage of time. We could refer to the former as user cost and treat the latter as time cost.

Example

A machine has a cost of $10,000 and a life of 5 years or 2,000 hours of work, whichever is shorter. It is used 600 hours in its first year of operation. Its depreciation thus might be measured to disclose the extra user cost, as follows:

Time depreciation $10,000/5	$2,000
User depreciation* [($10,000/2,000)600] − $2,000 =	1,000
	$3,000

These two measurements complement each other, and both should be used. Either one alone is an inadequate measure of utilization costs over several periods of time. In some periods of time, utilization costs may be satisfactorily measured by a fiat measurement based on the passage of time, but in another period only a fiat measurement based on work performed could reflect the actual amount of service used in that period. Both measurements are necessary in order to measure accurately the services used in a period of time.

---

* User depreciation refers to the extra utilization cost caused by using the machine.

As an aside, it may be noted that user cost (the cost of services consumed exclusively through use) should be measured and separately reported on a number of accounting statements. User cost, when considered in its original conception, should be evaluated in terms of the opportunity cost of the services used, but it does not have to be so valued. In the above illustration, user depreciation was measured as a portion of acquisition cost. The point is that the proper valuation of user cost may be treated as an issue separate from the determination of the services consumed exclusively through use. A solution to either problem would be a contribution to the accounting discipline.

User cost does not include all services used in production and distribution, for services which would have disappeared with the passage of time, even though they are in fact consumed by use, are not considered in calculating user cost. This is true even if the services used have an opportunity cost. User cost is precisely the cost—evaluated according to any appropriate valuation concept—of services used solely because of the activity on which they were used. Keynes [3] has said, "User cost has, I think, an importance for the classical theory of value which has been overlooked." One advantage of the user-cost concept is that it defines unambiguously certain costs of the production and distribution operation.

Time costs may be either costs of the recombination operation or an investment loss, depending on the circumstances. If the services which would have been consumed with the passage of time are in fact consumed in the recombination operation, they are costs of production and distribution, though they are not user costs. On the other hand, if the services are not used in the recombination operation, they represent losses due to the investment operation. Because it is difficult to divide time costs into recombination costs and investment losses, the notion of direct costing, which aims to separate investment operations from the recombination operation, excludes all time costs from the recombination operation. That is, direct costing developed because of the need to separate the results of the investment operation from those of the recombination operation. An understanding of the user-cost concept makes it possible to appreciate the results of the direct-costing procedure of eliminating all time costs from recombination costs.

8.4 VALUATION OF SERVICES USED

Let us turn to the second problem involved in developing realistic measures of utilization cost: determining the proper valuation of the services used. Note first that all formulas now in use tend to avoid the issue of determining the precise time services are used. Utilization costs are computed only for periods of time. Consequently they do not reveal the costs of services used on each activity. In addition, existing formulas assume that utilization cost will be measured in terms of acquisition cost. Actually, the cost of services used is not necessarily their acquisition cost, for utilization cost, like acquisition cost, is sacrifice. And there is little reason to assume that the sacrifice involved in using services is identical to the sacrifice involved in acquiring them. In theory, because of the existence of interest in our society, the two costs can never be equal if there is any time interval between acquisition and utilization.

Interest exists in our society. We cannot avoid it, either by ignoring it or by stating that it does not exist. By definition *interest is the cost of money*, and whether or not it is paid it exists. If it is not paid, it is lost interest. Businessmen are well aware of interest and consider it in making purchases, as we noted previously in the discussion of subjective and market values.

When a company makes purchases, the management recognizes that money tied up in service resources cannot earn explicit interest. Because of this, a higher price will be paid for services to be used immediately than for identical services to be used at a later date. This may be clarified by a hypothetical illustration.

Example

Company *A* needs the services of a machine which can either be rented for $10,000 a year or purchased immediately for $29,500 cash. The life of the machine is three years, and Company *A* can invest its funds at 4% interest. [It is not suggested that the 4% external rate of return is the proper interest rate to be used for this type of analysis. There are in fact three general rates which might be used and the proper one depends on the circumstances of the business decision: (a) *External rate of return*, or the rate that could be earned by using the funds for investment outside the business. (b) *Internal rate of return*, or the rate that could be earned by using the funds on other projects within the business. (c) *The cost of capital*, or the external rate that would have to be paid to acquire the funds. Since we are concerned here only with the fact that some interest rate exists, the reader is referred to books or articles on capital budgeting for a more detailed analysis of the discount rate.]

Company *A* wants to determine the most economical method of acquiring the services. Since revenue and expenses will be the same under either alternative except for the cost of the machine, the decision hinges on the cost of the machine. Typically, this comparison is made by discounting all payments to the present value, so that alternatives may be compared in terms of time-adjusted costs. But a crude comparison may also be made in terms of cash flow. For example, if Company *A* has

$30,000 cash on the date the machine is acquired, the cash flow of each method may be computed as follows:

	PURCHASE		RENT	
	Cash on hand	Outlay	Cash on hand	Outlay
Start of first year	$30,000.00	$29,500	$30,000.00	$10,000
Interest on unused cash 4%	20.00	—	800.00	—
Start of second year	$ 520.00		$20,800.00	$10,000
Interest on unused cash 4%	20.80	—	432.00	—
Start of third year	$ 540.80	—	$11,232.00	$10,000
Interest on unused cash 4%	21.63		49.28	
Cash balance, end of third year	$ 562.43		$ 1,281.28	

Because of the interest earned on unused cash, Company A would be better off in the amount of $718.85 ($1,281.28 − $562.43) by renting the machine.

The price at which Company A should buy rather than rent is that point where the purchase price drops below the present value of the future rents, discounted at 4% and computed as follows:

PV of first year's services	$10,000.00
PV of second year's services ($10,000/1.04)	9,615.38
PV of third year's services [$10,000/(1.04)^2]	9,245.56
	$28,860.94

Assume that the price is $28,860.94, and Company A does buy the machine. In effect the company purchased the services in the machine, and has paid the following prices for them.

For the first year's services	$10,000.00
For the second year's services	9,615.38
For the third year's services	9,245.56
Total	$28,860.94

If acquisition cost is used to measure utilization cost and the services are used as planned, depreciation each year should be $10,000, $9,615.38, and $9,245.56, respectively. If cost is below the present value of the future rents which the company anticipates, the same principle applies that a lower price will have been paid for the second and third year's services. It will be necessary, however, to compute the internal rate of return, which will equate cost and the future rents. The derived internal rate may then be used to calculate the cost of each year's services. For example, if the machine cost $25,000, the internal rate of return could be calculated on a trial-and-error basis. Since a 4% rate yields a present value of \$28,860.94, a higher rate will be needed to yield a present value of \$25,000. The results using 10%, 20%, 22%, and $21\frac{1}{2}$% as the discount rates are shown below:

	10%	20%	22%	$21\frac{1}{2}$%
PV of first year's services	\$10,000.00	\$10,000.00	\$10,000.00	\$10,000.00
PV of second year's services	9,090.90	8,333.33	8,196.72	8,230.45
PV of third year's services	8,264.45	6,944.44	6,718.62	6,774.03
	\$27,355.35	\$25,277.77	\$24,915.34	\$25,004.48

Since the rate of $21\frac{1}{2}$% yields approximately a present value equal to cost (\$25,004.48 versus \$25,000), depreciation each year should be approximately the present value of each year's services discounted at the $21\frac{1}{2}$% rate. Other depreciation methods are suspect. For example, in the data developed by discounting at 4%, straight-line depreciation of \$9,620.31 a year (\$28,860.94/3) would be an inaccurate measure of the acquisition cost of the services used each year.

Contrary to the normal assumption, however, acquisition cost does not measure utilization cost, except as a reasonable approximation of it in the first year. The correct utilization cost can only be determined by adding in the interest element as shown below:

	FIRST YEAR	SECOND YEAR	THIRD YEAR
Acquisition cost of services	\$10,000.00	\$ 9,615.38	\$ 9,245.56
Interest, second year (4%)	—	384.62	369.82
Interest, third year (4%)	—	—	384.62
Utilization cost of services	\$10,000.00	\$10,000.00	\$10,000.00

It should be noted that in theory, if market conditions were unchanged over the three-year period, \$10,000 would be the current market cost of each year's services if one-third of the services were purchased each year. That is, in theory, under ideal conditions where storage costs are not involved, utilization cost differs from acquisition cost by exactly the interest element over the time the services were held in storage.

Actually, interest is only one of several alternative uses of the funds. Under ideal conditions, interest may also be the opportunity cost if no higher return can be earned by using the funds elsewhere. Under imperfect conditions, however, there might be available to the firm some alternative which would permit the firm to earn a rate of return higher than the interest rate. The highest rate of return on the investment would represent the opportunity cost and, actually, the opportunity rate of return would more accurately account for the difference between acquisition cost and utilization cost. Practically speaking, however, the opportunity rate of return, though it is not known, tends to be reflected in changes in the current cost of the services. This means that a firm which wants to compute the difference between acquisition cost and utilization cost normally has to use current market replacement cost as a yardstick, though there may be situations in which the firm can measure utilization cost by adding the interest element to acquisition cost.

If a company uses a price level index to adjust acquisition cost to utilization cost, it must be careful to see that the adjustment provides for the interest element, though normally interest is automatically provided for in price changes. That is, if services purchased for $10,000 are held for one year before being used, the current replacement cost of the services at the end of the year could be due both to the interest factor and to other causes of price level changes. If the price level index is computed by comparing acquisition cost at the beginning of the year with replacement cost new at the end of the year, the index number adjustment of acquisition cost will adjust for both the interest element and the price level change. If the price level index is computed in some other way, it may not adjust acquisition cost for the interest element, and an additional adjustment of acquisition cost may be necessary to determine utilization cost.

Accounting fails to make a number of conceptual distinctions. Among these, the failure to distinguish utilization cost from acquisition cost is probably the most incomprehensible. Managers of businesses know that the distinction exists, and so do most other people. When sale of an asset is being considered, there are few people who are not more concerned with the current value of the asset than with its acquisition cost. No responsible investor would sell for $10,000 land having an acquisition cost of $8,000 if he felt the current replacement cost of it were $15,000, and replacement were necessary. The sacrifice involved in selling is measured not in terms of acquisition cost, but in terms of the current sacrifice involved. This is utilization cost. Despite the distinction between acquisition and utilization costs, contemporary accounting procedures seldom provide for the distinction in measuring the cost of using services. Almost universally, utilization cost is measured in terms of acquisition cost.

Attempts to justify the procedure have relied on two often-used accounting concepts. The justification is that *departures* and *expediencies* must be used in accounting because of the difficulty of the measurement problem. Expediencies represent attempts to follow the objectives set forth in accounting theory as closely as possible. Departures, on the other hand, ignore the dictates of accounting theory and follow authoritative pronouncements blindly.

At best, departures and expediencies merely represent explanations of current practice. At their worst, departures discourage the development of an effective, systematic information system capable of scientific advance. Expediencies, at their worst, encourage a tendency to label a contrary procedure as "impractical" without trial, even though the proposal may be approved as a theoretical objective. The result tends to be a hesitancy to refine and improve measurement methods. While accounting has not yet developed to the level of a science and we must expect expediencies and departures to be a part of accounting for some time, they constitute a weak defense for measuring utilization cost as a part of acquisition cost.

Because there is a distinction between utilization cost and acquisition cost, accounting must recognize it. Hence acquisition costing of service utilizations would have to be justified not on the grounds that it is correct but on the grounds that the distinction between utilization cost and acquisition cost is slight, and that acquisition costs properly allocated represent a reasonable measure of utilization cost. This is justification on the basis of *materiality*, another concept of imprecise meaning which has become an accepted part of the accounting discipline. One might defend materiality by the same reasoning as that suggested for expediencies and departures.

8.5 MEASUREMENT OF UTILIZATION COST

The preceding examination of the nature of utilization cost has emphasized the difference between acquisition cost and utilization cost, and has dealt with means for developing a measurement of utilization cost. Actually, there are three notions of the nature of the cost of utilization:

(1) *Net realizable value*, which is the price, less costs of selling, which could be obtained if the services were sold instead of used. In this sense utilization cost is the alternative receipts foregone by using the services. This concept of cost, in its complete development, refers not only to the immediate selling price but also to future selling prices, less cost of storing and selling, discounted back to the present time at a rate equivalent to that normally earned by the company. The highest present value of all these possible net selling prices represents the true "net realizable value." Practically, of course, it may be computed by reference to current selling price less cost of selling.

(2) *Current cost*, which is the current repurchase price of the services used. In this sense utilization cost is the sacrifice required to have the services available at the time of use. Should acquisition cost differ from current cost, the difference would represent a cost saving or loss due to

holding the services prior to use. Thus one could measure investment income by measuring utilization cost, for investment income would include, among other holding gains, the difference between acquisition cost and current cost at the time the services were used. Additional investment income might arise if the used services were held for an additional period prior to sale, and this income could be measured in a similar way, though the computation in this case would be the difference between utilization cost and a later current cost. It seems desirable to distinguish the resulting two types of investment income, for the former is more independent of the production and distribution activity and thus more controllable by management. The latter may be a noncontrollable investment gain or loss. In any event, the more controllable concept of investment income could be measured by matching current replacement cost of services used with their acquisition cost.

(3) *Replacement cost*, which is the sacrifice required to replace used services. If replacement is necessary, it measures the cost of the services used in that it is the sacrifice caused by using the services. It differs from current cost, in both its measurement and its meaning, only in that it refers to actual future replacement.

Both net realizable value and replacement cost are useful in planning future activities, but they do not represent the cost of using services in a long-range or normal sense. Both are short-run concepts, and while they may accurately reflect the immediate sacrifice if replacement is necessary or if a sale is foregone by using the services, they do not measure the normal sacrifice which would exist if the services were not already on hand. Assuming that services are not already on hand, the normal cost of using services would be their current acquisition cost at the time they are put to use. This appears to be the proper view of the sacrifice involved in using resources, and this conception of the valuation of utilization cost has the advantage of being independent of either past or future activities. It is independent of past acquisition cost and it is independent of future actions which management might take. It reveals effort which would have to be applied to carry out the production and distribution activities of the company if a prior investment operation had not been carried out.

Operationally, the use of current cost separates the acquisition operation from the utilization operation. In addition, it enables a distinction to be made between utilization operations and disposition operations. Finally, it permits one to separate the results of investment operations from other operations. These different operations are distinctive in a business, and thus accounting valuations should recognize these distinctions.

When we accept the idea that utilization cost should be valued without consideration of either past or future operations and recognize as investment income the difference between acquisition cost and current cost, we must consider two related problems.   First, if the proper valuation of utilization cost is the current cost of the services at the time they are "put to use," the question arises as to *when* services are put to use.   The answer provides not only a basis for determining utilization cost, but also suggests certain conceptually distinctive elements within investment income.

Although it has been suggested that the solution to the problem of measuring investment income might be simplified by treating all gains or losses from holding resources as investment income, separate elements of investment income may be disclosed somewhat as follows:

(1) Investment income from holding resources prior to the time the resources are put to use. This would be computed by comparing current cost on the date resources are put to use, which measures utilization cost, with acquisition cost.

(2) Investment income or loss arising during the necessary period of producing and distributing the goods and services. This would be the difference between current cost at the date services are put to use (utilization cost) and current cost at the date the services are distributed to customers.

(3) Investment income from holding finished goods and services beyond the normal time necessary for production and distribution. (This would be separated from investment income of type 2 only when objectively measurable.)

An attempt to measure investment income in this degree of detail makes the date services are put to use a significant point. The time services are "put to use" is a continuous process, ranging from the time management decides how to use specific services to the time when all services have been consumed. Therefore the selection of a point in time when services are to be recognized as having been "put to use" may have to be a conventional agreement. In general, in order to ensure uniform treatment, the point selected should not depart too far from the point when the services are physically used.

The second problem relates to the determination of the current cost of the services used. Since the services used may be acquired in different forms (labor or machine, for example), it seems desirable, in order to avoid the problem of determining precisely which services were used, to calculate the utilization cost of services in terms of the form containing the services at the time they are used. Thus if the service of "lifting materials" were provided by a machine and not by personal labor, the utilization cost of the services used is the current cost of the services as they exist in the machine and not as they might be available in the form of labor or another type of machine.

Procedurally, the valuation of utilization cost involves determining the amount of services extracted from a previously acquired resource. This is no simple matter. George Terborgh [4] has submitted some rather convincing evidence that current methods of measuring depreciation are inadequate. Raymond Hoffman [5] has called attention to the current accounting convention of emphasizing the flow of cost rather than the flow of goods to support various inventory valuation methods. Nevertheless, the conceptual approach to the problem of measuring utilization cost is to determine the amount of services used and then obtain the current cost of the services used. Practically, the determination of the amount of services used must often be expressed as a percentage of the total services in the resource. Utilization cost can then be computed by compiling the current cost of repurchasing the resources from which the services were drawn and applying the percentage to this amount. In other cases, other means for measuring the amount of services used will have to be devised.

In general, the procedure appears to be somewhat cumbersome and a simpler method is needed. Actually, current replacement cost may be readily available in some instances. In others, if price-level indexes are available, the procedure could be simplified by adjusting acquisition cost to utilization cost by means of the relative index values at different times.

The use of price-level indexes to determine current replacement costs requires the construction of specific price-level indexes for each type of resource used. The objective of the adjustment is to estimate current replacement cost of the resources used. This type of price-level adjustment should be distinguished from the general price-level index adjustment for changes in the purchasing power of money. The distinction may be clarified by the following illustration.

Example

Company X purchased, for $10,000, services which were held six months before being used. During the interval, prices of these services rose from 100 to 110; and the general price level rose from 100 to 102 in the six-month period. Utilization cost, and the investment income from the investment operation, might be computed as follows:

Utilization cost ($10,000 × 110)/100	$11,000
Acquisition cost ($10,000 × 100)/100	10,000
Price-level change	$ 1,000
General price-level adjustment [(102 − 100) × 10,000/100]	200
Investment income	$ 800

Effective use of price-change adjusted acquisition cost as a measure of utilization cost rests on an accurate determination of the acquisition cost of the services used. While formulas are used extensively in this process, no simple formula could ever accurately measure the acquisition cost of services used in any one period of time. Such is just not the way services are used by companies. Services are used to carry out plans; and plans change from time to time. Even if they did not change, it would be erroneous to assume that all plans require the use of services in such a way that any of the current accounting formulas would accurately reflect that flow. Considerable research is needed to develop procedures to measure the services used.

Effective measurement of the services used is only part of the problem, however, for it is the cost rather than the number of services with which any discipline concerned with personal or organizational values would be interested. In accounting, the need to distinguish between services and their cost is important because identical services may have different costs. The tacit accounting assumption that average cost represents the cost of each and every item in a bundle purchase is not necessarily valid. There is considerable evidence that a higher-than-average price is paid for the first items used and that a lower-than-average price is paid for the last items used.

Example

A buyer for a women's dress shop purchases 100 dresses for $10,000, expecting at the time he purchases that most of the dresses will be sold early in the season at $250 each, but knowing from past experience that some will have to be sold later at $125 and that some will have to be placed "on sale" for $75. At the time he buys, however, the buyer does not know which dresses will be sold at which prices. But he is willing to pay $10,000 for the 100 dresses, for only in this way can he be certain to have on hand the dresses which will be sold for $250. In effect, he pays a higher price for the dresses sold at $250 than for those dresses sold for $125 and $75, and the buyer's use of the average cost of $100 as the cost of each dress is probably not the best method of determining the cost of each dress sold.

In general, the uncertainty, the risk, and the cost of carrying services prior to the time they are used suggests that a lower-than-average price will be paid for services to be used later. For this reason also, the use of average cost as the cost of services used is suspect. In fact, the entire area of averaging, which is used so extensively in accounting procedures, needs to be reexamined.

8.6 MANAGERIAL PLANNING AND UTILIZATION COSTING

Determining utilization cost separately from acquisition cost makes for an improvement in the matching process, for production and distribution effort is then defined in terms of the sacrifice caused by using services. Separate determination of utilization cost precludes the existence of under-priced services due to a "lucky" purchase, and is a more realistic reflection of the cost of production operations. Most important, from a theoretical point of view, the concept of utilization cost suggests a conceptual basis for developing accounting data useful in making changes in management's plans. Once utilization cost is established as a distinct concept which may be measured in terms of net realizable value, as well as current replacement cost, it becomes possible to review existing plans and to make new ones by matching a constantly changing net realizable value against a continuous variety of possible courses of future action. Currently, however, the problem of measuring utilization cost in terms of current replacement cost is so involved that developing a method for constantly relating the net realizable value of various services to a variety of changing possible opportunities will have to be left for future research.

8.7 VENTURE INCOME

The accurate determination of utilization cost is necessary if we are to improve the measurement of investment income and the measurement of the effectiveness of production and distribution operations. In addition to these two operations of business, there is a third which is closely related to both. It is the operation of *innovation*, from which arises the gain or loss from new undertakings.

In most new ventures, it is difficult to distinguish the amount of income created by the holding, the production and distribution effort, and the innovation process. In general, it seems that most ventures result in all three types of income, but the measurement process may be so difficult that separate disclosure of each type is beyond the present capacity of accounting measurements. Because of the specialized use to which resources are put when innovation is involved, it is difficult to compute current replacement cost of services used. For the same reason, a meaningful specific price-level index could not be constructed. Consequently, the undertaking of new ventures involving innovation should be treated as a separate operation, and venture income should reflect the results of this distinct operation, although it may well represent a composition of holding, production and innovation incomes. Conceptually, holding and production incomes should be deducted from venture income to yield innovation income, and research might well be directed to this objective.

8.8 RELATIONSHIP OF UTILIZATION AND RECOMBINATION OPERATIONS

A significant part of planning is determining which services should be used to produce or distribute production, when the services should be used, and how they should be used. (For an analysis of the research involved in making these kinds of decisions, see [6].) Operationally we might think of this as the process of recombining services from one resource into another, as when we take services in the form of leather, labor, machinery, power, and a multitude of other resources, and recombine them into a new resource. Since a significant part of the holding operation is often terminated at the time services are used to produce or distribute a different type of resource or service, the recombination operation is very closely tied to the utilization operation. Nevertheless, it is well to treat it as a separate operation. That is, the amount of services used in a period of time falls within the utilization operation, but where the services were used is in the area of the recombination operation.

REFERENCES

1. STEPHEN C. TOURNAY, *Ockham: Studies and Sketches* (LaSalle, Ill.: Open Court Publishing Co., 1938), page 9

2. JOHN M. CLARK, "Aims of Economic Life as Seen by Economists," from *Goals of Economic Life*, edited by A. Dudley Ward (New York: Harper, 1953), pages 23–51

3. JOHN M. KEYNES, *The General Theory of Employment Interest and Money* (New York: Harcourt, Brace, 1936), page 66

4. GEORGE TERBORGH, *Realistic Depreciation Policy* (Chicago: Machinery and Allied Products Institute, 1954)

5. RAYMOND A. HOFFMAN, *Inventories* (New York: Ronald Press, 1962) Chapter 7

6. ROBERT FERBER and P. J. VERDOORN, *Research Methods in Economics and Business* (New York: Macmillan, 1962)

Chapter 9

Accounting for
Recombination Operations

9.1 THE ROLE OF THE RECOMBINATION OPERATION

In his 28-page bookkeeping treatise, *Particularis de Computis et Scripturis* ("Details of Accounting and Recording"), which was originally a part of *Summa de Arithmetica, Geometria, Proportioni et Proportionalita,* Fra Luca Paciolo in 1494 suggested that "more skills are required to make a successful businessman than are required to make a good lawyer."

Be that as it may, it is true that the function of business in modern society is a complex activity. So complex, in fact, that people in their efforts to simplify matters tend to formulate and accept inadequate or too-generalized conceptions of the business function. Many people, for example, intuitively accept the notion that all business operations are encompassed in the recombination operation of a business entity. This state of mind is reflected in our acceptance of the assertion that "the function of business in society is to recombine or mix services, producing goods and services for consumers in such a way that value, which represents income, is added." People consider the other business operations as operations which facilitate the advancement of the basic recombination activity. Accountants in their professional role, however, should deal with the facts of business activity, and consider the recombination operation as one of several business operations. The relationship of the recombination operation to other business operations is revealed in Diagram 6.

Note that the recombination operation, though very important, is only one of several business operations which could create income. In essence,

Diagram 6 | THE SIX BASIC BUSINESS OPERATIONS

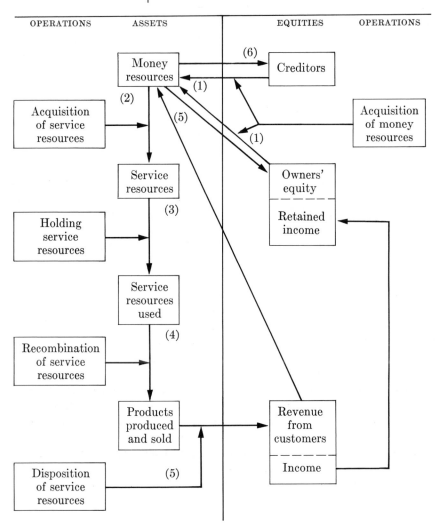

Explanation of business operations:

(1) Acquisition of money resources from creditors and owners
(2) Acquisition of service resources by investing money resources
(3) Holding service resources prior to use
(4) Recombining services to produce and deliver a product to customers
(5) Disposition of services, from which comes revenue in the form of money resources
(6) Distribution of money resources, which include income elements to creditors and owners

recombination refers to the mixing of the various services extracted from service resources in the utilization process. Traditionally, it has included deciding what to produce and distribute, developing efficient means for joining the various services, and distributing the finished product to customers. But there is reason to think that it should now also include using services to motivate customers to want the product, and to buy it.

9.2 THE MOTIVATION FUNCTION

In terms of accomplishment, the recombination operation includes the creation of a good or service in its physical form at the time and place needed. Economists have referred to the activity as the process of creating form, time, and place utility   Marketing authorities have referred to it as the "creation of time, place, and possession utilities." [1] In modern times, the recombination operation has begun to encompass more than these three, for it now includes the demand-creation or motivational function: causing customers to want the products. The role of advertising in our society provides dramatic evidence that the motivational (demand-creation) function is a most important aspect of business operations. Despite the obvious existence of a substantial motivational function in business operations, in the form of high- and low-pressure salesmen as well as advertising, accounting theory lags in that it fails to recognize this function as a distinct aspect of the recombination process. We need, therefore, to reorient accounting thought to take cognizance of the changing economic environment in which business operates.

Historically, business has operated to produce the basic economic goods and services needed by society for food, clothing, and shelter. Gradually, this activity has expanded to meet less basic economic needs for such items as style-oriented clothing, work-saving food products, and modernized shelter. Following in the wake of this product-improvement process, business activities have expanded further to meet new economic needs on the periphery of man's needs, such as the want for travel, recreation, and culture. As business operations have expanded into the new area, businessmen have realized the need to awaken the latent economic desires of man and bring these peripheral wants to the threshold of needs. Thus the motivational function, though always existing to some degree, has now become a significant aspect of business operations.

The insertion of the motivational function into the recombination operation has resulted in a new method for creating value. That is, it is now possible to add value to goods or services by changing the minds of customers regarding the desirability of the services in a product or service. Initially, the demand-creation function sought to change the mind of customers by acquainting them with new services in products or informing them of particularized services in a specific good. This is still the primary objective, but students of business often contend that the motivation function has advanced (or fallen) to the place where superficial, unreal, temporary, and even undesirable values are insinuated into the human mind by this business function. There seems to be no compelling evidence to support this latter view, and no reason for accounting theory to deal with this aspect of the motivation function at the present time. Accounting theory does need, however, to recognize the existence of the motivation function in the recombination operation.

So long as business operations were directed to meeting an existing and self-determined human demand, the recombination operation was confined to producing and distributing services to customers. Production was defined as the process of creating form utility; distribution dealt with place utility; and both contributed to time utility. From these concepts, there grew the notion of production effort, for which one set of accounting procedures was adopted, and distribution effort, for which another set of accounting procedures was appropriate. Thus one set of measuring principles could not govern the whole recombination operation, a failure which aroused some discontent. But lackings in the state of the measurement art led to the continuance of the distinction. (However, W. A. Paton [2] has remarked that "an occasional indication is found in business practice of a realization of the fact that there is nothing inherently unreasonable in an accumulation of elements of distribution costs as a type of deferred charge or cost inventory to the extent that the charges incurred are clearly incurred on account of future sales rather than on account of current business.")

As the motivation function increased, the procedures used to account for distribution costs began to be applied to motivation costs. Consequently motivation effort became, in accounting theory, part of distribution effort.

As a result of the lag in the adjustment of accounting theory to the new business environment and the inability of accounting research to improve accounting measurements to deal with the motivation aspect of the distribution function, accurate methods of accounting for recombination operations are lacking. For accounting purposes, the distinction between production and distribution is actually less pronounced than their similarity to each other. Both activities add value to services, and it is usually difficult to state precisely when production ends and distribution begins.

Although separate disclosure of services recombined in the distribution operation (place utility) and those recombined into a new physical product (form utility) is undoubtedly desirable, the use of different measurement procedures for assigning the amount of services recombined may be questioned. Most urgent, however, is the need to disclose separately the services recombined in the performance of the motivation function, thereby extracting them from the general classification of distribution activities. Such is the import of George O. May's statement [3]:

> Certain costs, the benefit of which are expected to extend over more than one accounting period, are customarily charged against revenue as incurred on prudential grounds. Among these costs are those of selling and promotion, experimental work and research. As already noted, the constantly growing importance attached to intangible assets has raised the question whether some modification of existing practice in the treatment of such items should receive consideration.

9.3 RECOMBINATION OF UTILIZED SERVICES

The preceding analysis has enumerated three distinct activities within the recombination operation:

(1) *The production activity:* the creation of a good in its physical form, or the development of a service to be rendered to customers.
(2) *The distribution activity:* the physical distribution of a good or service to customers. It might be referred to as the delivery function, except that it includes taking orders from customers and other necessary distribution activities which are not technically part of delivery.
(3) *The motivation activity:* the efforts to induce a customer to order a good or service, which might be referred to as the activity of creating a demand for a good or service. Effective performance of this activity may be measured in terms of the number of orders received.

Bearing this summation in mind, we can examine the overall recombination operation as one accounting issue, for there is much similarity among the three separate activities.

9.3.1 The need for recording recombinations

The first issue involved in accounting for recombination operations is whether it is necessary or desirable to record recombinations at all. The question is, should accounting measurements provide for the reclassification of services used into new accounts which describe the product or services created by the use of the services? The answer is not an obvious yes. One can easily find authoritative statements questioning the need for tracing the cost of services used to products produced. Direct costing implies that full tracing is not appropriate, either because it cannot be done accurately or is not necessary. One study on cost behavior [4] concludes, "For the determination of total income, for instance, only total costs are required; their allocation among 'products' is entirely immaterial."

Operationally, however, unless the six basic operations of a business entity have been stated incorrectly, the recombination operation is a distinct business operation, and the effectiveness with which that operation is performed should be measured and communicated. That is, we need to know what has been produced, the cost of producing it, and its market value or worth if we are to recognize efficient or inefficient performance of the operation. From the point of view of income determination also, the measurement of expense is simplified if recombinations are recorded. Unless the cost of services used to make a product are assigned to the product, it is difficult to determine when the services have been used to provide revenue. Even more fundamental is the fact that services have been shifted from one resource to another by the recombination operation, and this fact should be recorded. Evidence could be submitted to support the view that conceptually all services recombined (which excludes losses) should be recorded or reclassified as part of the product or service created. But the evidence is not needed, for current practice does endeavor to trace the flow of costs of services through business operations. Excluding the cost of certain services from the reclassified accounts appears to be due to measurement problems rather than conceptual confusion.

The problem of accounting for the recombination operation is not solved by merely stating that services should be reclassified, for we must determine how to cost these services properly. Present accounting practice is restricted to recording and tracing the acquisition cost of services. Emphasis is on the tracing of cost and not on the flow of services. Therefore it is not customary to trace cost-free services used in the recombination operation to product-recombination accounts. Furthermore, the emphasis on costs rather than the flow of services has caused losses to be treated as recombination costs and reclassified as part of the cost of producing and distributing a product.

Since the term "relevant cost" has been introduced into accounting literature, let us use this notion as a basis for selecting the costs of services to be traced to products, the idea being that only the services actually recombined are relevant to the production and distribution activity, and that their cost alone should be recorded as the cost of products. Presumably both direct costers and conventional costers would be satisfied with this conclusion. Losses of services would not be recombined, which should please the direct costers. On the other hand, the costs of all sacrifices caused by producing and distributing a product would be recombined. This should please conventional costers.

9.3.2 The method of recording recombinations

The preceding analysis indicates that recombinations should be recorded. This raises a second question: How should the recombinations be recorded in terms of the three distinct recombination activities of production, distribution, and motivation? Current accounting practice decrees that accounting measurements should trace the flow of costs through an entity. But, in accordance with this principle, under the system for reclassifying the cost of the services used, services could be reclassified by departments, (where the services were used), by functions (the specific activity performed), or by any other characteristic. In these accounts, the cost of the services used could be held in abeyance for income-determination purposes until the underlying services were transferred to customers.

Thus the principle of tracing the flow of cost, although it shows the desirability of reclassifying services to disclose business operations, does not indicate how the services should be reclassified. Our search for an answer to the question of how to record recombination must therefore be directed to areas other than the stated principles of accounting.

It is normally assumed that the reclassification of used services should be in terms of the values created by their use, the thought being that income determination is facilitated by such a classification. This has been interpreted to mean that it is a good idea to recombine or reclassify services used in terms of the product or service created because the value of the product or service is enhanced by the recombination process. This interpretation has considerable theoretical support.

Critics of this interpretation, however, have pointed out that services used in advertising to create a demand for a product add value to a product by changing the minds of potential customers as to the worth of the product. They conclude that the value point of view would require a recombination, as part of the cost of the product, of the services used in distribution and motivation, as well as those used in production. Because this procedure is not followed in contemporary accounting practice, the critics contend that this omission is evidence that reclassification in terms of the created object of value is presumably not a valid criterion of how services used should be reclassified.

The justification for recombining services, however, may be found in the objective of income determination, for the recombination of services into product accounts facilitates the matching procedure. This recombination includes services used in distribution and motivation activities, as well as those used in production. In fact, the services used in motivation efforts may precede the production effort, which suggests that mismatching will result unless the services used in motivation are traced to products and held in abeyance until the revenue from the sale of the product is recognized.

Since this is not done in practice, the problem of accounting for the recombination operation obviously needs considerable attention. We need to determine whether theory is right and practice is wrong, or practice is right and theory is wrong. There is no evidence now to indicate which is correct. The initial problem is to determine how services used in the recombination operation should be classified for income-determination purposes.

Although one might question present procedures of accounting for the recombination operation, there are defenses for current practice. One justification for contemporary reclassification procedures which generally reclassify production costs as costs of the product, but treats distribution, motivation, and administration costs as expenses is that the cost of services used in distribution, motivation, and administration are about equal each period of time. Thus the results of the matching process are not weakened by the fact that not all utilization costs are included as product costs. The validity of this justification must be questioned, however. Distribution and motivation costs *do* vary from year to year. Nor is it necessarily valid to assume that all services used in distribution and motivation are used only for the benefit of the product delivered to customers in one particular period of time. These services benefit several types of products and activities delivered in many periods of time.

9.4 THE MEASUREMENT PROBLEM

In the preceding section we suggested that the measurement of income by the matching process would be improved if all services used in the recombination operation were reclassified according to the product or service created by the activity. By this process accounting measurements would correspond with business operations. In other words, all recombination operations are directed to the production, motivation, and distribution activities, and these are tied ultimately to some product or service. [We did not include administration in this list, in order to call attention to efforts now being made to treat all administration costs as basically costs of production, motivation, or distribution.]

Despite the desirability of such a reclassification, implementation of it is not easy. Under normal conditions it is impossible to measure precisely all the services used on each product. The difficulty is referred to as the *joint and common cost problem*. But the issue involves more than this, since the notion of a "product" is an elusive concept. For practical classification purposes, it is often necessary to adopt something of an intuitive description of different products. At times, where intuition is not adequate, arbitrary demarcations of products may be necessary. There are a considerable number of authoritative statements, however, to the effect that a product can be acceptably defined by intuition. This is not true when it comes to the accounting measurement of joint costs.

Broadly, there are two problems involved in measuring the services used in the recombination operation. The first is the valuation of the services used; the second is the assignment of the valuation to different products and services. We can solve the first measurement problem by accepting the cost or sacrifice involved in using the service—the utilization cost—as the proper measure. This indicates, if our previous arguments are accepted, that the current replacement cost of the services is the proper valuation of the recombination operation. Opportunity cost or net realizable value are rejected on the grounds that they represent a short-run gain foregone and are more appropriate for short-term planning.

Current replacement cost is considered appropriate for evaluating the long-run ability of the firm to buy services, to recombine them so that value is added, and to dispose of the products at a profit. The concept of current replacement cost is more useful for long-term planning, in which a decision is made to produce and sell a specific type of product over a long period of time—such as a decision by a shoe company to manufacture and sell shoes—than either opportunity cost or net realizable value.

9.4.1 Expected and unexpected losses

Before we accept current replacement cost as the proper valuation of services used in the recombination operation, we need to determine whether these costs should include the cost of those services which were originally intended to be used in the recombination operation, but which were lost. That is, to use only the current replacement cost of the services actually used might tend to understate the managerial effort directed to the recombination. Since these losses exist only because of the recombination operation, it follows that they should be included as part of the cost of the recombination operation.

To analyze this proposition, let us first note four possibilities.

(1) *The losses may be expected by all producers,* so that the market price of all the services is forced down to a price which is equivalent to that which would be paid for only services which are expected to be used. That is, the price of a machine having a capacity of 10,000 hours of work which are "worth" $20,000 would be forced down to the price which would be paid for only those services which all producers expect to use in the recombination operation. If only 6,000 hours of work are anticipated, the maximum price of the machine might be $12,000. No cost would be attached to the 4,000 potential hours of work which all producers expect to lose.

(2) *The losses may be expected by one particular producer*, but not by all producers, so that one producer pays a higher price than other producers for the services in a resource which are to be used in the recombination operation. That is, if all producers pay the same price for the resource and one particular producer expects to lose more of the services in the resource than other producers, it is apparent that he is paying a higher price than other producers for each service unit to be used.

(3) *The losses may be unexpected by all producers;* for example, losses from an earthquake or other acts of God.

(4) *The losses may be unexpected by one particular producer*, but not by other producers. Into this category would fall a producer who did not expect a fire and did not insure his property to protect the services acquired.

Obviously no cost is attached to the losses expected by all producers. Hence, in determining current replacement cost of the services used, one should not assign current replacement cost to the expected losses.

Losses expected by one but not by all producers can seldom be objectively determined. But if they could, it would be appropriate to assume that no cost was attached to such losses and to determine the current replacement cost of services used according to this assumption. This procedure, however, may result in different costing of the recombination operation by different producers, because different producers might well have different ideas as to what is expected and what is unexpected. Consequently, costing services according to the losses expected by one particular producer would have to be supported by objective evidence that his loss expectation, though perhaps differing from that of other producers, was appropriate. Normally, the current costing process excludes only those services which all producers expect will be lost.

Unexpected losses, of course, do have a cost; but any implication that the recombination operation causes unexpected losses is contrary to the normal view of an unexpected loss. An unexpected loss could take place whether or not the recombination operation were performed. For this reason, one does not have to include the current replacement cost of these lost services as a cost of the recombination operation. If it came to a choice between the unexpected losses of one particular producer and those of all producers, only objective evidence would warrant accepting the unexpected losses of the one particular producer as the criterion when one was determining the current cost of the recombination operation.

9.4.2   Assigning value to specific products

To conclude that the current replacement cost of the services used—carefully computed by considering expected losses—is the appropriate valuation for the recombination operation is to solve only part of the measurement problem. The valuation must be assigned to specific products or groups of products. By and large there are two techniques used to accomplish this objective:

(1) *Direct assignment*, based on an intuitive feeling that an accurate observation of the flow of services to specific products is possible.
(2) *Indirect assignment*, based on an assumption that certain observed activities are representative of the flow of services to products.

Neither of these techniques is applied particularly well. Even when an observation of service used appears to be quite objective, such as in the case of packaging or delivery costs, these costs are often not assigned to products. On the other hand, indirect assignments are often based on questionable activities; for example, power costs are sometimes assigned to products on the basis of the direct labor costs of various products. In general, therefore, at the present time the assignment of costs to products is very unsatisfactory, and at best can serve only as a rough general measurement.

9.4.3 Debatable concepts of cost

Because of the difficulty of assessing the recombination operation in accordance with accounting theory, and because the mind of man is ingenious when he needs to justify an existing situation, some questionable concepts have been proposed to the accounting profession. Typical of these are the following:

(1) Not all costs of services used in production and distribution are costs of products, because "fixed costs are costs of having capacity to produce and . . . they expire with the passage of time. . . . The same costs have no determinable relationship to product units. . ." [5]

(2) Distribution costs, including motivation costs, used in the recombination operation are in the main applied to products sold in the period. This notion is seldom expressed in the literature, but it exists in the minds of many accountants.

(3) Direct costs are different from indirect costs. This concept exists despite Devine's analysis and conclusion that "the distinction between direct and indirect costs is so vague that building service costs may be viewed either as direct or indirect. Space hours are not essentially different from materials. . . . For costing purposes, machine hour utilization is on the same conceptual level as direct labor services." [6]

(4) Motivation costs are not costs of products or services, for "in many fields ads aim primarily at building up the company's name and prestige in the consumer's mind, rather than at selling a particular product." [7] Actually this point of view merely calls attention to the difficulty of the

measurement problem. It does not deny that the effort is made to sell some additional products at some time, although it has been interpreted as denying that this selling objective exists. Even if the interpretation were true and the advertising were directed to a nonincome objective, the effect would be to remove the services so used from the income-determination problem, and the motivational effort would have to be treated as a disposition of services not related to the income objective.

These suggestions express the accountant's approach to the measurement problem, an approach characterized accurately by Alexander [8]:

> Faced with a choice between precision of operations and precision of concept, the accountant has chosen the former, the economist the latter. That is, the accountant has chosen a concept of income which permits precise measurements but which yields misleading results under conditions of fluctuation and uncertainty. The economist has sought to construct a concept that would stand up under fluctuating conditions, but such a concept cannot easily be applied in practice.

The problem of accurately assigning the one cost of services recombined into a product by the recombination operation may be unsolvable, because the correct cost is not one cost. Rather, cost may be a probability. That is, the cost may not be single-valued, but may have multiple values clustered around a central tendency. In other words, the cost of services recombined into product A, being drawn from a variety of other goods and services, could perhaps be better computed by statistical methods. The result might be a range or class-interval measure of the cost of the services recombined. We should not reject the use of a statistical method to measure the cost of recombined services for the reason that it must give only a range of measurements and will include a probable range of error for any single measure. Perhaps measurement by statistical methods would be more reliable, though less precise, than measurement by the conventional accounting methods of allocating costs.

Vatter [9] has expressed the opinion that conventional measurements must fail. He says, "Despite the effort of the cost accountant to trace the effects of joint services to specific sales and deliveries, the result can never be attained in any theoretically acceptable sense, however useful these operations may be in practice." He refers, of course, to single valuation, and the implication is that only multiple valuations can be supported in any theoretically correct sense.

9.5 PROBABILITY MEASUREMENTS

Since we have shown that the recombination operation is more involved than normally recognized in accounting theory and that conventional measurements fail to correctly assign utilized costs to products and services, let us now propose both a theoretical framework and methods of improving accounting for the recombination operation.

Let us first accept the fact that we live in an uncertain world. Consequently cause and effect relations are not constant; there is a variable aspect to all things in which people deal. The golf score varies each time we play the course. The time it takes to run a mile varies with each runner and each race. Students vary from time to time in their level of performance. Workers fail to produce uniformly each period of time. Therefore we might say that the services used to perform an activity vary from time to time and from situation to situation. In fact, detailed time studies indicate that services contribute to results in a way which does not exhibit constancy. There is evidence, minute in many instances and large in others, that there is a constant variation in the services used to perform activities. Thus the accounting problem of assigning the utilization costs of a period to the goods and services produced during the period is a most difficult task.

Fortunately, there is one aspect of this problem which we do not have to consider: the fact that the services extracted from one resource differ from one another, that they vary and have no homogeneity. If we did have to consider this aspect, we could not trace costs to products. Sands [10] has noted and explained the situation in the following terms. "Some assets provide more than one kind of service simultaneously. . . . Fortunately the services provided by most business assets are fairly easily determinable and subject to reasonable estimation by reference to the value of other assets which provide the same or similar services."

To return to the task of improving accounting for the recombination operation, let us say that it is possible, by an intuitive process, and with varying degrees of confidence, to assign the cost of utilized services to goods and services produced. Some costs can be assigned with an intuitive confidence of nearly 100%, while others have to be allocated with considerably less intuitive confidence, and some cannot be assigned at all because they do not have the support of any intuitive confidence. The various levels of confidence are illustrated in Table 9–1 on page 160.

This intuitive process of assigning services used to products implies two things: Either the degree of confidence required to make assignment should be specified, or interval measurements should be developed for all assignments. Both involve statistical measurements derived from sampling, and both yield somewhat unsatisfactory results. That is, the first would not enable one to assign all the costs to goods and services produced, since it excludes those costs which could not be assigned because there was a *minimum* degree of confidence. The second would give a range of possible costs instead of one valuation. In addition, the mere fact that there was a range would not imply the existence of a normal curve dispersion around a central tendency, and this would hamper the interpretation of the

TABLE 9–1

LEVEL OF CONFIDENCE TABLE FOR
ASSIGNING UTILIZATION COSTS TO PRODUCTS*

Degree of intuitive confidence	Type of source of services used	Basis for intuitive confidence
100%	Raw materials	One can observe the physical product used in the finished goods
80–100%	Direct labor	One can observe the use of the services directly on the finished goods, even though one cannot observe the services used in the finished product.
30–80%	Indirect labor and production overhead (certain distribution services, such as delivery charges, could also be assigned with this same degree of confidence)	One can reason that all services used in production are for the purpose of creating products, and that the relative amount used on any one finished product may be estimated by allocating the cost of services used on the basis of some other activity which is assumed to correspond with the use of the services.
10–30%	Joint costs (certain motivation and distribution services have this same degree of confidence)	One assumes that the purpose of the recombination process is to produce a product for sale, and that the value of the product is directly related to the amount of services used. Hence the joint services used may be allocated to finished goods on the basis of the relative sales value of the finished product.
Below 10%	General advertising, income taxes	One assumes that no measurable relationship can be established between the services used and the finished goods and services.

* These results do not, of course, represent the intuition of all accountants. The table was derived from a sample composed of twelve practicing accountants and 23 graduate students of accountancy.

range measurement. For example, if the range were to be computed by tabulating the minimum and maximum utilization cost which would be assignable to each product under a variety of assignment bases, there would be no reason to assume any uniform dispersion within the range. Different costs would be assigned to a product as the allocation of utilization cost was made on several selected bases, such as direct labor cost, machine hours, and number of salesmen's calls; but there would be no way to evaluate the most reasonable single measure.

Nevertheless, both the process of specifying the degree of confidence required for an assignment to be made and the method of developing interval or range measures of product cost remove the assignment process from the area of intuition and place the measurement on a more objective basis. (For an attempt to advance the accounting measurement technology in this direction, see [11].) Further, the assignment process would be applicable in both production, motivation, and distribution.

Practically speaking, however, present statistical sampling techniques may not yield sufficiently precise results to justify departure from the intuition basis. Moreover, a range of measurements, even though more objectively determined, would not necessarily represent improved data for determining income.

Example

An assignment to products A and B of $10,000 of costs used in production, motivation, and distribution, as shown below, would not facilitate the determination of one overall operational income amount. The knowledge that the $10,000 should be assigned somewhere within the range of $8,000 to A and $2,000 to B to $3,000 to A and $7,000 to B would be of no help.

COSTS ASSIGNED TO	RANGE OF AMOUNTS		
	Maximum	Average	Minimum
Product A	$8,000	$ 5,500	$3,000
Product B	7,000	4,500	2,000
Total		$10,000	

Despite the less than ideal results of using presently available statistical measurement methods, such methods represent the most promising area for the study of the problem of measuring recombination operations. The trouble with relying on intuitive feelings is that different people may have different intuitive feelings about similar services. And, similarly, the trouble with depending on the convention that services used in motivation and distribution need not be recombined as a cost of the goods and services is that the generalization is too broad. There are some distribution and motivation services that *can* be assigned to goods and services.

9.6 ACCOMPLISHMENT OF THE RECOMBINATION OPERATION

Operationally, much can be said to support the matching concept as the criterion for measuring the effectiveness of the recombination operation. In a very real sense management strives to attain goals, and there is a need for a measurement of the extent to which the goal of the recombination operation has been attained. Ideally this measurement would disclose the value of a product after each stage in the recombination operation. According to convention, this has been measured by standard costs. When standard costs are kept up to date, such a measure of accomplishment is fairly satisfactory, although it does not enable us to measure the income created by the recombination operation. If a "normal" profit is added to the standard cost, it may be possible to measure the income from the recombination activity. It is this idea which perhaps underlies the valuation of inventory according to net realizable value before deducting normal profit. The effect of this procedure is that income on the recombination operation is recognized at the time of the recombination. Certainly the concept of net realizable value is not new to accounting; therefore the idea of measuring the effectiveness of the recombination operation should not be thought far-fetched.

Another suggestion is that the accomplishments of the recombination operation should be measured in terms of the ultimate sales price of the product produced. Not only would such a process provide no means for measuring goods-in-process when no sales price existed, but also sales prices fluctuate due to non-recombination factors, and generally lack stability. If something of a long-run average immediate sales price could be established, it might serve to measure the accomplishments of the recombination operation. Variations of ultimate sales price from immediate average sale price would represent non-recombination income.

Our inability to measure satisfactorily the accomplishments of the recombination operation is probably the best example of a situation where difficulties in measurement hold back the development of the accounting determination of income. Research on this topic is needed. The format for the measurement of effectiveness exists, for matching is operationally a correct representation of business activity. But the matching concept provides only a criterion for reclassifying services. It does not fully answer the question of how to reclassify the services used, nor does it dictate how accomplishment is to be measured. It may well be that the further develop-

ment of means for measuring the effectiveness of the recombination operation will have to await the development of measurement methods. But
crude as current measurement methods may be, they should be used in
discussions in accounting literature, for the need to improve the means of
measuring the recombination operation is pressing.

REFERENCES

1. WROE ALDERSON, *Marketing Behavior and Executive Action* (Homewood, Ill.:
Richard D. Irwin, 1957), page 68–69

2. W. A. PATON, *Essentials of Accounting* (New York: Macmillan, 1949), page 531

3. GEORGE O. MAY, *Business Income and Price Levels, an Accounting Study*
(New York: Study Group on Business Income, 1949), page 28

4. Committee on Price Determination, *Cost Behavior and Price Policy* (New
York: National Bureau of Economic Research, 1943), page 172

5. N.A.C.A. Committee on Research, "Direct Costing," *N.A.C.A. Bulletin*,
XXXIV (April 1953), 1118

6. CARL T. DEVINE, *Cost Accounting and Analysis* (New York: Macmillan,
1950), page 562

7. G. L. BACH, *Economics, an Introduction to Analysis and Policy* (Englewood
Cliffs, N.J.: Prentice-Hall, 1960), page 451

8. SIDNEY S. ALEXANDER, "Income Measurement in a Dynamic Economy,"
Five Monographs on Business Income (New York: Study Group on Business
Income, 1951), page 9

9. WILLIAM J. VATTER, *The Fund Theory of Accounting and Its Implications for
Financial Reports* (Chicago: University of Chicago, 1947), page 24

10. J. E. SANDS, *Wealth, Income and Intangibles* (Toronto: University of Toronto,
1963), page 68

11. ZENON S. ZANNETOS, "Standard Costs as a First Step to Probability Control:
A Theoretical Justification, an Extension and Implications." *Accounting Review*,
39 (April 1964), page 296

Chapter 10

Accounting for the Disposition of Services

10.1 EXPECTED DEMAND AS A FACTOR IN DISPOSITION

A concept central to accounting thought is *exchange*, which may be defined as the activity of transferring interests in goods from one accounting entity to another. It is distinguished from the production and distribution operation in that those operations merely provide the goods to be transferred. Although the bulk of the production and distribution operation is for the purpose of exchange and not consumption, the actual exchange operation must be recognized as distinct. Particularly is this so for *disposition exchanges*, although it is desirable also to treat acquisition exchanges as a distinct operation.

The recombination operation encompasses those activities of creating and delivering a product or service to customers. The value added by the recombination function is created by producing that which is called for by both an existing consumer demand and a demand created by the motivation function. The existing or created demand to which the recombination operation is directed, however, is not the specific demand into which the product will be sold. This demand is unknown. Rather, it is the expected, normal or typical demand.

Because demand fluctuates constantly and the production process normally takes time, production has to be undertaken with the expectation of a demand. Actual demand will not be known until the production is

164

available for sale. The longer the recombination process, the more necessary such an expectation is, for it becomes more difficult to predict the
specific demand into which the production will be sold. From this it follows
that, since the demand into which a company sells is a specific demand
which may be above or below the expected demand, the company has an
additional opportunity for gain or loss. A gain would result when specific
demand exceeded expected demand, and a loss would take place under
the opposite condition.

Some part of this gain or loss resulting from the changing demand for
the product would be attributed to the holding operation. But a holding
gain or loss emanates from shifts in demand that are beyond the control
of the selling company. This leaves unassigned any gain or loss resulting
from effective pricing in a given demand schedule. That is, an effective
disposition operation would result from selecting a price within the demand
schedule which would maximize net income, not necessarily revenue.
The price selected might involve a withholding of production from the
market in order to sell a smaller quantity at a higher unit price. Or it might
involve variable pricing to different customers, rather than following the
one-price policy, for a number of reasons.

The point is that the total periodic income of a company may be
influenced significantly by pricing policy and sales control. The gain or
loss is due neither to the holding operation nor to the recombination
operation, but to the disposition operation. Gains or losses come about
both because demand fluctuates over time and is therefore sensitive or
insensitive to price changes, and also because the individual demand for a
product is a schedule of price ranges rather than a schedule of specific
prices. (For a more detailed discussion of the nature of demand, see [1].)
If we define demand in the customary way as the amount of a good or
service which consumers will buy at different prices, we can illustrate the
fluctuating nature of the demand facing a selling company over any specific
period of time, and its elasticity to price, as follows.

Example

A company conducted a market survey of the demand for its products on
Jan. 1 and July 1, with results as set forth below and in Diagram 7. During
the interval from Jan. 1 to July 1, the demand for product A increased,
since the same volume can be sold at a higher price on July 1, although
the degree of elasticity remains relatively stable. On the other hand, the
demand for product B has become more inelastic, with the result that a
price change on July 1 does not change volume as much as a corresponding
price change on Jan. 1. At both dates, the demand for product B is far
less sensitive to price changes than the demand for product A.

Diagram 7 | **THE FLUCTUATING NATURE OF DEMAND**

January 1

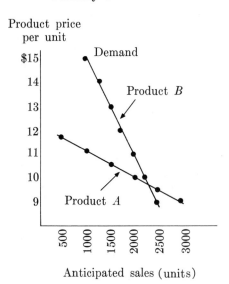

July 1

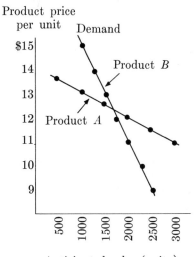

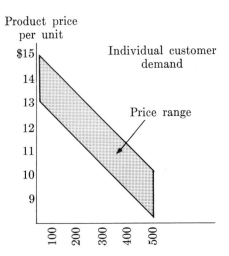

Units which would be purchased

For any one customer, however, the demand curve takes a broad band rather than a narrow line. This is so because seldom does any one customer know precisely the quantity he will purchase at various prices. For example, the demand of customer A for the products of Company X at any one time is portrayed in the manner shown at the bottom of Diagram 7. This means that the quantity which customer A will purchase at any one price may vary for reasons other than price. To the selling company, this represents an opportunity for multiple pricing to secure the maximum income from each customer.

10.2 THE DISPOSITION OPERATION

Because the demand curves for a company's products have varying degrees of elasticity which fluctuate over time, the sales prices of finished products depend on the conditions under which the products are sold and on the volume sold. Thus the final price at which a product is sold will depend on activities other than the recombination operation. The other activities involved are those included in the operation of disposing of the services. For example, assume that Company X sold 10,000 units of product A for $23,000. The price might be explained in the following manner.

Sales price	$23,000
Price explained by specialized desire for the particular product by one customer (lucky sale)	2,000
Regular company sales price	$21,000
Price explained by ignorance of customers of prices of competitors (imperfection in the market)	1,500
Regular industry sales price	$19,500

The two items of lucky sales and market imperfections are merely typical of a host of causes of variations between normally expected sales prices—to which production is geared—and actual sales prices. Causes range from nonrational conduct of customers to monopoly price control, and include such items as effective bargaining, fluctuating demand, and noneconomic factors. Therefore, in modern business, effective pricing may lead to significant gains or losses.

The importance of the disposition operation as a distinct aspect of business operations has been overlooked in accounting theory. With the development and growth of administered prices in the United States, including both public utility pricing and monopolistic competition pricing, we can no longer assume that prices adjust automatically to short-run changes in supply and demand. The fact is that business managements do have the power, within certain ranges, to set prices. Moreover, they exercise this discretionary power and even consider it a desirable form of pricing, as the following testimony [2] of an executive of the United States Steel Corporation indicates:

> It has been suggested that when demand is temporarily in excess of supply, steel mill products should be sold to the highest bidder. During such periods this type of expedient pricing might indeed yield a handsome quick profit. However, this would be a short-sighted policy and would surely lead to serious discrimination among our customers.

The significance of discretionary pricing power to accounting theory is that it firmly establishes the disposition operation as a distinctive business activity of some importance. (For a more complete discussion of the nature and implications of the discretionary pricing power of business, see [3].) There must be means for measuring the effectiveness of the disposition operation. This necessity may require a distinctive type of accounting research, if effectiveness is defined in terms of income or loss, for the disposition operation is a most complex activity. For example, a large business entity may recognize a loss on disposition in the short run, by setting prices below those which could be set in the short-run supply and demand situation, in order to be assured of an income in the long run. Alternatively, pricing policy may be established without regard to the long-run maximum income, so that long-run income will not serve as a measure of effectiveness either.

However, a company might restrict volume by setting a high price; the company would thus obtain a higher net income than it would if it set price at the point where the total supply of production would equal demand. In such a situation, a distinct and apparently continuous income could be attributed to the disposition operation. This income would not necessarily represent a type of income arising from the adding of services to the product. Instead it would represent a means of allocating the products and services created to their highest economic use; for only those consumers in a position to extract the greatest amount of services from the finished products or services would pay the higher price. To the extent that the income thus recognized is in excess of that amount which would be recognized if the market were cleared by market pricing rather than administered pricing, the question arises as to the social desirability of this type of income. That is, the disposition operation must be justified as being responsible and in the public interest. Business firms, in their own interest, and to allay consumer suspicions as well as serve the public interest, should require that this type of income be separately disclosed.

But it is difficult to separate the value added by the recombination operation from the price increase added by the disposition operation.

Indeed certain income derived from the disposition operation may be a constant amount each period of time. Thus much of the increase or decrease in the income from the two operations would be due entirely to the recombination process. The underlying idea is that, under administered pricing, a constant price eliminates most gains and losses from the disposition operation, because short-term changes in demand and supply factors are not allowed to influence income. This point of view is not valid, however, since demand may change over time. If price is fixed, as it is under conditions of administered prices, volume will change, and income will fluctuate not because of price changes but because of volume changes.

Because motivation activities may change the demand curve for a company's products, and because the changes in the demand curve with which the disposition operation is concerned are often caused by forces beyond the control of the company, it is impossible to examine the disposition operation strictly in terms of changes in demand. In a sense the disposition operation represents the efforts of a company to conform and advantageously adjust to its changing environment. Since the motivation activities are part of the recombination operation and thus excluded from the disposition operation, measuring the distinction between the "created" and the "natural" demand is necessary, but yet not possible in any precise sense. Thus it may not always be possible to measure the effectiveness of the disposition operation separately from the effectiveness of the recombination operation.

Various measurement possibilities come to mind, of which the following is typical. Let us say that the motivation activity represents effort to dispose of services. By this reasoning, it could therefore be included as part of the disposition operation rather than the recombination operation. This would enable disposition effectiveness to be measured, but it would limit the recombination operation to the creation and physical distribution of services. On the surface this appears to be a good idea, since it would avoid certain measurement problems. But, operationally, the disposition operation, unlike the recombination operation, does not involve the use of services to create values, not even those services used in the motivation activity. Disposition is primarily a specialized planning activity, and the effectiveness with which it is performed should be measured whenever possible, and be commented on when measurement is not possible.

10.3 TYPES OF DISPOSITIONS

Many authorities would contend that the disposition operation, in the sense previously described, does not exist as a separate business operation. These authorities consider that, except for occasional, unusual marketplace relationships, the disposition activity is passive, with both voluntary and involuntary increments or decreases in "value" being the result of the holding, production, and other operations. For many practical purposes they may be correct, but the framework of income determination theory should be conceptually broad enough to encompass the possibility that the disposition operation is or could be a significant aspect of modern business.

Whether disposition is considered broadly or in the conventional manner, measurement problems arise in accounting for the transfer of goods and services to customers. Basically, the disposition activity involves both the transfer of services to customers and the loss of services. In a sense, it is the opposite of the acquisition activity, since it involves the same three accounting problems of recognition, classification, and valuation. The problems of determining when to recognize that a disposition has taken place, of grouping the results of the various dispositions so that the activities of all types of operations are significantly revealed, and of valuing the services disposed of represent the basic accounting issues involved in accounting for the disposition activity. Thus the problems involve:

(1) *Selecting a point or time to recognize an expense or loss*, both of which represent an outflow of services in the form of a disposition. Currently, expenses are recognized at the time revenue is recognized, while losses are recognized at the time services are judged to have disappeared.

(2) *Classifying the expenses and losses in sufficient detail* and according to categories which reveal most appropriately the underlying activity. Thus expenses and losses may be classified according to the function performed, the person responsible for the disposition, the form in which the services were contained, or any other satisfactory classification system.

(3) *Valuing the expense or loss.* Customarily, dispositions have been measured in terms of acquisition cost, and such valuations do reveal the starting point for all business operations.

There is no reason to accept without question the conventional procedures now used to recognize, classify, and value dispositions in the determination of overall operational income. At least the framework for the theoretical examination of accounting for dispositions should be broader than just a description of current solutions to the problem.

If we wish to account for the effectiveness of the disposition operation, another dimension is added to the problem; for it becomes necessary to have valuations of both the input and the output of the disposition operation. This problem of input valuation, like the acquisition operation, although in the reverse, is best solved in terms of the value created by the preceding operation, the recombination operation. That is, the valuation of the accomplishment of the recombination operation may be treated as the valuation of the input to be used in the measurement of the effectiveness of the disposition operation, but this requires a more satisfactory measure of the accomplishment of the recombination operation than is now available.

The analogy of the disposition operation being the opposite of the acquisition operation has its limitations. It is true that acquisition is the activity of acquiring services for use, and disposition is the activity of disposing of the services after they have been used in the recombination operation. But disposition includes involuntary as well as voluntary dispositions, whereas acquisition is essentially a voluntary activity. The problem of measuring all the services which have been disposed of is very real, and the process cannot be confined to those dispositions which are voluntary. There are some theorists who imply that the involuntary losses should be insured against, thus permitting us to confine the measurement of the disposition activity to the voluntary dispositions; but the fact is that some companies do not or cannot insure against all involuntary losses. Thus measurement of the effectiveness with which the disposition operation is performed requires an evaluation of all dispositions.

10.4 INSURANCE AND DISPOSITIONS

Insurance has often been considered as a process of smoothing income. For this reason we cannot measure the effectiveness with which the disposition operation is performed in one short period of time if a company decides to insure itself against certain losses. The idea is that a loss is an irrational waste of resources. According to this line of reasoning, an insurance premium is based on both efficient and inefficient experiences, for the premium must be high enough so that the insurance company can cover all losses. An efficient company—that is, one in which dispositions due to losses are below those of other companies—does not benefit from insurance in the long run. However, there is presently no means to measure this efficiency, because an inaccurate measure of loss in the form of insurance premiums is spread over several periods of time. Some accountants feel that all losses are caused and can be controlled and prevented. The concept of chance as a phenomenon of business is excluded. This conception of the nature of the disposition operation is quite broad. Thus preventing dispositions of services at an inopportune time or in an inappropriate manner is considered to be part of the disposition function.

Other accountants support the proposition that losses are due to chance alone, and that no direct causal relationship exists between specific losses and specific actions. To these accountants, an insurance premium in no way represents a smoothing of income, for the risk exists during each period of time. Risk represents an equivalent disposition of services. According to this extreme school of thought, risk is a phenomenon of nature and must be paid for either by insurance premiums, by protective measures, or by absorption of the loss. Since it is a continuous on-going phenomenon, risk is a cost of the services used in the holding and recombination operations, and has nothing to do with the disposition operation.

10.5 LOSSES AS DISPOSITIONS

Actually, losses probably include both causal and chance elements, and the earlier theoretical suggestion that insurance premiums might be treated as a type of "protective" cost to be attached to the services protected may represent a suitable way of handling insurance. In this sense insurance premiums represent an acquisition activity, and not a disposition of services.

For the company which does not insure and proposes to absorb its losses, the loss is a disposition activity and should be evaluated. This includes the so-called *losses of uncertainty*, i.e., those losses for which no probability of loss may be computed due to limited information, as well as the *losses of risk*, for which a probability may be computed and by reason of which insurance opportunities exist. In addition to these two types of involuntary losses, there is a third which may be referred to as *losses of change*, or the disappearance of services due to the impact of change on all activity.

Although these losses are often included as part of the losses of uncertainty, it seems preferable to confine uncertainty losses to those which occur without a basic change in the nature of the environment. Losses of change are becoming a significant aspect of the disposition operation, because of the rapidity with which change is taking place in modern society. As an aside, it may be noted that the phenomenon of change has never been dealt with in an adequate manner in accounting theory, and theorists ought to direct their attention to it. The following description of change by Hawley [4] might well represent a suitable starting point.

> The workings of change, however, whether it concerns social phenomena or phenomena of any other kind, has long been a philosophical problem for which as yet there is no final solution. The issue involves a number of perplexing questions; for example: What are the units of change? How much difference must there be in before and after states to constitute a change? And what is the context in which change is to be observed? Such questions are differ-

ently resolved in two views of the matter that occupy the center of attention in most debates. They may be described as the continuous and discontinuous conception of change.

According to the one view, change is a continuous and uninterrupted process. It proceeds constantly and inexorably by infinitely small alterations. In short intervals of time, therefore, change is often imperceptible. Still, nothing is at rest; nothing is the same in successive instants. And the changes we observe are but cumulative effect of innumerable modifications which together form a continuum.

In the second view, the discontinuous conception, change is regarded as a cyclical process in which variation alternates with stability. It is the assumption of this conception that every phenomenon is so constituted as to be resistant to modification for limited periods of time. Each object or combination of objects represents an equilibrium of mutually sustaining forces. External pressures build up against that equilibrium until eventually it is broken and change follows rapidly. The modifications which ensue work toward the reestablishment of equilibrium on a new or different basis. Inertia sets in again and a new cycle is begun.

The problem of accounting for losses, whether they are due to change, to uncertainty, or to risk is most involved. Like the distinction between the value added by the recombination operation and the price increase arising from the disposition operation, the distinction between the losses due to holding services and the losses due to the disposition operation is difficult to make. Moreover, the losses may not be measurable unless the measurement arts are better developed. Fortunately the bulk of the disposition activity involves voluntary and purposeful releases of services. For example, fixed asset replacement studies represent purposeful disposition activities, and so do pricing studies to establish the most appropriate price.

10.6 RECOGNITION OF DISPOSITIONS

Accounting for the disposition operation involves selecting a point at which to recognize that a disposition has taken place. In the case of dispositions to customers, the issues are similar to those involved in accounting for the acquisition operation. But special problems arise in the disposition of services involving losses, both because physical disposition of goods containing services lags behind the loss of the services, and because physical disposition is an option of management. Accurate accounting for the disposition of services would require that disposition of services in the form of losses be recognized as soon as the services disappear. The main (practical) issue is one of consistency, though the greater the correlation between the loss of the services and their recognition, the better the measurement. An inconsistent or varying recognition point tends to preclude interpretation of measured amounts. In general, the recognition of losses is one of the areas in which accounting research is badly needed.

One promising area of research is the measurement of losses due to risk. These losses are predictive, on a probability basis, because experience has shown that they will occur. The incidence or time when the loss will take place, however, is not known precisely. There is available only a range within which the loss may occur.

Example

Assume that a company makes a study of breakdowns of its machines and finds that breakdown and repair costs are as follows:

(a) Running time before breakdown		(b) Repair cost	
0– 30 hours	10%	$ 0–15	10%
30– 60 hours	20%	15–30	20%
60– 90 hours	40%	30–45	40%
90–120 hours	20%	45–60	20%
120–150 hours	10%	60–75	10%
Total	100%	Total	100%

These figures show an average running time of 75 hours and an average repair cost of $37.50. The company has one machine which it plans to use for only 60 hours, but does not know for certain, of course, whether it will have a breakdown. If the machine does break down, the repair cost could range from zero to $75. Provided with an opportunity to insure against any loss by paying an hourly insurance premium of $18\frac{3}{4}$ cents per hour (10% + 20% = 30% times $37.50 = $11.25 divided by 60), the company might elect to self-insure by setting up a reserve at the $18\frac{3}{4}$-cents-per-hour rate. If the machine broke down after 50 hours of operation, the reserve would have accumulated to $9.37. Assume that repair costs were $46. The difference between the two ($46.00 less $9.37) would represent a risk loss not adequately measured in advance. In the long run, of course, such differences would be eliminated, but for short periods there is a need to determine losses due to risk.

Losses due to change could be measured in a manner similar to the measurement of risk if the means for determining a rate of change could be found. Attempts to do so are encouraging. For example, accountants have been able to estimate obsolescence of equipment on the basis of the rate of technological change. If research can develop an improved measurement of the impact of change, it may be possible to recognize these losses as it becomes evident that the services are being lost.

There has not yet evolved an objective process for recognizing uncertainty losses prior to the time of the physical disposition of the resource formerly containing the services lost. On a judgment basis, however, one can usually estimate some losses prior to the physical disposition date. Judgment may be improved by noting that uncertainty is caused by lack of control over events. These events may be due to (1) the acts of another person or (2) a natural occurrence. Systematic consideration of each of these possible causes of unexpected developments is an aid to rough planning for uncertainty losses.

10.7 CLASSIFICATION OF DISPOSITIONS

Services disposed of to customers are customarily classified both as "sales" and "expenses," though neither classification normally includes dispositions of unusual items where only the gain or loss on disposition is recognized. For the unusual items, the general classification of gains and losses is in terms of the object disposed of. Thus such classifications as "loss on sale of machinery," "gain on sale of land," and "loss due to abandonment of property" are widely used. (We have already discussed the need for a more useful classification of dispositions to customers and the general nature of the classification problem.) In general, however, we need a more meaningful classification of losses. The three-way division of losses (risk, change, and uncertainty) seems to be a minimum requirement.

10.8 VALUATION OF DISPOSITIONS

Because of the dual valuation of dispositions, revenue and expense or accomplishment and effort, the valuation of dispositions is most important for the determination of income, either for the disposition operation separately or for all business operations combined. This is true because the final accomplishment, the revenue, completes both the disposition operation and the total business income operations. While expense may be measured in terms of acquisition cost if total operational income only is to be computed, it must be valued differently if the effectiveness of the disposition operation is to be determined; we have discussed both types of expense measurement.

On the other hand, the proper revenue valuation of dispositions is the cash or cash equivalent received in exchange when the disposition occurs. This principle is identical with the principle for valuing service acquisitions, and is valid even though the cash or cash equivalent received in exchange is well below the value at which the services are carried on the accounting records. Only when no cash or cash equivalent is received, as in the case of a loss, may the revenue valuation of dispositions be omitted.

Diagram 8 | RELATIONSHIP AMONG MEASUREMENTS OF BUSINESS OPERATIONS

ACTION	ACQUISITION OPERATION	UTILIZATION OPERATION	RECOMBINATION OPERATION	DISPOSITION OPERATION	TOTAL
(5) *Total operations*					
(a) Value of products on hand at end of period					$152,000
(b) Acquisition cost of services acquired					95,000
Total income					$ 57,000
(4) *Disposed of services*					
(a) Products created and resources acquired				$100,000	
(b) Value of resources disposed, including $8,000 in motivation				98,000	
Disposition operation income				$ 2,000 →	$ 2,000
(3) *Used 50% of services in production and distribution*					
(a) Value of products created			$90,000		
(b) Utilization cost of services recombined			60,000		
Recombination operation income			$30,000		30,000
(2) *Held acquired services*					
(a) Current cost		$120,000			
(b) Acquisition valuation		100,000			
Utilization operation income		$ 20,000			20,000
(1) *Purchased services*					
(a) Value acquired	$100,000				
(b) Cost	95,000				
Acquisition operation income	$ 5,000				5,000
Total operational income					$ 57,000

10.9 RELATIONSHIPS AMONG OPERATIONS EFFECTIVENESS

As we noted previously, the measurement of the effectiveness with which the disposition operation is performed involves deducting the accomplishment valuation of the recombination operation from the total revenue provided by dispositions during the accounting period. This procedure illustrates the relationship of the various operations of a business to each other, for the accomplishment of one operation represents the effort applied to the following operation. Diagram 8 on the facing page uses illustrative figures to summarize this relationship.

REFERENCES

1. PAUL A. SAMUELSON, *Economics* (New York: McGraw-Hill, 1951)

2. Hearings Before the Subcommittee on Antitrust and Monopoly of the Committee on the Judiciary, U. S. Senate, 85th Congress, *Administered Prices* (Washington, D. C., Government Printing Office, 1957), pages 353–355

3. GARDNER C. MEANS, *Pricing Power and the Public Interest* (New York: Harper, 1962)

4. AMOS H. HAWLEY, *Human Ecology* (New York: Ronald Press, 1950), pages 319–320

Chapter 11

The Distribution of Operational Income

11.1 ACCOUNTING FOR THE DISTRIBUTION OF INCOME

We have classified the operations of business which constitute a general framework of accounting income-determination theory as follows:

(1) *Acquisition of money resources,* or means to acquire service resources.
(2) *Acquisition of service resources* to be used in the income-generation process.
(3) *Utilization of services,* in the sense of extracting the services for use or holding the services for the investment gain.
(4) *Recombination of extracted services* into goods and services to be delivered to customers.
(5) *Disposition of services,* including both sales to customers and losses.
(6) *Distribution of money resources* to creditors, stockholders, and others.

We have examined the accounting problems involved in measuring the middle four, the income-generating operations, in some detail in an effort to develop meaningful concepts of accounting income. It might be noted that this approach to the study of income-determination theory also has historical support. C. E. Knoeppel [1] suggested in 1922 as an axiom of industrial efficiency that "profit accounting should be so classified as to reflect the results of the three major sections of a business (buying, making, and selling), that it may be known which contributes to the success or failure of an enterprise, and to what extent."

Actually, both the first and the last operations—the acquisition and distribution of money resources—may also be examined in terms of the three accounting tasks of recognition, classification, and valuation of activities. The only distinction is that it is the acquisition and disposition of money resources rather than service resources to which the three tasks are directed.

Thus we have covered the basic problems of accounting for business operations. There is, however, one aspect of business operations which needs special consideration in any discussion of business income. It is the problem of accounting for the distribution of income. It has been pointed out [2] that the amount of dividends paid is related to the amount of reported income. But this feature is only part of the problem of accounting for the distribution of income, for the issue is more involved.

Most discussions of the distribution of income tend to assume that income is composed of a constitutive element, and that accounting for the distribution of operational income involves accounting for the distribution of that element. This intuitive feeling needs to be examined, for a distribution of income is in fact a distribution of assets or rights to assets, and only by convention may specific distributions be labeled distributions of income. Before proceeding with an examination of the issue, however, let us look at certain constitutive conceptions of operational income in more detail than we did in Chapter 5, and from a slightly different point of view.

11.2 CONSTITUTIVE CONCEPTIONS OF OPERATIONAL INCOME

Constitutive interpretations of overall operational income vary widely, ranging from the notion that it represents taxable income to the view that it reflects the excess of cash receipts over cash disbursement. While many of the interpretations do not agree with the operational measurement, there are many which are approximated by operational income. The following three interpretations illustrate the concept that operational income is a reasonable representation of various types of constitutive income.

(1) Operational income, in a constitutive sense, may be visualized as *the extent to which an entity has increased its assets through operations.* It does not include all gains accruing to all parties having an interest in the entity. It need not be and is not—as it has been described—a measure of the increase of the stockholders' equity in the entity. Nor is it even a measure of the increase in the equity of all creditors and investors, for, to conform to that idea, gifts and other nonoperational items would have to be included in the concept of income. But in a general sense operational income may be thought of as the increase in assets resulting from business operations. In

this constitutive sense, it excludes both capital contributions and withdrawals by stockholders and creditors.

(2) Operational income, in another constitutive meaning, may be considered more of a social concept than a measure of increases in individual or group rights, for it may be held to reflect *the economic contribution which an entity has made to the economy in which it operates*. This concept of the nature of total operational income is quite crude, and its use in this constitutive meaning should be undertaken cautiously. The fact is that operational income does include elements of gain which are losses to other entities and not net contributions to the economic wealth of society. The proportions of operational income which should be considered contributions to society and which should be considered gains or winnings from other entities have not been reliably estimated. Some authorities feel, however, that the bulk of operational income represents an economic contribution to society. [This was the conclusion of a conference of leading accounting educators and practitioners in late 1962.] One obvious measurement error in this point of view is that there is an element of double-counting when a summation of the operational incomes of all business entities is assumed to reflect a type of social income, because interest and dividends received are treated as operational income, while interest and dividends paid are not deducted from it. In spite of this measurement limitation, this conception of the constitutive nature of operational income appears to be growing more popular.

(3) Since society has assigned to business certain responsibilities for the economic development of society, operational income may be conceived of as *a measure of the efficiency with which a business entity has carried out these responsibilities*. That is, operational income may be treated as an index of the efficiency with which inputs have been used to accomplish outputs. An income would reflect efficiency, while a loss would represent inefficiency. This notion of the constitutive nature of operational income implies that operational income, computed by the matching procedure, is a measure of effectiveness, and need not be either a measure of all the increase in assets through business operations or a measure of the economic contribution to society. The controversy which raged a few years back over the "current-operating" income concept versus the "all-inclusive" income concept suggests the divergent conceptions of the constitutive nature of operational income, for the former supports the view that income reveals the effectiveness of the business entity, while the latter reflects the notion that income is the increase in assets.

Some people contend that perhaps overall operational income may be defined in terms of all these divergent constitutive meanings, providing that its constitutive nature is changed to agree with the use to which the income figure is put. This possibility points up the fact that these and other generalizations of the constitutive nature of overall operational income have limited accuracy. In fact, the nature of accounting income, which has been defined as an operational income concept, is somewhat akin to a statistician's description [3] of the nature of index numbers:

> It ought to be conceded that index numbers are essentially arbitrary. Being at best rearrangements of data wrenched out of original market and technological contexts, they strictly have no economic meaning. Changes in tastes, technology, population composition, etc., over time increase their arbitrariness. But, of course, there is no bar to the use of indexes "as if" they did have some unequivocal meaning, provided that users remember that they themselves made up the game and do not threaten to "kill the umpire" when the figures contradict expectations.

The true meaning of operational income is evident only by reference to the nature and purpose of the operations underlying the accounting computation of it. That is, if one wants to know what operational income truly means, one must examine the manner in which it is computed and not rely on what someone says has been measured. If business operations changed so that different measurement methods were used, operational income would then reflect another constitutive meaning. Because business operations and accounting measurements do vary, it is evident that the constitutive meaning of operational income varies.

11.3 DETERMINATION VERSUS DISTRIBUTION OF INCOME

We have noted previously that the determination of operational income should be distinguished from the measurement of the allocation or distribution of the income, because the concept of allocating or distributing income implies a constitutive income element. That is, if operational income is a measurement without a constant constitutive definition, it can hardly be allocated or distributed to anyone.

Actually, the notion of a distribution of income is something of a misnomer, for many of the so-called "distributions of income" are not income distributions at all. For example, gain on the retirement of preferred stock below its book value is automatically allocated to common stockholders, yet it is not income according to the accounting conception of income. Nevertheless, it is at times referred to as a distribution of income when the cash saved by the advantageous preferred stock retirement is paid to common stockholders as a dividend. The statement that a company "ought to distribute some of its income to customers by reducing prices" is another illustration of the confusion surrounding the term. Furthermore, references to income taxes and to employee "profit"-sharing plans as distributions of income indicate that the confusion as to the meaning of distribution of income is widespread.

Normally, "distribution of income" refers to distributions to stockholders, but lately several authorities in the finance area include distributions to creditors within the term. This is a realistic point of view, since both types of distributions are made in accordance with the contractual rights of the various suppliers of funds to the entity. In fact [4], the origin of the distinction between interest and profit distributions is obscure. The classical distinction that interest is certain whereas profit is uncertain came after religions banned interest-taking and sanctioned profits. The ambiguous distinction between interest and profit is revealed by the reasoning of the Malay fisherman, who contends that payment for the use of money to buy a boat is profit-sharing, and not a "tax on money" (interest) because the return is uncertain. The 1300-year-old condemnation of *riba* (interest or usury) in the Koran appears to be based on the assumption that borrowing was for personal consumer needs under conditions of stress. Out of the mist and haze surrounding the word emerges the notion that "interest" is a carry-over from the past, which does not fit well in modern industry, where borrowing is primarily for production rather than consumption and where the contractual arrangements for interest and dividend payments may run counter to the classical certainty-uncertainty distinction. (Cumulative preferred dividends may be more certain than interest on income bonds.)

The notion that interest is a payment for the use of money while profit is an excess payment for innovation or the return for entrepreneurship may be a valid distinction. But this notion is not used in accounting for interest and profit distributions. Were it used, dividends to stockholders would be broken down into interest and profit elements. Since both interest and dividends are a payment for the use of money, such a breakdown is not particularly significant.

The implication of the proposal that income distributions should include both interest and dividend payments is that operational income refers to income before interest payments. It indicates that operational income is a measure of the gain accruing to both creditors and stockholders. Although this may be true, accountants have never clearly identified whose income should be computed and designated as the income of the business. The conceptual material presented here indicates that income, in its most accurate constitutive meaning, is a measure of asset increases before any share of the increase is distributed to creditors or stockholders. However, the more general practice is to deduct the interest charges from the total of asset increases, and to imply that business income represents stockholders' income. However, there are various stockholder groups; to which does this notion apply? The possible groups whose income could be reported as business income may be classified in the following manner:

(1) *Economic entity income*, which refers to the increase in assets from all types of operations.

(2) *Total equity-group income*, which is entity income plus gifts to the entity.

(3) *Total original-stockholder group* (the group which originally acquired the stock directly from the corporation). This is normally a nonexistent group, because some of the original stockholders will have sold their stock to other investors at a price other than the original issue price. This income would be computed by deducting creditors' interest from total equity-group income, and adding or deducting any gains or losses which resulted from settling creditors' claims above or below their booked value.

(4) *Total present-stockholder group* (the group which people usually assume is the group whose income is reported). This group will have paid varying prices for varying amounts of equity, and the amount paid is not equal to the funds received by the corporation. In the sense that a share of capital stock is a share of the underlying assets of the corporation, the present stockholder has paid a price for these assets different from the price paid by the corporation. Different valuation of assets means different expenses, and different income as the assets are used to produce revenue. Because different stockholders have paid varying prices for the stock, it is not possible to compute one total present-stockholder group income.

(5) *Total original junior-stockholder group income*, which normally would be computed by deducting preferred stock dividends from the total original-stockholder group income, and adding or deducting gains and losses on senior treasury stock transactions. This group, like the total original-stock-holder group, normally does not exist, because some of the original stock-holders retire from the group by selling their stock to another investor.

(6) *Total present junior-stockholder group*, which might be an ideal group if it could be measured but, like the total present-stockholder group, it cannot be computed in a meaningful sense. If it could be computed, the gains and losses on retiring common stock above or below booked value would be included as a gain to the presently remaining junior stockholders.

(7) *Managerial-entity income*, which is the balance of the increase in assets from all operations after all equity holders have been paid for the use of their funds. Procedurally, this would represent the undistributed earnings of the corporation plus or minus the gains or losses arising on retire-ment of equities above or below book value. Over the life of the corpo-ration—since legally all income accrues to equity holders—it may be contended that this type of income will be zero. For long periods of time,

however, a substantial balance of managerial-entity income will exist in the form of retained earnings.

Despite all the quibbling over whose income should be reported as business income, there is considerable logic to the notion that the constitutive concept closest to operational income is the economic entity income. In line with this concept, payments to both creditors and stockholders for the use of funds represent distributions of income. Creditors receive interest and stockholders receive dividends, and the accounting problems involved are to determine when and in what amount these distributions take place.

Conceptually, however, there is also the problem of determining which distributions to stockholders and creditors are distributions of earned assets and which are distributions of capital. There is no inherent reason why distributions to stockholders should reduce retained income rather than contributed capital. A stockholder could be refunded contributed capital just as easily as he could be paid funds earned by the entity. The main fact is that companies distribute assets to creditors and stockholders. But the fiction of distributing earned assets before contributed capital is refunded— which has been referred to as the application of the LIFO principle to equities—is well established in accounting thinking. Let us, therefore, confine this analysis to certain problems which arise when attempts are made to measure these distributions, assuming that they can be distinguished from the general problem of asset distribution.

11.4 INTEREST AND THE SEVERANCE CONCEPT

The distribution of income to creditors, both short- and long-term, is made according to the contractual rights of the creditors. Normally the contract between the borrower and the lender requires specific explicit or implicit cash interest payments, or both, though there are instances where the amount is not specific. (For an example, see [5], in which a company covenanted to pay 3% fixed interest and, in addition, 3% interest income for each year in which net income was sufficient.) As a result the main problem of accounting for the payment of interest to creditors is one of determining when the distribution has taken place.

A distribution of income, when it refers to interest and dividend payments, implies a severance of assets from the entity, and the distribution of these assets to the individuals or groups claiming the entity's income. But the word "severance" is not restricted to physical severance; it also refers to the allocation and establishment of the right to the assets. This is significant to accountants, for the *right* to assets is not, conceptually, the same as the physical *receipt* of assets. Possession of an object is only one of two irreducible aspects of asset. In addition, there must be the right to use the object. This right to possess the object, with others recognizing a duty not to use or take it, is established by social custom and sanction, both legal and nonlegal in nature. (For a description of the basic nature of ownership, see [6].)

But where the right to assets ends and the receipt of assets begins is no simple decision, because the right to assets, except in a legal connotation, is an emerging process rather·than a discrete step. For example, a creditor may have the "right" to receive an interest payment, but if the paying company does not have the means to make the payment, the "right" is not a strong right. The strength of the right increases if the paying company has the means to make the payment. But even this "right" is not without its weaknesses, because the paying company may decide not to pay or to delay in making the payment. Thus the "right" to assets is a claim which grows in strength until normally it culminates in the physical receipt of the assets. But even this act may not represent a conclusive right, for there is always the possibility that for some reason the received assets may have to be returned to the paying company.

The preceding example calls attention to the continuous nature of the seemingly distinct activities of allocating rights to assets and distributing assets. For accounting purposes, it is appropriate to treat both activities as one operation and to consider the issue to be one of selecting the proper time to recognize the severance. In this sense "severance" means that assets will be physically severed at some future date and assigned to particular individuals or groups.

In the case of explicit interest, the contractual arrangement normally provides for the accrual of interest over time, although payment is periodic; and accounting, following business operations, recognizes distributions of interest on the accrual basis. [The tendency to impute a continuous aspect to what has previously been considered discrete business actions is a growing, although subtle and almost subconscious, feature of accounting thinking. It may be a reflection of the process by which accounting adjusts to a new environment.] For convenience, the amount of accrued interest may also be booked periodically. But, contractually, interest accrues continuously and severance may be considered to take place as it accrues. Accounting for the distribution involves recognizing a liability for the amount of the accrued interest.

Implicit interest differs from its explicit counterpart, in that the physical severance of assets normally does not occur until the principal loaned is repaid. The contract for implicit interest typically does not distinguish between principal and interest, and provides for only one sum to be paid at maturity of the loan. Although the severance or the income distribution involved might not be recognized until the terminal date of the loan, the contractual provision for the ultimate physical severance is considered so definite that recognition of the implicit interest is also provided for on an accrual basis by periodic increases in the liability to the lender.

So strongly entrenched in accounting thinking is the notion of "interest accrual" that these distributions of income have been recognized in accounting records, even though evidence may exist that no physical payment can be made, a situation which might exist in the case of an insolvent company. This process of allowing the rules of accounting, rather than ultimate reality, to govern accounting action suggests a need to review the accounting notion that the legal contract for interest governs accounting action, even though failure to carry out the contract will result in a loss to the owner of the right to the assets. On the surface, it would seem that the accrual process should be governed by ultimate economic reality rather than legal rights.

11.5 DIVIDENDS AND ALLOCATION OF RIGHTS

Unlike distributions in the form of interest, distributions to stockholders in the form of dividends are seldom considered definite enough for the accrual process to be used, although the consistency and reliability of the regular quarterly dividends of certain companies is such that this might be possible. Conceptually, the list of possible dates for recognizing a distribution to stockholders could range as follows:

(1) Constant accrual, on the reasoning that dividends are regular and may be anticipated.
(2) The date the board of directors declares the dividend will be paid.
(3) The date the declaration is announced.
(4) The date the company prepares a list of the stockholders who are to receive the dividend.
(5) The date the dividends are mailed to stockholders.

Normally, dividend distributions are recognized on the accounting records at the time the declaration is publicly made that physical severance will take place. This recognition point is used for all types of dividends, including dividends in kind, scrip dividends, note and bond dividends, and preferred stock dividends on common stock, as well as cash dividends in both domestic and foreign currencies. This statement is based on the following classification of dividends.

A. Dividends involving immediate severance of assets
   (1) Cash dividends, paid in either domestic or foreign currency

    (2) Noncash (kind) dividends
        (a) Paid in securities of other companies (stocks or bonds)
        (b) Paid in merchandise*
        (c) Paid in other assets
B. Dividends involving delayed severance of assets
    (1) Credit in accumulative accounts†
    (2) Scrip dividends
    (3) Notes payable of the paying corporation
    (4) Bonds of the paying corporation
    (5) Senior stock (preferred stock) of the paying corporation
    (6) Junior stock (common stock) of the paying corporation
C. Optional (on the part of the recipient) severance of assets
    (1) Consent dividends (cash dividends which may be reinvested in stock of the paying corporation)
    (2) Cash or stock dividends (normally used for fractional shares under a stock dividend)
    (3) Other options, such as agreements among stockholders to take different assets as their dividends (more often used by small closely held corporations)

The recognition of dividend distributions at the time the declaration is made that physical severance will take place is used even though the lag between the declaration date and the time for the future physical severance of assets differs with each type of dividend. For a cash dividend, the lag between the cash payment date and the declaration date is slight. But in the case of bond dividends, the physical cash distribution which pays off the bond at maturity may take place years after the date the bonds were issued.

This variation in the lag between the time dividends are declared and the date physical severance of assets takes place has been used as a justification for realization recognition rather than point recognition as the basis for accounting for dividends. It is believed that realization recognition would provide the flexibility needed to record different kinds of dividends at different times. Logically speaking, if realization recognition is appropriate for recognizing revenue, it is equally appropriate for dividends. But since realization recognition may perhaps allow emotional factors to

---

* This is not a modern development. In 1678, the London East India Company made a distribution "in damaged calico which could not be sold." See [7].

† This method was used by the Cities Service Company from 1921–1925. See [8].

influence the selection of the realization date, it is rejected now as a solution to the problem of recognizing dividend distributions. Instead, the lag between the dividend declaration date and the final severance of cash should be adjusted for by the discounting process, which brings the future value of a severance back to the present.

In the case of a stock dividend, the assumption that the nature of a dividend distribution is a severance of assets may be questioned, because of the indefiniteness of the date when the physical severance will take place. If the stock issued as a dividend is never retired, asset severance will never occur. On the other hand, if the company were liquidated, severance would take place at that time. Because the physical severance date is indefinite, one may contend that there has been no statement of intention to sever assets. In fact, there is logic in the idea that a stock dividend is more of an allocation or reallocation of *rights* to assets than it is a severance of assets. If the result of the stock dividend were to increase the rights of one group of stockholders and decrease the rights of other stockholders, this would represent a reallocation or transfer of rights to assets. The following example serves to illustrate the reallocation feature of a stock dividend.

Example

A company has outstanding 1,000 shares of no-par common stock valued at $100,000, 500 shares of preferred stock valued at $50,000, and retained earnings of $4,000. It decides to issue 100 shares of common stock to the preferred stockholders as a stock dividend. If the market value of the common stock is $40 a share, the effect of the dividend is to reduce retained earnings and increase common stock by $4,000. The effect of the stock dividend is as follows.

RIGHT TO ASSETS		ORIGINAL PREFERRED STOCKHOLDERS	ORIGINAL COMMON STOCKHOLDERS
Before stock dividend		$50,000	$100,000
After stock dividend			
Preferred stock	$50,000		
Common stock			
$\frac{1}{11}$ of 104,000 =	9,454	59,454	
$\frac{10}{11}$ of 104,000 =			94,546
Increase in rights		9,454	(5,454)
Allocation of rights		4,000	0
Reallocation of rights		5,454	(5,454)
Total		$ 9,454	($ 5,454)

Although conventional accounting procedures take no cognizance of the reallocation aspect, there are three distinct aspects of dividend distributions with which accounting theory should deal.

(1) Severance of assets
(2) Allocation of rights to assets
(3) Reallocation of rights to assets

In particular there is a need to account for the reallocation process, since the reallocation of rights to assets is now a well-established business practice. It exists in the form of employee stock options, resource acquisitions for capital stock, and treasury stock activities, all of which are activities which should be reported.

11.6 RECOGNITION OF THE DISTRIBUTION

Broadly speaking, the three problems of accounting for dividend distribution are:
(1) *Determining the action which represents a dividend distribution*
(2) *Determining when the distribution takes place*
(3) *Determining the amount of the distribution*

We have discussed the first of these three problems. The second must be examined, for the time to recognize the distribution is central to the problem of distribution of assets.

There is nothing inherently right or wrong about the selection of any date as the recognition point for dividend distribution. Presumably, the date selected should provide the most useful information to various interested parties. In any respect, inconsistency in the recognition date should be avoided. Seemingly, however, inconsistency exists in two cases: the conception of preferred and common stock dividends on common stock and the treatment of creditor and stockholder reallocation distributions.

When a common stock dividend is paid on common stock, accounting does not define such a dividend as a distribution of income, but a preferred stock dividend *is* so defined. It is contended that the common stockholder is neither better nor worse off after the common stock dividend than he was before. He has merely received a formal certificate of rights previously represented as retained earnings. On the basis of this type of thinking, the Supreme Court of the United States held that common stock dividends on common stock did not constitute a distribution of income. [Eisner vs. Macomber, 252 U.S. 189 (1920).]

In fact, however, all income not claimed by others accrues to common stockholders at the time it is earned by the business entity. And the common stockholder is better off at that time than he was before. Although the gain may be described as "retained earnings," it represents operational income the constitutive element of which is a created but unrecognized gain claimed by stockholders. Because "retained earnings" represents future dividend claims of both common and preferred stockholders, there is a basis for not recognizing the income distribution until the allocation of "retained earnings" to either common or preferred stockholders is more definitely determinable. But there does appear to be a definite distribution of income when a common stock dividend is issued in recognition of the common stockholder's right to the income which has been previously earned for him. By this reasoning, a common stock dividend, if it is to be treated consistently with preferred stock dividends, should be defined as a distribution of income, and so recognized.

In the case of the reallocation of rights to assets, an inconsistency exists in accounting thought. Although the reallocation transaction concerning stockholders only is not recognized as a distribution of income, a reallocation is recognized when losses of creditors are treated as a special component of stockholder income. In a sense, the distribution of accumulated retained earnings to preferred stockholders as a dividend is merely a reallocation of rights formerly belonging to the common stockholders, and this points to the similarity of the distribution and reallocation activities. In fact, it may be contended that all allocations and distributions of income are reallocations of earnings previously accruing to the common stockholders. Acceptance of this view would eliminate the inconsistency which arises when some reallocation gains are treated as income while others are not. Basically, reallocations of rights to assets are similar to allocations and severance of assets, and should be so recognized.

11.7   AMOUNT OF THE DISTRIBUTION

Let us now turn to the problem of determining the amount of the distribution. For cash dividends and interest charges, the amount of the distribution is normally the amount of cash to be distributed. But for cases in which the cash payment is delayed substantially or the dividend is in non-cash form, determining the amount of the distribution may be more difficult. A dividend in kind may have a book value of one amount and a market value of another at the time the distribution is recognized. Stock dividends may be valued at a par or stated value, at book value of other shares outstanding, or at the market value of the shares issued. Practice varies, but as a general principle, market value reflects the amount of the distribution whether or not it all represents an income distribution. This is accepted practice in the case of stock dividends, but is not used for dividends in kind or delayed cash dividends. The following example will clarify the issue which is involved whenever dividends are evaluated in kind.

Example

A company owns securities of other companies which cost $10,000, and carries a $28,000 merchandise inventory. The securities have a market value of $35,000, and the merchandise has a sales value of $39,000. If the company were to issue both the securities and the merchandise as a dividend in kind, a valuation of the distribution at cost would not require that the unrecognized gain be recognized as income, while a valuation at market value would imply that the company could recognize an income by a forced distribution of assets to stockholders. The rationale for market valuation of such distributions is that the stockholder has received the market value—though this might be questioned if the merchandise is valued at an unrealistic sales price—and that the issuing company has merely recognized that previously created but unrecognized income is now claimed by stockholders. In general it is difficult to justify one valuation for stock dividends and another valuation for dividends in kind. Market valuation of both is realistic.

The problem of valuation of distributions extends into the area of valuation of reallocations of rights to assets. In this case, however, the valuation of a reallocation should be computed from the relative rights of the various creditors and stockholders before and after the reallocation. Since reallocation involves no valuation of assets, the proper valuation of reallocation should therefore be in terms of relative rights to booked values.

Delayed cash dividends represent a special valuation problem. Normally their market price may be computed by discounting the future payment by an appropriate bank rate of discount. For short-term delays, such as scrip and note dividends, the short-term discount rate is used. For longer-term instruments, such as bonds, another rate may be used. Even in the case of stock dividends, it may be possible to approximate the present value of an indefinite future payment date by discounting the stream of anticipated perpetual dividends which will be paid or received on the stock dividend. In many cases an existing market for these rights is available for valuation purposes.

11.8 PRE- AND POST-DISTRIBUTION OF OPERATIONAL INCOME

The lag between the recognition of operational income and the distribution of assets to which it is related is significant only in the case of distributions to common stockholders. For creditors and holders of non-participating preferred stock—where the time of the distribution (monthly, quarterly, or annually) is normally specified—income distributions may be recognized prior to, concurrent with, or after the income has been recognized.

For example, interest charges may be recognized before income is computed. In some instances in which losses rather than income are recognized, interest and preferred dividends may be paid several years prior to the recognition of income. In the main these pre-distributions of income are treated as reallocations of the common stock rights, so that any "deficit" is assumed to apply against common stockholder rights. For creditors and preferred stockholders, the problem of a gap between the recognition of income and the distribution is not one of a lag. Rather it is a problem of advance distributions, and the solution of charging pre-distributions to the common stock seems to be a reasonable solution. For those cases in which a lag does exist, it is not so great that any particular accounting problem exists.

This is not true in the case of common stock, however, for the lag may be substantial. Recognition of income may precede distribution by several years. The accumulated income is normally accounted for as "retained earnings," but an assumption does exist that there should be some explanation to justify the non-distribution, and this assumption led to the concept of "surplus reserves." Procedurally, retained earnings may include provisions for contingencies, possible losses, sinking fund investments, market price declines, building expansion programs, investments in treasury stock, and a host of others. The singular aspect of this situation is that there is no conceptual framework to indicate when such reserves should be set up or even what types of reserves should be provided. In fact, so divergent are the policies of different companies that it has been suggested that no segregation of retained earnings is appropriate [9]. Retained income would, as it does now for unappropriated earnings, represent the amount of income not distributed for any possible number of reasons. Such a retreat from the needs of proper accounting for income cannot be justified, and there is a great need for standards to indicate which reserves should be established. This is an accounting problem of no little concern.

Summary

From an operational point of view, the notion of a distribution of income tends to lose its meaning. Only when income is defined in a constitutive sense is it correct to refer to the distribution of income. The shift to the operational concept tends to broaden the problem into one of accounting for the allocation, reallocation, and distribution of rights to assets. Accounting research on this overall problem is needed.

REFERENCES

1. C. E. KNOEPPEL, "Axioms of Industrial Effectiveness," *Administration*, **IV** (September 1922), page 319

2. JOHN LINTNER, "Distributions of Incomes of Corporations Among Dividends, Retained Earnings, and Taxes," *American Economic Review*, **XLVI** (May 1956), page 97

3. I. H. SIEGAL, "Letter to the Editor," *The American Statistician* (February 1952)

4. RAYMOND FIRTH, *Elements of Social Organization*, third edition (London: Watts & Co., 1961), Chapter 4

5. "The Philadelphia Transportation Company Case *Re:* Income Interest on Bonds," *Cases in Public Accounting Practice*, Volumes 3 and 4 (Chicago: Arthur Andersen & Co., 1961)

6. E. ADAMSON HOEBEL, *Man in the Primitive World* (New York: McGraw-Hill, 1958), pages 431–449

7. WILLIAM R. SCOTT, *The Constitution and Finance of English, Scottish and Irish Joint-Stock Companies to 1720*, Volume 2 (Cambridge: 1910)

8. WILLIAM C. WARING, JR., "Fractional Shares Under Stock Dividend Declarations," *Harvard Law Review*, **44** (1930–1931), page 422

9. Committee on Concepts and Standards Underlying Corporate Financial Statements, *Reserves and Retained Income, Supplementary Statement No. 1* (Columbus, Ohio: American Accounting Association, December 31, 1950)

Chapter 12

The Communication of Operational Income

Of all the needs of a modern scientific world, the need to improve communications is probably the most pressing. Specialization and widespread activities coupled with a growing interdependence have made it quite necessary, and yet almost impossible, for us to know what others are doing. Testimonials of this need and inadequacy could go on indefinitely, ranging from the need for information on the complex activities of the business community to the need for information on the developments in scientific disciplines. The basic problem has been with us for ages, for it spans both time and space. Cherry [1] has noted the importance of communication to civilization:

> "Man's development and the growth of civilization have depended, in the main, on progress in a few activities—the discovery of fire, domestication of animals, the division of labor; but, above all, in the evolution of means to receive, to communicate, and to record his knowledge . . ."

12.1 NATURE OF COMMUNICATIONS IN ACCOUNTING

Communication is the process of developing an impression, a map, or a picture of an activity or situation and conveying it to another person or group in such a way that the activity or situation is understood. Thus it encompasses an observation by a communicator, the recording or the symbolizing of the observation in meaningful terms, the transmission of the symbolized information to the receiver, and the comprehension by the receiver of the activity or situation represented by the impression, map, or picture. Let us now examine accounting concepts and methods in the light of modern communication theory.

For the present, the accounting communication of income is confined to one part of the communication process: transmitting information to receivers in such a way that the information and its implications are understood. More precisely, the accountant is concerned with the transmission of information about operational income activity. But even this somewhat restricted area of interest involves a number of assumptions and objectives which we should enumerate in order to understand the relationship of accounting reports to the general theory of communication.

To this end, let us note that the communication of income is somewhat related to the steps involved in its measurement. That is, because an accounting income communication must not only report the income but also convey to a receiver a picture or description of the operations of an organization, this description must be of such a nature that the operations by which income is generated are understood by the receiver. The task of the accountant may be summed up by the exclamation of the young accountant surveying from the vantage point of a high tower the broad expanse of a large industrial firm: "You mean I have to reveal all this activity for an entire year on one sheet of paper—the income statement?"

If a description of operations were not the accounting objective, there would be no need to report anything except the final income figure. But because a description of operations *is* the objective, the detailed measurements must be reported, since the accounting description rests on measured data. Unmeasured, non-quantitative data are not used in the accounting description of economic activity. Activities or operations must therefore be quantified in some way so that they may be communicated by accounting. The process by which this is done represents the accounting mechanism.

The advantage of measured or quantified descriptions is that they lend to the map or picture a precision not available in non-quantitative descriptions. However, this advantage is also a limitation, because the communication description in accounting cannot be fully comprehended unless the measurement methods used in developing the description are revealed. That is, the amount of a measurement depends on how it is measured. For example, a report that depreciation expense is $12,000 is of limited significance unless the receiver of the report knows whether the measurement was computed by the straight-line formula, by a declining-balance technique, or by some other method. Actually, the problem of revealing measurement methods should be extended to include a consideration of such issues as how information of all types is collected, the reluctance or willingness with which information is provided, and any other aspect which might suggest a measurement bias in the information. In other words, the communication of business operations in quantitative terms provides a more precise description than non-numeric descriptions. But the description in quantitative terms may be improved by revealing the measurement methods used.

Although the transmission of measured income descriptions is only part of the communication process, people tend to think of transmission as the substance of the accounting communication problem. There is nothing wrong with this view if one understands that the transmission is not of signs or numbers but of *ideas*, and that transmission is not complete unless the receiver understands the idea represented by the signs and numbers; only then can one say that a communication on operational income has taken place.

Unfortunately, communication in accounting too often consists of the transmission of signs and numbers rather than the underlying idea, which leads to numerical accuracy and rigid classification categories, but narrows the scope of the accounting report. When accountants strive toward communication of ideas, the stress is on media for transmission, on classification, and on arrangement of data so that the underlying "significant" ideas will stand out. Even these efforts, however, seldom assume the breadth necessary to improve the transmission of data on operational income. The medium of transmission remains fixed, in that an income statement is always used, and there is a tendency to look down on the efforts made in other fields to transmit the picture of operational income in other terms. Yet these other fields do make inroads, as is evidenced by the proportion of a corporation's annual report which is prepared by its public relations department. Even within the income statement, few proposals for revolutionary new methods of classification and arrangement have been proposed.

12.2 COMMUNICATION THEORY AND ACCOUNTING REPORTS

Within the framework of communication theory, all accounting for operational income may be included, for communication is concerned with conveying a picture, a map, or a description of an event to another party. It includes the following activities:

(1) An event, happening, or situation exists or occurs in the world. Actually, this is a rather nebulous notion, since what is an event or happening to one person is nothing to another. That is, what constitutes an activity or situation depends on the frame of reference of the observer. A psychiatrist observing a group of people would undoubtedly note events or situations entirely different from those observed by the accountant. About

all we can really say is that changes of all types are constantly taking place, and, as accountants, we shall have to select whatever changes we think significant for the users, present and prospective, of the accounting report.

(2) An observer (the accountant) views the changes and selects the appropriate events (exchanges) and records them by means of a symbolic representation (numbers and classifications) understood by the accountant and the users of his reports. These accounting symbols represent the language of accounting; and accountancy has thus been termed the "language of business," though the language really covers more than business. Procedurally, the accountant, in performing the activity, records the events in terms of numbers according to preconceived classifications.

(3) The observer (accountant), using symbolic representation, reports on a number of events over a period of time. The report is good, in the technical sense, if the symbolic representations accurately reflect the events. It is lacking if it does not reveal symbolically the significant aspects of the event(s).

(4) The observer (accountant) transmits his report to receivers. The report is good, in the transmission sense, if the receiver understands the reality underlying the symbolic representation, which means that the receiver must understand the symbols used. In many cases the accounting terminology is misunderstood (this is a problem in need of special attention). On the other hand, a report is bad, in the transmission sense, if the receiver who understands the symbolic representations does not comprehend the reality underlying the report. In such a situation the fault lies with the transmission process.

(5) The receiver (reader of the accounting report) who understands the reality underlying the symbolic representation of the event then takes action which will modify future events. If he takes desirable action—whatever that might be—communications have been effective. If he takes undesirable action, communications have been ineffective. As a general standard, when it comes to evaluating communications, "desirable action" is that which is best for society.

Diagram 9 on the following page is a schematic diagram of a generalized communication conception of accountancy. Let us analyze this diagram in some detail [2].

(1) *The matrix of communication situation* is indicated by the large circle. It represents the composition and workings of the economic system in which the communication of accountancy takes place.

(2) *The four basic elements of the communication situation*

    (a) *Circle EE* represents the world of economic events of a business enterprise.

Diagram 9 | THE MATRIX OF COMMUNICATION

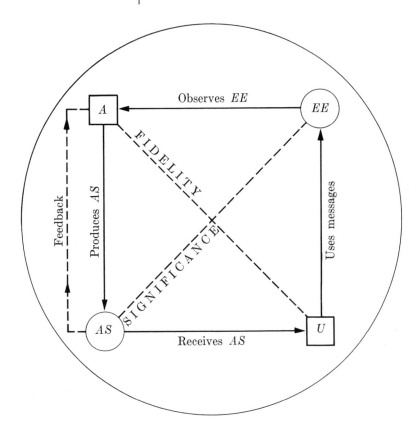

EE = Economic events of a business enterprise
 A = Accountant of a business enterprise
AS = Accounting statements of a business enterprise
 U = Users of accounting statements

  (b) *Square A* represents the accountant. (The accountant is to be
      thought of as comprising the entire accounting staff as well as
      the external auditors of a firm.)
  (c) *Circle AS* represents the accounting statements of an entity.
  (d) *Square U* represents the user of accounting statements.
 (3) *Information flow*, the direction of which is indicated by the arrows along
      the horizontal and vertical lines (counterclockwise).

(4) *The relationships among the elements*
    (a) $A \leftarrow EE$. The relationship between the accountant (A) and the world of economic events (EE) of a business enterprise.
    (b) $A \rightarrow AS$. The relationship between the accountant (A) and the accounting statements (AS).
    (c) $U \leftarrow AS$. The relationship between the user of accounting statements (U) and the accounting statements (AS).
    (d) $U \rightarrow EE$. The relationship between the user of accounting statements (U) and the world of socioeconomic events (EE) of the related business enterprise.
(5) *Fidelity.* The correspondence between what is understood by the user of accounting statements (U) with what the message(s) expressed by the accountant (A) is (are), or is (are) intended to be.
(6) *Significance.* The degree of relevance and adequacy which accounting statements (AS) have in relation to the world of economic events (EE) which they represent.
(7) *Feedback.* The ability of the accountant (A) to make corrections by interpreting to himself the accounting statements (AS) he has encoded but not yet released.

Effective transmission of operational income information requires that the symbolic representation (the measurements, classifications, arrangements, and terminology) disclose the operations performed during the accounting period, and this is the objective of the accountant's income statement. Until recent years, when the importance of the non-recombination operations became evident, this objective was pursued on the assumption that all operations were homogeneous and could be reported on as one operation. It is surprising that accountants tried to accomplish such an objective on one sheet of paper. Surely the very complexity of the operations of even a small firm would require more than one simple formalized statement supported by a limited number of footnotes. Surely brevity was not forced on accountants by the incapacity of the human mind to comprehend. Supplementary statements in the form of summaries could have provided the necessary overall view.

Possibly the desire for secrecy may have caused those past accounting reports to be so skeletal. However, it is no longer reasonable to withhold disclosure blindly for fear of revealing information to competitors. Much of the information is now being disclosed informally in the president's section of both quarterly and annual reports to stockholders.

Based on his study with the Long Range Objectives Committee of the American Institute of Certified Public Accountants, John L. Carey [3], executive director of the AICPA, has remarked, "Managements which desire to preserve a good market for their securities and a good line of bank credit are far more frank than they were in earlier days. Purchasers of securities may be obtaining from other sources more information, of greater value to them, than that which appears in the formal financial statements audited by independent CPA's." In fact, there appear to be no real barriers to a complete and full disclosure of operational income; no barriers, that is, outside of emotional aspects, the social instability which accompanies changes, and the cost of producing the information. Efforts to expand the function of accounting reports are common, but there is, of course, the aversion to change on the part of managers and accountants. However, this is a barrier which time and education can remove.

12.3 INCOME COMMUNICATION PROBLEMS

If we accept the objective of complete and full disclosure of operational income, we must consider the following questions:

(1) What operations shall be communicated?
(2) In what degree of detail shall each operation be reported?
(3) How shall the communication be made?

12.4 INFORMATION TO BE TRANSMITTED

The answer to the first two questions would seemingly require disclosure of efforts and accomplishments in each of the areas of business operations—acquisition, utilization, recombination, and disposition—disclosure sufficiently detailed to reveal all distinctive elements of expense and revenue during the period. In many instances, a detailed report would include information on significant subgoals as well, which would entail a disclosure of the effort applied, in terms of specific functions and resources, in pursuit of all goals. It would also be necessary to disclose the effectiveness of different types of operations, which could be accomplished by recognizing the non-homogeneous nature of income as reflected by measures of different types of constitutive income as well as total operational income. Finally, it would be necessary to disclose the various components of operational income in such detail that many constitutive concepts of income could be developed from the one operational income report.

In the process of achieving these disclosure needs, one should recognize the fact that the meaning of specific, constitutive concepts changes subtly and slowly over time. Thus one should try to anticipate the change, and provide details of operation so that various changes in each constitutive concept of income will not require a revision of the basic format for reporting operational income.

Although it is impossible, without empirical verification, to state categorically and precisely all the operational income data which should be revealed, let us suggest that the disclosure should include the following information:

(A) Effectiveness of business operations should be disclosed for:
  (1) Acquisition and utilization operations combined, if separate measurement is not possible.
  (2) Recombination operation separately, if measurement is possible, for (a) production activities, (b) distribution activities, and (c) motivation activities.
  (3) Disposition operation separately, if measurement is possible, for (a) pricing, and (b) losses.
(B) The following elements of operational incomes should be disclosed to clarify various measurement points of view:
  (1) Money income (a) realized (at different recognition points), and (b) unrealized (at different recognition points).
  (2) Real income (a) realized (at different recognition points), and (b) unrealized (at different recognition points).
(C) The following sources of operational incomes should be disclosed to reveal factors underlying business operations:
  (1) Types of customers.
  (2) Nature of economic activity, which would include (a) innovation, or ventures if separate disclosure of innovation is not measurable, (b) investment (both current and "windfall"), and (c) combined operating activities, by types of products and by geographic areas.
(D) The distribution of income should be disclosed:
  (1) By types of recipients (stockholders, creditors, governments).
  (2) By nature of distribution (dividends, interest, and taxes).
  (3) By a statement of the reallocation of rights.
(E) Measurement techniques and methods used should be disclosed in sufficient detail to preclude misunderstandings.

In addition, accountants may someday include in the operational income report measurements of some type of managerial subjective income. For the present, let us bear in mind that the substance of accounting should not exceed by too much the measurement techniques of the accounting discipline, and let us therefore stay within the realm of the possible and not include subjective income in operational income.

In fact, speaking of the realm of the possible, even the standard we have proposed represents something of a long-run objective, to be approached by a series of steps. The size of these steps will vary with the beliefs and wishes of the profession, but each step, once taken, will then become the current standard to which operational income reporting should adjust. The suggested standard set forth in this study must be considered a big step. Others may prefer shorter steps. Whichever proposal is followed, however, there is ample evidence, in the SEC standards for reports and in many criticisms of accounting reports, to indicate that more complete disclosure of income is now being sought. Because some sort of steps must be taken, it seems desirable to have an ideal objective standard of reporting toward which the profession can move.

12.5 THE TRANSMISSION PROCESS

The third problem of transmitting income information—how shall the communication be made?—is one that is neglected in current accounting theory. That is, there is no theory of how to transmit accounting information, and few developments at the basic philosophical level which would aid accountants in developing such a theory. Some research is being done, however, to develop tools which will determine whether two communicators misinterpret each other. (Naess [4] has expressed the hope "that many fields . . . may directly profit by investigation within the broad limits of a theory of interpretation and preciseness . . .") But nothing of use to accountants has yet been developed. In view of this situation, we may assume that any substantial advances in transmission methods will have to be made by the trial-and-error process, though there are undoubtedly areas where a more scientific approach may be possible.

The problem of transmission is a knotty one, for it involves such factors as communication media, redundancy, and semantics, as well as words, numbers, forms, and arrangements. The issue is becoming more and more involved every day, as the economy broadens its base and the general public—stockholders, employees, creditors, suppliers, and customers, both present and prospective—become financially interested in the daily activities of business firms. So widespread has this economic involvement become that not only annual and quarterly financial reports, but monthly, weekly, and even daily reports will probably be needed in the future. Accounting information is needed not only because of the preciseness of the information which the discipline is capable of producing, but because such data are subject to independent confirmation. Therefore, just as the weather map, using rather technical terms, is now published daily in newspapers, so may reports on operational income of companies whose stock is publicly held be a daily feature of all large newspapers and financial magazines in the future.

Continuous reporting of income is not an unattainable dream. After all, continuous auditing now exists, and it would be entirely feasible to issue

annual reports monthly, each one covering the past twelve months'
operations. Many large companies issue daily reports internally to their top
management, and much of this information could be made public after
attestation by independent auditors. In addition, abbreviated quarterly
data are now reported in certain financial newspapers and many periodicals
now provide daily information on stock prices.

Yearly reports will undoubtedly prove inadequate for a rapidly moving
economy, and hence the notion of annual reporting must be reexamined.
There was a time, thirty years ago, when it was adequate, but this is no
longer true. The very abundance of that which is referred to as "financial
news" is evidence of the need for a great increase in accounting communications on economic activity. Thus let us hope that accountants will break
from the tradition of yearly reporting, and think in terms of *continuous*
reporting.

12.6 SEMANTICS

Another major problem of transmitting accounting information is *semantics*.
(For a brief, more formal exposition of the role of semantics in accounting,
see [5].) The difficulty lies in the fact that the words, numbers, and forms
used to transmit information do not convey the meaning intended. Much
misunderstanding has arisen because most recipients of the accounting
message have never taken the time to find out what the accounting symbols
are intended to signify. However, it is unfortunately true that no signs
(words, numbers, etc.) used to transmit a message can convey the message
as clearly as can the underlying action or object which the signs signify.

For example, the word "cash" is not the same as the money; and to a
recipient of a message, the sign (the word "cash") is not the same stimulus
as the object it signifies (money). Nevertheless, there is a relationship
between the sign (the word) and the significate (the money), but this
relationship is not known precisely and varies from sign to sign. For some
signs, the relationship is quite high; in other words, the recipient of the sign
reacts just as he would if he had direct contact with the significate. For
other signs, the relationship may be very weak, and the recipient of the sign
may not react as he would if he had direct contact with the underlying
object or action which the sign is supposed to represent.

Accountants need to seek means to improve the relationship between
accounting signs and their significates. To do this, however, they must
first develop a means for measuring the relationship in a scientific manner [6]. At a lower level of analysis, there is a need for a vast inductive
study of the reaction of recipients to accounting signs. The meaning of
accounting signs is revealed by what the recipient *does*, not by what he

maintains that the sign means; for he may know the verbal definition of the sign, but not understand the action or object which it signifies. The study is needed because quite evidently the relationship between accounting signs and their significates is weak. The term *"delinquent* account,*"* for example, may be a term which carries a significance not intended by the transmitting accountant, and proposals to drop such terms as "reserves" and "surplus" show that such signs do not represent well the underlying significates.

12.7 REDUNDANCY

Closely allied to the problem of semantics is that of *redundancy*. Redundancy, as defined in Webster's Third International Dictionary, is "the part of a communication that can be eliminated without loss of essential information; *specif:* the number arrived at by subtracting from one the ratio of the actual information content of a communication to the maximum information content and expressed as a percentage."

Communication by number symbol is an involved problem, for although number symbols increase the preciseness of meaning, which is desirable, they also require reading which is much more careful than that which readers of accounting reports generally accord to them. Consequently, redundancy may be necessary in accounting reports. That is, accountants may have to repeat numerical presentation in different arrangements in order for the reader to comprehend the implications of the numbers. For example, one means of inserting redundancy into accounting reports on operational income would be supplementary statements in percentage form. Alternatively, various relationships among different numbers may be shown in ratio form, or by a graph, map, or chart presentation. The problem with numbers, unfortunately, is that overlooking one digit of a number completely changes the meaning of the information. Words do not have this precision of meaning and, in fact, often take their meaning from the context of the sentence and paragraph in which they are used. Thus a reader may skip a word in a report and still grasp the meaning of the report, because of the fact that words have a unique meaning in each context.

Both semantics and redundancy are essential considerations in the development of accounting means for transmitting operational income effectively, and these two factors should be included in any accounting framework of income determination theory.

12.8 THE COMMUNICATION FORM

Let us turn from conceptual issues to current forms of reporting in the income statement, since this undoubtedly has to be the starting point of any proposal for changes in methods of transmitting operational income.

Before proposing a new and more comprehensive reporting form, let us examine the nature and implications of the three conventional types of income reports: (1) the single-step report, (2) the multi-step report, and (3) the activity report.

The *single-step income report* is based on the assumption that it is not possible to distinguish clearly different operations, and that it is therefore impossible to report on accomplishments, efforts, and effectiveness of the various operations of a business. In the face of evidence that the operations can be and are differentiated to a satisfactory degree for organizational and other purposes, advocates of single-step reporting contend that it is impossible to distinguish operations, and also impossible to assign effort and accomplishment to any selected set of business operations. According to this view, one can at best only disclose all accomplishments, all efforts, and the total effectiveness of the entity. It is considered unwise to disclose any specific relationship among parts of one operation because of the low state of the accounting art of measurement. As a result, total revenues are grouped as one sum from which total expenses are deducted, and thus income is computed in one step. The single-step income report takes the following form.

THE ILLUSTRATIVE COMPANY

INCOME REPORT FOR THE PROPER ACCOUNTING PERIOD

Revenue

Sales of "regular" goods and services		$xx,xxx
By-product sales		x,xxx
Investment revenue		xxx
Total		$xx,xxx

Expenses

Cost-of-goods-sold expense (detailed)	$ x,xxx	
Distribution expenses (detailed)	x,xxx	
Administration expenses (detailed)	x,xxx	
Other expenses (itemized)	xxx	$xx,xxx
Income		$ x,xxx

The *multi-step income report* assumes that certain activities of a company are sufficiently distinct from the basic objective of the company so that income from "normal" operations may be computed separately from other activities. Historically, because the primary purpose of each business entity was usually to produce and distribute one basic product for an existing demand, and because the relative importance of the recombination operation usually far exceeded that of all other operations, this multi-step type of an income report served well the function of reporting on all income operations. But when the complexity and size of modern business began to render this form of income report inadequate, the accounting reaction resulted in the single-step income report form. The multi-step report has not disappeared from use, however, and for many companies, particularly smaller, specialized ones, it may be the most appropriate income-reporting form. This income report takes the following form.

THE ILLUSTRATIVE COMPANY

INCOME REPORT FOR THE PROPER ACCOUNTING PERIOD

Sales		$xx,xxx
Cost of goods sold		x,xxx
Gross margin		$ x,xxx
Operating expenses: (itemized)	$ xxx	
	xxx	x,xxx
Operating income		$ x,xxx
Nonoperating items:		
By-product sales	$ xxx	
Investment revenue	xxx	
Nonoperating expenses	(xxx)	xxx
Regularly recurring income		$ x,xxx
Extraordinary gains and losses (itemized)		xxx
Income		$ x,xxx

The *activity report*, which is conceptually more related to operational income reports than the other two income-report forms, endeavors to disclose in more detail the objectives of a company, and to reveal the effectiveness and extent to which each objective is attained. While the activity report does not attempt to report minutely on each separate venture, it does group activities in more detail than the multi-step report. Essentially, it is based on the premise that the objectives of a business may be stated, in a broad sense, in terms of the final output of a company. That is, it endeavors to disclose the effectiveness with which broad groups of products and services are produced and delivered to customers. Typically, this results in a four-way classification of products or services rendered to customers (*principal activities, minor activities, ancillary activities,* and *gains and losses*), a classification further subdivided by areas of responsibility within a company.

The activity report is more widely used internally than externally, and thus has no uniform format. Similarly, it goes by so many titles that one hesitates to generalize them all under the one title of "activity reports." Activity reports do, however, disclose revenue, expenses, and incomes by segments of the business. Conceptually, they take something of the following form.

THE ILLUSTRATIVE COMPANY

INCOME REPORT FOR THE PROPER ACCOUNTING PERIOD

Principal activities

	Division A	Division B	Division C	Total
Revenue from operations	$ x,xxx	$ xxx	$ x,xxx	$xx,xxx
Operating expenses (detailed)	xxx	xxx	xxx	x,xxx
Income	$ xxx	$ xx	$ xxx	$ xxx

Minor activities

	Type A	Type B		
Operating revenues	$ xxx	$ xxx		
Operating expenses	xxx	xx		
Income	$ xx	$ xx		xxx

Ancillary activities

			Company	
Incidental revenues			$ xxx	
Incidental expenses			xx	xxx
Gains and losses (detailed)				xxx
Total income				$ x,xxx

12.9 OPERATIONAL INCOME REPORTING

One can find support for each of the three preceding income-reporting forms, but actually none of them is adequate for reporting the income of a modern business entity. These income-reporting forms do not reveal enough information to permit effective decisions to be made by the investing public, or by employees, creditors, and others. Therefore additional information must be provided, if our free-enterprise system is to operate effectively. Further, business operations have changed in subtle ways, and top management itself needs to know the effectiveness with which the various operations of the entity have been performed.

As noted in earlier chapters, disclosure of certain basic income components allows a variety of constitutive income concepts to be computed. This fact is the cornerstone of operational income reporting, for the objective of the operational income report is to reveal *components* of income, and the relationships that exist among them. In addition, however, a report must be more than a mere itemization of income components.

Therefore there must be an accounting format which reveals all activities of a business, as well as the component elements of income. As yet this format has not been developed, and proposals for its proper arrangement will have to meet the test of general acceptance.

Although we do not intend to propose a prescribed form for reporting operational income, the following form indicates the minimum disclosure.

THE ILLUSTRATIVE COMPANY

OPERATIONAL INCOME REPORT FOR THE PROPER ACCOUNTING PERIOD

Operation	*Schedule*		*Income*
Acquisition operation	A		$ 10,000
Utilization operation			
General price-level change	B	$ 8,955	
Specific price-level change	B	55,045	64,000
Recombination operation	C		186,000
Disposition operation	D		75,000
Distribution operation			—
Total operational income			$335,000

Schedule A: acquisition operation

	Acquisition cost	Current (replacement) cost on acquisition date	Acquisition income
Item *A*	$ 6,000	$ 6,000	$ 0
Item *B*	12,000	13,000	1,000
⋮	⋮	⋮	⋮
Total	$150,000	$160,000	$10,000

Schedule B: utilization operation

	Current (replacement) cost				
	Acquisition date	Start of period	Disposition date	End of period	Utilization income
Item *A*	—	$ 15,000	$ 6,000	$ 14,000	$ 5,000
Item *B*	$ 5,000	12,000	19,000		2,000
Item *C*	14,000	—	3,000	15,000	4,000
⋮	⋮	⋮	⋮	⋮	⋮
Total	$160,000	$170,000	$200,000	$194,000	$64,000
General price level, %	101	100	102	105	
General price level elimination	—	—	$ 2,922	$ 6,033	8,955
Specific price changes					$55,045

Schedule C: recombination operation

Immediate sales price of products completed		$479,000
(Work in process valued at current replacement cost)		
Services used at current replacement cost		
Disposed of during the period	$200,000	
On hand at end of period	93,000	293,000
Total recombination income		$186,000

Schedule D: disposition operation

Sales	$275,000
Sales at immediate sales prices	200,000
Total disposition income	$ 75,000

The preceding operational income statement is based on measurement techniques which are as yet not well developed. In addition, the proposed format will have to be condensed and adjusted to fit the needs of each reporting company. It does, however, represent a format which is a desirable objective. It is also possible to compute, from the information presented, a variety of component elements of operational income. This permits a variety of constitutive concepts of income, to be calculated.

12.10 OTHER INCOME-COMMUNICATION PROBLEMS

The problem of communicating income is, sad to say, not restricted to effective formats for disclosing periodic income. Other issues include such problems as the length of the reporting time period and the need to separate non-homogeneous elements in each income measurement. Some analysts say that the concept of periodic income is inadequate if one is reporting on any period less than five years. They insist that, if periodic income reports are to be rendered, the annual income report should be based on an average of five-year operations. Such a procedure would, of course, allow a better allocation of expenses to particular segments of the business, and would convert a number of unexpected short-term gains and losses into expected items of expense and revenue. But the usefulness of such a measure of income would be restricted; because, within five years, a company could so change direction that a description of average operations might not be particularly useful.

The implicit assumption underlying most income statements is that income is a homogeneous element. Such an assumption is hardly justified, for income may be distinguished on several bases. It may be separated in its constitutive approximation, according to the groups to whom it accrues (preferred and common stock), according to its source (government contracts and ventures), according to its nature (realized in the form of cash, accrued, or market appreciation), and by a number of other systems. In fact, it appears that the framework within which income may be reported is fully as broad as the framework underlying income-determination theory.

12.11 QUALIFICATIONS OF OPERATIONAL INCOME REPORTING

The problem of precisely measuring effectiveness in each business operation is beyond the present capacity of the measurement technology of accounting. The framework presented in this text has been submitted to provide guidance to efforts to improve the measurement side of the discipline. On the other hand, we have not attempted to suggest non-income goals which business entities may, or may not, have. To the extent that these non-income goals exist, the recommendations we have submitted for the structure of accounting thought are inadequate. With these qualifications, however, we submit this framework as a reasonable articulation of the conceptual accounting problems involved in the determination of income, and the filling-in of this framework is an area in which accounting research and theory could contribute significantly.

REFERENCES

1. COLIN CHERRY, *On Human Communication* (New York: Science Editions, 1961), page 31
2. NORTON M. BEDFORD AND VAHE BALADOUNI, "A Communication Theory Approach to Accountancy," *Accounting Review*, **XXXVII** (October 1962), pages 653–54
3. JOHN L. CAREY, *The CPA Plans for the Future* (New York: American Institute of Certified Public Accountants, 1965), page 143
4. ARNE NAESS, "Toward a Theory of Interpretation and Preciseness," *Semantics and the Philosophy of Language*, edited by Leonard Linsky (Urbana: University of Illinois Press, 1952), page 249
5. DAVID H. LI, "The Semantic Aspect of Communication Theory and Accountancy." *Journal of Accounting Research*, **I** (Spring 1963), 102–107
6. CHARLES E. OSGOOD, GEORGE J. SUCI, AND PERCY H. TANNENBAUM, *The Measurement of Meaning* (Urbana: University of Illinois Press, 1957), Chapter 1

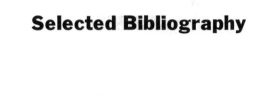

Selected Bibliography

Selected Bibliography

CHAPTER 1

Books

BENJAMIN, A. CORNELIUS, *Operationism.*   Springfield, Ill.: Charles C. Thomas, 1955

BRAY, F. SEWELL, *The Accounting Mission.*   Melbourne: Melbourne University Press, 1951

BRIDGMAN, P. W., *The Logic of Modern Physics.*   New York: Macmillan, 1927

Committee on Research Planning and Accounting Development, *The Field of Management Accounting.*   New York: National Association of Accountants, 1963

DEVINE, CARL THOMAS, *Essays in Accounting Theory.*   DeLand, Florida: private publication, 1962

FRANK, P. G., editor, *The Validation of Scientific Theories.*   New York: Collier's Books, 1961

LEVITT, T., *The Twilight of the Profit Motive.*   Washington, D.C.: Public Affairs Press, 1955

LITTLETON, A. C., *Structure of Accounting Theory.*   Columbus, O.: American Accounting Association, 1953

MOONITZ, M. *Basic Postulates of Accounting.*   New York: AICPA, 1961

SPROUSE, R. T., AND M. MOONITZ, *A Tentative Set of Broad Accounting Principles for Business Enterprises.*   New York: AICPA, 1962

WILLIAMS, THOMAS H., *An Investigation of the Mathematical Dimension of Accountancy,* Ph.D. dissertation, University of Illinois, 1961

Articles

ARROW, K. J., "Utilities, Attitudes, Choices: A Review Note." *Econometrica,* **26** (January 1958), 1–23

CHAMBERS, R. J., "Conditions of Research in Accounting." *Journal of Accountancy,* **110** (December 1960), 33–39

DEIN, R. C., "The Future Development of Accounting Theory." *Accounting Review,* **XXXIII** (July 1958), 389–400

DEVINE, CARL T., "Research Methodology and Accounting Theory Formation." *Accounting Review,* **XXXV** (July 1960), 387–399

HARSANYI, J. C., "Cardinal Welfare, Individualistic Ethics, and Interpersonal Comparisons of Utility." *Journal of Political Economy*, **LXIII** (August 1955), 309–321

KLEEREKOPER, I., "The Economic Approach to Accounting." *Journal of Accountancy*, **115** (March 1963), 36–40

KOPLIN, H. T., "The Profit Maximization Assumption." *Oxford Economic Papers*, **15** (July 1963), 130–139

MEHTA, J. K., "The True Nature of Economic Generalizations." *Indian Journal of Economics*, **XXXIX** (April 1959), 371–382

SAWYER, B. E., "Influence on Accounting by Concepts in Allied Fields." *Accounting Review*, **XXXIII** (April 1958), 267–268

SCHRADER, W. J., "Inductive Approach to Accounting Theory." *Accounting Review*, **XXXVII** (October 1962), 645–649

STEWART, JAMES C., "The Future of the Accounting Profession." *The Chinese Accountant*. Hong Kong: Society of Chinese Accountants and Auditors, 1963, 35–42

CHAPTER 2

Books

Staff of Joint Economic Committee, *Productivity, Prices and Incomes*. Washington, D.C.: Superintendent of Documents, 1957

EDWARDS, E. O., AND P. W. BELL, *The Theory and Measurement of Business Income*. Berkeley: University of California Press, 1961

HEILBRONER, R. L., *The Quest for Wealth*. New York: Simon & Schuster, 1956

MAY, G. O., *Financial Accounting*. New York: Macmillan, 1943

PARSONS, TALCOTT, *The Social System*. Glencoe, Ill.: The Free Press, 1951

PIGOU, A. C., *The Economics of Welfare*. London: Macmillan, 1938

POLANYI, K., *The Great Transformation*. New York: Farrar and Rinehart, 1944

RAY, DELMAS D., *Accounting and Business Fluctuations*. Gainesville, Florida: University of Florida Press, 1960

Articles

ALEXANDER, SIDNEY, "Income Measurement in a Dynamic Economy." *Five Monographs on Business Income*. New York: AICPA, 1950, 1–95

BAXTER, W. T., "The Accountant's Contribution to the Trade Cycle." *Economica*, **XXII** (May 1955), 99–112

FROEHLICH, W., "Moral Judgments in Income Concepts." *Review of Social Economy*, **XIII** (March 1955), 1–19

GATOVSKII, L., "The Role of Profit in a Socialist Economy." *Problems of Economics*, **V** (February 1963), 10–18

POWLISON, KEITH, "The Profit Motive Compromised." *Harvard Business Review*, **28** (March–April 1950), 102–108

CHAPTER 3

Books

BIET, B., *Théories Contemporaines du Profit: Essai de Micro et Macroanalysis*. Paris: Librairie de Médicis, 1956

EDWARDS, E. O., AND P. W. BELL, *The Theory and Measurement of Business Income*. Berkeley: University of California Press, 1961

FISHER, IRVING, *The Nature of Capital and Income*. London: Macmillan, 1912

FOULKE, R. A., *A Study of the Theory of Corporate Net Profits*. New York: Dun & Bradstreet, 1949

GREFTEGREFF, K., *Inntekt og Beslektede Begreper i Økonomisk Teori* (Income and Related Concepts in Economic Theory), with an English summary. Oslo: Oslo University Press, 1962

HANSEN, P., *The Accounting Concept of Profit*. Amsterdam: North Holland Publishing Co., 1962

KEYNES, J. M., *The General Theory of Employment Interest and Money*. New York: Harcourt, Brace, 1936

KIERSTEAD, B. S., *Capital, Interest and Profits*. New York: John Wiley & Sons, 1959

KNIGHT, F. H., *Risk, Uncertainty and Profit*. London: London School of Economics and Political Science, 1933

LAUTERBACH, A., *Man, Motives and Money*, second edition. Ithaca: Cornell University Press, 1959

LINDAHL, ERIK, *Studies in the Theory of Money and Capital*. London: Allen & Unwin, Ltd., 1939

MARSHALL, ALFRED, *Principles of Economics*, eighth edition. New York: Macmillan, 1948

SCHLAIFER, R., *Introduction to Statistics for Business Decisions*. New York: McGraw-Hill, 1961

SCHNEIDER, ERICH, *Wirtschaftlichkeitsrechnungtheorie der Investition*. Tübingen, Germany: J. C. B. Mohr (Paul Siebeck), 1961

SHACKLE, G. L. S., *Expectations, Investments, and Income*. London: Oxford University Press, 1938

Study Group on Business Income, *Five Monographs on Business Income*. New York: AICPA, 1950

Articles

ALCHIAN, ARMEN A., "The Rate of Interest, Fisher's Rate of Return Over Cost, and Keynes' Internal Rate of Return." *American Economic Review,* **XLV** (December 1955), 938–943

AMES, EDWARD, "Research, Invention, Development and Innovation." *American Economic Review,* **LI** (June 1961), 370–381

BODKIN, R., "Windfall Income and Consumption." *American Economic Review,* **XLIX** (September 1959), 602–614

BRAY, F. S., "The Nature of Income and Capital." *Accounting Research,* **1** (January 1949), 27–49

BREAK, G. F., "Capital Maintenance and the Concept of Income." *Journal of Political Economy,* **62** (February 1954), 48–62

FELLNER, W. J., "Profit as the Risk-Taker's Surplus." *Review of Economics and Statistics,* **XLV** (May 1963), 173–184

FERBER, R., "The Accuracy and Structure of Industry Expectations in Relation to Those of Individual Firms." *Journal of American Statistical Association,* **53** (June 1958), 317–335

FETTER, F. A., "Reformulation of the Concepts of Capital and Income in Economics and Accounting." *Accounting Review,* **XII** (March 1937), 3–12

FISHER, IRVING, "Income in Theory and Income Taxation in Practice." *Econometrica,* **5** (1937), 1–55

FRANKEL, S. H., "'Psychic' and 'Accounting' Concepts of Income and Welfare." *Oxford Economic Papers,* **4** (February 1952), 1–17

HEWITT, W. W., "The Concept of Income." *Journal of Political Economy,* **XXXIII** (April 1925), 155–178

HORWICH, G., "Real Assets and the Theory of Interest." *Journal of Political Economy,* **LXX** (April 1962), 157–169

LINDAHL, ERIK, "The Concept of Income." *Economic Essays in Honor of Gustav Cassel.* London: Allen & Unwin, 1933, 399–407

LITTLETON, A. C., "Contrasting Theories of Profit." *Accounting Review,* **XI** (March 1936), 10–18

LITTLETON, A. C., "What Is Profit?" *Accounting Review,* **III** (September 1928), 278–288

MEEK, R. L., "The Physiocratic Concept of Profit." *Economica,* **XXVI** (February 1959), 39–53

MURAD, ANATOL, "An Uncertainty Theory of Profit." *American Economic Review,* **XLI** (March 1951), 164–169

REID, MARGARET G., "Consumption, Savings and Windfall Gains." *American Economic Review,* **LII** (September 1962), 728–737

ROBINSON, J., "Some Problems of Definition and Measurement of Capital." *Oxford Economic Papers,* **XI** (June 1959), 157–166

THOMAS, A. L., "Discounted Services Again: The Homogeneity Problem." *Accounting Review*, **XXXIX** (January 1964), 1–11

TISDELL, C. "Uncertainty, Instability, Expected Profit." *Econometrica*, **31** January–April 1963), 243–247

TUCKER, G. S. L., "The Origin of Ricardo's Theory of Profits." *Economica*, **XXI** (November 1954), 320–333

WESTON, J. F., "A Generalized Uncertainty Theory of Profit." *American Economic Review*, **XL** (March 1950), 40–60

CHAPTER 4

Books

Staff of Accounting Research Division, AICPA, *Reporting the Financial Effects of Price-Level Changes*. New York: AICPA, 1963

CHURCHMAN, C. W., *Prediction and Optimal Decision*. Englewood Cliffs, N.J.: Prentice-Hall, 1961

CHURCHMAN, C. W., AND P. RATOOSH, editors, *Measurement: Definition and Theories*. New York: John Wiley & Sons, 1959

DEAN, ARTHUR H., *An Inquiry into the Nature of Business Income Under Present Price Levels*. New York: AICPA, 1949

EUCKEN, W., *The Foundations of Economics: History and Theory in the Analysis of Economic Reality*. Chicago: University of Chicago Press, 1951

HONKO, JAAKKO, *The Annual Income of an Enterprise and Its Determination*. Helsinki, Finland: Yrityksen Vuositulos, Lüketaloustieteellinen Tutkimuslaitos, 1959

JONES, R. C., *Effects of Price-Level Changes on Business Income, Capital, and Taxes*. Columbus, O.: American Accounting Association, 1956

KATANO, ICHIRO. *Accounting for Changing Money Value*. Tokyo: Dobunkan Publishing Co., 1962

MASON, PERRY, *Price-Level Changes and Financial Statements*. Columbus, O.: American Accounting Association, 1956

MAY, G. O., *Business Income and Price Levels: An Accounting Study*. New York: Study Group on Business Income of American Institute of Accountants, 1949

NAGEL, ERNEST, *Principles of the Theory of Probability*. Chicago: University of Chicago Press, 1939

RUSSELL, B., *Principles of Mathematics*, second edition. New York: Norton & Co., 1938

SMITH, D. T., AND J. K. BUTTERS, *Taxable and Business Income*. New York: National Bureau of Economic Research, 1949

TERBORGH, GEORGE, *Realistic Depreciation Policy*. Chicago: Machinery and Allied Products Institute, 1954

TORGERSON, WARREN S., *Theory and Methods of Scaling*. New York: John Wiley & Sons, 1958

WALSH, FRANCIS J., JR., *Inflation and Corporate Accounting*. New York: National Industrial Conference Board, 1962

WOOLF, H., editor, *Quantification—A History of the Meaning of Measurement in the Natural and Social Sciences*. Indianapolis: Bobbs-Merrill, 1961

Articles

AVERY, H. G., "Economic Value Versus Original Cost." *NAA Bulletin*, **XL** (February 1959), 5–14

BAUMOL, W. J., "The Cardinal Utility Which Is Ordinal." *Economic Journal*, **LXVIII** (December 1958), 665–672

CONKLIN, W. D., "Judgment in the Determination of Net Income." *Arthur Young Journal*, **I** (January 1954), 8–12

DEAN, A. H., "Relation of Law and Economics to the Measurement of Income." *Accounting Review*, **XXVIII** (July 1953), 328–342

ENGELMANN, K., "The Realization Basis of Determining Income Would Eliminate Distortions Caused by Inflation." *Journal of Accountancy*, **90** (October 1950), 321–323

FROEHLICH, WALTER, "The Role of Income Determination in Reinvestment and Investment." *American Economic Review*, **XXXVIII** (March 1948), 78–91

GERSCHENKRON, A., "Problems in Measuring Long-Term Growth in Income and Wealth." *Journal of American Statistical Association*, **52** (December 1957), 450–457

GRAHAM, W. J., "The Effect of Changing Price Levels on the Determination, Reporting, and Interpretation of Income." *Accounting Review*, **XXIV** (January 1949), 15–26

GREENHUT, M. L., "A General Theory of Maximum Profits." *Southern Economic Journal*, **XXVIII** (January 1962), 278–285

HICKS, J. R., "The Measurement of Real Income." *Oxford Economic Papers*, **10** (June 1958), 125–162

MAJUMDAR, T., "Armstrong and the Utility Measurement Controversy." *Oxford Economic Papers*, **9** (February 1957), 30–40

NIGAM, R. K., "The Measurement of Profits." *Accounting Research*, **7** (January 1956), 1–41

REYNOLDS, I. N., "Selecting the Proper Depreciation Method." *Accounting Review*, **XXXVI** (April 1961), 239–248

SMITH, C. A., "The Effects of Combinations of 'Fast' and 'Slow' Depreciation on Reported Net Income." *NAA Bulletin*, **XLII** (April 1961), 31–42

SORTER, G. H., "Reported Income and Inventory Change." *Journal of Business*, **XXXII** (January 1959), 47–51

VATTER, W. J., "Fund-Theory View of Price-Level Adjustments." *Accounting Review*, **XXXVII** (April 1962), 189–207

WELLISZ, S., "A Note on the Measurement of Real Income." *Oxford Economic Papers*, **12** (February 1960), 112–121

CHAPTER 5

Books

American Institute of Accountants, *Changing Concepts of Business Income.* New York: Macmillan, 1952

CANNING, JOHN B., *The Economics of Accountancy.* New York: The Ronald Press, 1929

CARTER, C. F., AND B. R. WILLIAMS, *Investment in Innovation.* London: Oxford University Press, 1958

CHAMBERLIN, E. H., *Toward a More General Theory of Value.* New York: Oxford University Press, 1957

GILMAN, L., *Accounting Concepts of Profit.* New York: The Ronald Press, 1939

GOETZ, BILLY E., *Management Planning and Control.* New York: McGraw-Hill, 1949

GORDON, M. J., *The Investment, Financing and Valuation of the Corporation.* Homewood, Ill.: Richard Irwin, 1962

KARLIN, ARTHUR D., *An Inquiry into the Psychological and Philosophical Antecedents of an Asset Concept.* Unpublished Ph.D. dissertation, University of Illinois, 1964

RIVERIN, ALPHONSE, *Le Profit Comptable: Fiction ou Réalité?* Quebec: Les Presses de l'Université Laval, 1961

Articles

ANTON, H. R., "Activity Analysis of the Firm: A Theoretical Approach to Accounting (System) Development." *Lüketaloudellinen Aikakauskirja* [1961 (4)], 290–305

BACKER, M., "Accounting Theory, Objectives and Measurements." *Journal of Accountancy*, **116** (October 1963), 57–63

BAUMOL, W. J., "Speculation, Profitability, and Stability." *Review of Economics and Statistics*, **XXXIX** (August 1957), 263–271

BEDFORD, NORTON M., "Critical Analysis of Accounting Concepts of Income." *Accounting Review*, **XXVI** (October 1951), 526–537

BEDFORD, NORTON M., "Nature of Business Costs, General Concepts." *Accounting Review*, **XXXII** (January 1957), 8–14

BODENHORN, D., "A Cash-Flow Concept of Profit." *Journal of Finance*, **XIX** (March 1964), 16–31

BOMELI, E. C., "The Accountant's Function in Determination of Net Income." *Accounting Review*, **XXXVI** (July 1961), 454–459

BRETT, F. A., "Reevaluation of Accounting Concepts to Meet the Requirements of a Dynamic Economic Measurement." *Accounting Review*, **XXXV** (October 1960), 692–693

BRONFENBRENNER, M., "A Reformulation of Naïve Profit Theory." *Southern Economic Journal*, **XXVI** (April 1960), 301–309

CERF, A. R., "Diverse Accounting Procedures, Price-level Changes and Financial Statement Ratios." *Journal of Business*, **XXX** (July 1957), 180–192

CHANG, E. C., "Business Income in Accounting and Economics." *Accounting Review*, **XXXVII** (October 1962), 636–644

CHIPMAN, J. S., "The Foundations of Utility." *Econometrica*, **28** (April 1960), 193–224

CHURCHMAN, C. W., AND R. L. ACKOFF, "Operational Accounting and Operations Research." *Journal of Accountancy*, **99** (February 1955), 33–39

(DEVINE, CARL T.) "Accounting," *Encyclopedia Britannica* (1963 edition), **I**, 78–80

FEIGEL, HERBERT, "Operationism and Scientific Method." *Psychological Review*, **52** (September 1945), 250–259

GOLDBERG, L., "A Distinction Between 'Profit' and 'Income'." *Accounting Research*, **3** (April 1952), 133–139

GORDON, M. J., "Scope and Method of Theory and Research in the Measurement of Income and Wealth." *Accounting Review*, **XXXV** (October 1960), 603–618

HUSBAND, GEORGE R., "Rationalization in the Accounting Measurement of Income." *Accounting Review*, **XXIX** (January 1954), 3–14

JOHNSON, C. E., "Case Against the Idea of an All-Purpose Concept of Business Income." *Accounting Review*, **XXIX** (April 1954), 224–243

KELLEY, A. C., "Can Corporate Incomes Be Scientifically Ascertained?" *Accounting Review*, **XXVI** (July 1951), 289–298

LATANE, H. A., "Criteria for Choice Among Risky Ventures." *Journal of Political Economy*, **LXVII** (April 1959), 144–155

MARGOLIS, J., "The Analysis of the Firm: Rationalism, Conventionalism, and Behaviorism." *Journal of Business*, **XXXI** (July 1958), 187–199

MOONITZ, M., "Should We Discard the Income Concept?" *Accounting Review*, **XXXVII** (April 1962), 175–180

ORR, D., "A Stochastic Income Model Using Optimal Inventory Rules." *Review of Economic Studies*, **XXX** (June 1963), 84–92

PHILIPS, G. E., "The Accretion Concept of Income." *Accounting Review*, **XXXVIII** (January 1963), 14–25

POOL, A. G., "The Economic and Accounting Concepts of Profit." *Accounting Research*, **4** (April 1953), 144–152

RAUN, D. L., "Income: A Measurement of Currently Added Purchasing Power Through Operations." *Accounting Review*, **XXVII** (July 1952), 352–358

SOLOMONS, D., "Economic and Accounting Concepts of Income." *Accounting Review*, **XXXVI** (July 1961), 374–383

CHAPTER 6

Books

BRAY, F. S., *The Measurement of Profit*. London: Oxford University Press, 1949

CURTIS, EDWARD T., *Company Organization of the Finance Function*. New York: American Management Association, 1962

CYERT, RICHARD M., AND H. JUSTIN DAVIDSON, *Statistical Sampling for Accounting Information*. Englewood Cliffs, N.J.: Prentice-Hall, 1962

DIVINE, T. F., *Interest—An Historical and Analytical Study in Economics and Modern Ethics*. Milwaukee: Marquette University Press, 1959

GOLD, BELA, *Foundations of Productivity Analysis: Guides to Economic Theory and Managerial Control*. Pittsburgh: University of Pittsburgh Press, 1955

Institute of Cost and Works Accountants, *A Report on Marginal Costing*. London: Gee & Co., 1961

MAJUMDAR, T., *The Measurement of Utility*. New York: St. Martin's Press, 1958

NAA Research Report 34, *Classification and Coding Techniques to Facilitate Accounting Operations*. New York: National Association of Accountants, 1959

STUDENSKI, PAUL, *The Income of Nations: Theory, Measurement, and Analysis: Past and Present*. New York: New York University Press, 1958

Articles

ANDERSON, P. S., "The Apparent Decline in Capital–Output Ratios." *Quarterly Journal of Economics*, **LXXV** (November 1961), 615–634

BOWERS, RUSSELL, "Tests of Income Realization." *Accounting Review*, **XVI** (June 1941), 139–155

COPELAND, M. A., "Accounting Conventions Should Determine Business Income." *Journal of Accountancy*, **87** (February 1949), 107–111

DAVID, P. A., "The Deflation of Value Added." *Review of Economics and Statistics*, **XLIV** (May 1962), 148–155

DAVIDSON, S., "Depreciation and Profit Determination." *Accounting Review*, **XXV** (January 1950), 45–57

DEAN, JOEL, "Measurement of Profits for Executive Decisions." *Accounting Review*, **XXVI** (April 1951), 185–196

FERRARA, W. L., "Idle Capacity as a Loss—Fact or Fiction?" *Accounting Review*, **XXXV** (July 1960), 490–496

HAWKINS, L. C., "Measurements of Efficiency." *Oxford Economic Papers*, **2** (January 1950), 30–50

MAY, G. O., "Concepts of Business Income and Their Measurement." *Quarterly Journal of Economics*, **LXVIII** (February 1954), 1–18

MAY, GEORGE O., "Postulates of Income Accounting." *Journal of Accountancy*, **86** (August 1948), 107–111

MORGAN, J. N., "The Measurement of Gains and Losses." *Quarterly Journal of Economics*, **LXII** (February 1948), 287–308

MYERS, J. H., "The Critical Event and Recognition of Net Profit." *Accounting Review*, **XXXIV** (October 1959), 528–532

RASCH, G., "A Method of Indirect Measurement in Productivity Studies." *Productivity Measurement Review*, **10** (August 1957) 23–44

RENSHAW, E. F., "A Note on the Measurement of the Benefits from Public Investment in Navigation Projects." *American Economic Review*, **XLVII** (September 1957), 652–662

ROY, A. D., "The Valuation of Random Income Streams." Genoa, Italy: *Metroeconomica* (December 1958), 136–154

SEIDMAN, N. B., "Determination of Stockholder Income." *Accounting Review*, **XXXI** (July 1954), 494–499

SHARITS, E. C., "Business Income and the Cash Basis." *Accounting Review*, **XXXI** (July 1954), 494–499

STOREY, R. K., "Matching Revenues with Costs: An Analysis of Accounting Adaptation to Uncertainty." *Accounting Review*, **XXXV** (April 1960), 310–312

STOREY, R. K., "Revenue Realization, Going Concern and Measurement of Income." *Accounting Review*, **XXXIV** (April 1959), 232–238

WINDAL, F. W., "Accounting Concept of Realization." *Accounting Review*, **XXXVI** (April 1961), 249–258

WIXON, R., "The Measurement and Administration of Income." *Accounting Review*, **XXIV** (April 1949), 184–190

WRIGHT, F. K., "Measuring Project Profitability: Rate of Return or Present Value." *Accounting Review*, **XXXVII** (July 1962), 433–437

CHAPTER 7

Books

ALCHIAN, ARMEN A., *Economic Replacement Policy*. Santa Monica, Calif.: The Rand Corporation, 1952

COMMITTEE ON PRICE DETERMINATION, *Cost Behavior and Price Policy*. New York: National Bureau of Economic Research, 1943

FITZGERALD, A. A., AND L. A. SCHUMER, *Classification in Accounting*. Sydney, Australia: Butterworth, 1952

GIESE, JAMES W., *Classification of Economic Data in Accounting*. Unpublished Ph.D dissertation, University of Illinois, 1962

HODGES, H. G., *Procurement: the Modern Science of Purchasing*. New York: Harper, 1961

Lutz, F. A., and V. Lutz, *The Theory of Investment of the Firm.* Princeton: Princeton University Press, 1951

NAA Research Report No. 40, *Techniques in Inventory Management.* New York: National Association of Accountants, 1964

Osgood, C. E., G. J. Suci, and P. H. Tannenbaum, *The Measurement of Meaning.* Urbana: University of Illinois Press, 1957

Paton, W. A., and A. C. Littleton, *An Introduction to Corporate Accounting Standards.* Chicago: American Accounting Association, 1940

Research Series No. 30, *Accounting for Intra-Company Transfers.* New York: National Association of Cost Accountants, 1956

Turvey, R., *Interest Rates and Asset Prices.* New York: Macmillan, 1960

Articles

Edgerton, R. A. D., "Investment, Uncertainty and Expectations." *Review of Economic Studies,* **XXII** (1954–55), 143–150

Goobey, G. H. R., "The Use of Statistics in the Investment of Funds." *Applied Statistics,* **V** (March 1956), 1–11

Gordon, M. J. "Valuation of Accounts at Current Cost." *Accounting Review,* **XXVIII** (July 1953), 378–384

Gregory, J. C., "Capital Expenditure Evaluation by Direct Discounting." *Accounting Review,* **XXXVII** (April 1962), 308–314

Heinritz, Stuart F., "Measuring Purchasing Performance." *Purchasing.* Englewood Cliffs, N.J.: Prentice-Hall, 1947, pages 635–656

Hirshleifer, J., "On the Theory of Optimal Investment Decision." *Journal of Political Economy,* **LXVI** (August 1958), 329–352

Iino, Toshio, "Accounting Concept of Asset." *Hitotsubashi Journal of Commerce and Management,* **2** (November 1962), 21–29

Luce, R. D., "A Probabilistic Theory of Utility." *Econometrica,* **26** (April 1958), 193–224

Modigliani, Franco, and Merton H. Miller, "The Cost of Capital Corporation Finance and the Theory of Investment." *American Economic Review,* **XLVIII** (June 1958), 261–297

Solomons, D., "The Determination of Asset Values." *Journal of Business,* **XXXV** (January 1962), 28–42

Stockfisch, J. A., "The Relationships Between Money Cost, Investment, and the Rate of Return." *Quarterly Journal of Economics,* **LXX** (May 1956), 8

Thurstone, L. L., and L. V. Jones, "The Rational Origin for Measuring Subjective Values." *Journal of American Statistical Association,* **52** (December 1957), 458–471

White, W. H., "The Rate of Interest, the Marginal Efficiency of Capital and Investment Programming." *Economic Journal,* **LXVIII** (March 1958), 51–59

CHAPTER 8

Books

DEVINE, C. T., *Inventory Valuation and Periodic Income.* New York: The Ronald Press, 1942

FERBER, ROBERT, AND P. J. VERDOORN, *Research Methods in Economics and Business.* New York: Macmillan, 1962

GILLMAN, J. M., *The Falling Rate of Profit.* New York: Cameron Associates, 1958

GOLDBERG, LOUIS, *Concepts of Depreciation.* Sydney: Law Book Co. of Australasia, 1960

GRANT, E. L., AND P. T. NORTON, JR., *Depreciation.* New York: The Ronald Press, 1955

HOFFMAN, RAYMOND A., *Inventories.* New York: The Ronald Press, 1962

Research Series No. 33, *Current Practice in Accounting for Depreciation.* New York: National Association of Accountants, 1958

TERBORGH, GEORGE, *Realistic Depreciation Policy.* Chicago: Machinery and Allied Products Institute, 1954

WARD, A. DUDLEY, *Goals of Economic Life.* New York: Harper, 1953

WEBB, G. T., *Depreciation of Fixed Assets in Accountancy and Economics.* Sydney: Law Book Co. of Australasia, 1954

Articles

BUTLER, WILLIAM F., "Capacity Utilization and the Rate of Profitability in Manufacturing." *American Economic Review,* **XLVIII** (May 1958), 239–248

COUGHLAN, JOHN W., "Guises of Replacement Cost." *Accounting Review,* **XXXII** (July 1957), 434–447

Council of Institute of Chartered Accountants in England and Wales, "Treatment of Investments in the Balance Sheets of Trading Companies." *Recommendations on Accounting Principles.* London: Institute of Chartered Accountants in England and Wales, 1961 (*N* 20), 1–10

DAVIDSON, S., AND Y. YASUBA, "Asset Revaluation and Income Taxation in Japan." *National Tax Journal,* **XIII** (March 1960), 45–58

DIACHKOV, M., "Methodological Questions of Revaluing Fixed Capital." *Problems of Economics,* **II** (November 1959), 41–46

DORFMAN, R., "Waiting and the Period of Production." *Quarterly Journal of Economics,* **LXXIII** (August 1959), 351–372

EDGERTON, R. A. D., "The Holding of Assets: 'Gambler Preference' or 'Safety First'?" *Oxford Economic Papers,* **8** (February 1956), 51–59

FLEWELLEN, W. C., JR., "Concept of Depreciation Accounting Held by the United States Supreme Court." *Accounting Review,* **XXXV** (July 1960), 413–421

GOUDEKET, A., "An Application of Replacement Value Theory." *Journal of Accountancy,* **110** (July 1960), 37–47

HORVAT, B., "The Depreciation Multiplier and a Generalized Theory of Fixed Capital Costs." *Manchester School of Economic and Social Studies*, **XXVI** (May 1958), 136–159

LOVELL, M. C., "Buffer Stocks, Sales Expectations, and Stability: A Multi-Sector Analysis of the Inventory Cycle." *Econometrica*, **30** (April 1962), 267–296

LOWE, H. D., "The Essentials of a General Theory of Depreciation." *Accounting Review*, **XXXVIII** (April 1963), 293–301

McANLY, H. T., "The Case for Lifo." *Journal of Accountancy*, **95** (June 1953), 691–700

PENNOCK, J. L., AND C. M. JAEGER, "Estimating the Service Life of Household Goods by Actuarial Methods." *Journal of American Statistical Association*, **52** (June 1957), 175–185

PREINREICH, G. A. D., "The Economic Life of Industrial Equipment." *Econometrica*, **VII** (January 1940), 12–14

REYNOLDS, ISAAC N., "Selecting the Proper Depreciation Method." *Accounting Review*, **XXXVI** (April 1961), 239–248

RHODES, E. C., "Earned and Investment Incomes, U. K. 1952–53." London School of Economics, *Economica*, **XXIII** (February 1956), 62–66

ROSS, M. H., "Depreciation and User Cost." *Accounting Review*, **XXXV** (July 1960), 422–428

SELZER, L. H., "Interest as a Source of Personal Income and Tax Revenue." *Journal of American Statistical Association*, **50** (December 1955), 1248–1330

VANEK, J., "An Afterthought on the 'Real Cost–Opportunity Cost' Dispute and Some Aspects of General Equilibrium Under Conditions of Variable Factor Supplies." *Review of Economic Studies*, **XXVI** (June 1959), 198–208

WRIGHT, F. K., "Toward a General Theory of Depreciation." *Journal of Accounting Research*, **II** (Spring 1964), 80–90

CHAPTER 9

Books

ARROW, KENNETH J., SAMUEL KARLIN, AND HERBERT SCARF, *Studies in the Mathematical Theory of Inventory and Production.* Stanford: Stanford University Press, 1958

BOWMAN, E. H., AND R. B. FETTER, *Analysis for Production Management.* Homewood, Ill.: Richard D. Irwin, 1957

BRUMMET, R. L., *Overhead Costing.* Ann Arbor, Mich.: Bureau of Business Research, 1957

BUZZELL, R. D., *Value Added by Industrial Distributors and Their Productivity.* Columbus, O.: Ohio State University Bureau of Business Research, 1959, Monograph No. 96

Committee on Price Determination, *Cost Behavior and Price Policy*. New York: National Bureau of Economic Research, 1943

Research and Technical Committee, *Cost Reduction*. London: Institute of Cost and Works Accountants, 1956

Council of the Institute of Chartered Accountants in England and Wales, *Notes on the Allocation of Expense*. London: Institute of Chartered Accountants in England and Wales, 1951

DAVIS, HIRAM S., *Productivity Accounting*. Philadelphia: University of Pennsylvania Press, 1955

HEGAZY, A. M., *Accounting for Managerial Control*. Cairo: El-Esnawy Press, 1960

PATON, W. A., *Essentials of Accounting*. New York: Macmillan, 1949

RESEARCH SERIES No. 30, *Accounting for Intra-Company Transfers*. New York: National Association of Accountants, 1956

SANDS, J. E., *Wealth, Income, and Intangibles*. Toronto: University of Toronto Press, 1963

VATTER, WILLIAM J., *The Fund Theory of Accounting and Its Implications for Financial Reports*. Chicago: University of Chicago Press, 1947

Articles

AUMAN, R. J., AND S. B. KRUSKAL, "Assigning Quantitative Values by Qualitative Methods in the Naval Electronics Problem." *Naval Logistics Research Quarterly*, **6** (1959), 1

AVERY, H. G., "Accounting for Joint Costs." *Accounting Review*, **XXVI** (April 1951), 232–238

BARCLAY, ALASDAIR G., "The Practicing Accountant's Contribution to Productivity." *Eleventh Summer School at the University of St. Andrews*. Edinburgh: Institute of Chartered Accountants of Scotland, 1963, 36–60

BIERMAN, H., "Pricing Intracompany Transfers." *Accounting Review*, **XXXIV** (July 1959), 429–432

BROCHET, R., "Use of Productivity Measurement for Inter-Firm Comparisons in the French Jute Industry." *Productivity Measurement Review* (November 1961), 40–46

CASTENHOLZ, W. B., "What Constitutes Material Cost of Production." *Accounting Review*, **XXXIII** (October 1958), 650–653

EARLY, J. S., "Recent Developments in Cost Accounting and the Marginal Analysis." *Journal of Political Economy*, **LXIII** (June 1955), 227–242

ERNST, H., "Accounting for Productivity Changes." *Harvard Business Review*, **34** (May–June 1956), 109–121

LORIG, ARTHUR N., "Joint Cost Analysis as an Aid to Management." *Accounting Review*, **XXX** (October 1955), 634–637

LOWE, H. D., "The Essentials of a General Theory of Depreciation." *Accounting Review*, **XXXVIII** (April 1963), 293–301

MEYER, JOHN R., "Some Methodological Aspects of Statistical Costing as Illustrated by the Determination of Rail Passenger Costs." *American Economic Review*, **XLVIII** (May 1958), 209–222

MISHAN, E. J., "A Reappraisal of the Principles of Resource Allocation." *Economica*, **XXIV** (November 1957), 324–342

NACA Committee on Research, "Direct Costing." *NACA Bulletin*, **XXXIV** (April 1953), 1077–1132

PADDOCK, H. E., "Production Waste—Its Nature and Its Accounting." *Accounting Review*, **XXXIII** (January 1958), 50–55

PFOUTS, R. W., "The Theory of Cost and Production in the Multi-Product Firm." *Econometrica*, **29** (October 1961), 650–658

RUIST, E., "Production Efficiency of the Industrial Firm." *Productivity Measurement Review* (December 1961), 3–79

SHILLINGLAW, G., "Guides to Internal Profit Measurement." *Harvard Business Review*, **35** (March–April 1957), 82–94

SMITH, R. J., "Analysis of Current Theory and Practice Regarding the Elements of Cost Included in Inventory by Manufacturers." *Accounting Review*, **XXXIV** (October 1959), 628–630

SMITH, V. L., "The Theory of Investment and Production." *Quarterly Journal of Economics*, **LXXIII** (February 1959), 61–87

STONE, W. E., "Intracompany Pricing." *Accounting Review*, **XXXI** (October 1956), 625–627

WALTERS, A. A., "The Allocation of Joint Costs with Demands as Probability Distributions." *American Economic Review*, **L** (June 1960), 419–432

WALTERS, A. A., "Marginal Productivity and Probability Distributions of Factor Services." *Economic Journal*, **LXX** (June 1960), 325–330

WILLIAMS, N., "The Allocation of Scarce Materials Between Products." *Applied Statistics*, **V** (November 1956), 166–176

ZANNETOS, ZENON S., "Standard Costs as a First Step to Probability Control: A Theoretical Justification, an Extension, and Implications." *Accounting Review*, **XXXIX** (April 1964), 296–304

CHAPTER 10

Books

ALDERSON, WROE, *Marketing Behavior and Executive Action*. Homewood, Ill.: Richard D. Irwin, 1957

ATHEARN, J. L., *Risk and Insurance*. New York: Appleton-Century-Crofts, 1962

BONBRIGHT, J. C., *Principles of Public Utility Rates*. New York: Columbia University Press, 1961

KAPLAN, A. D., JOEL B. DIRLAM, AND R. F. LANZILLOTTI, *Pricing in Big Business: A Case Approach*. Washington, D.C.: Brookings Institution, 1958

Lucas, D. B., and S. H. Britt, *Measuring Advertising Effectiveness.* New York: McGraw-Hill, 1963

Means, Gardner C., *Pricing Power and the Public Interest.* New York: Harper, 1962

Mossman, Frank H., *Differential Distribution Cost and Revenue Analysis.* East Lansing: Michigan State University, 1962

Schultz, H., *The Theory and Measurement of Demand.* Chicago: University of Chicago Press, 1957

Articles

Adelman, M. A., "The 'Product' and 'Price' in Distribution." *American Economic Review,* **XLVII** (May 1957), 266–273

Bund, H., and J. W. Carroll, "The Changing Role of the Marketing Function." *Journal of Marketing,* **XXI** (January 1957), 268–325

Corden, W. M., "The Calculation of the Cost of Protection." *Economic Record,* **XXXIII** (April 1957), 29–51

Gamble, F. R., "The Role of Advertising in Today's Economy." *Boston University Business Review,* **3** (Spring 1956), 9–12

Hartogensis, A., "The Art and Practice of Pricing." *NAA Bulletin,* **XXXIX** (March 1958), 63–74

Hahn, F. H., "The Theory of Selling Costs." *Economic Journal,* **LXIX** (June 1959), 293–312

Lanzillotti, R. F., "Pricing Objectives in Large Companies." *American Economic Review,* **XLVIII** (December 1958), 921–940

McAnly, H. T., "Administrative Expense and Profit in Product Pricing." *Journal of Accountancy,* **116** (August 1963), 33–38

McClelland, W. G., "Pricing for Profit in Retailing." *Journal of Industrial Economics,* **VII** (July 1959), 159–174

Oxenfeldt, A. R., and W. T. Baxter, "Approaches to Pricing: Economist Versus Accountant." *Business Horizons,* **4** (Winter 1961), 77–90

Shillinglaw, G., "Profit Analysis for Abandonment Decisions." *Journal of Business,* **XXX** (January 1957), 17–29

Woods, Richard S., "Theory and Practice in the Capitalization of Selling Costs." *Accounting Review,* **XXXIV** (October 1959), 564–569

CHAPTER 11

Books

Arthur Andersen & Co., *The Philadelphia Transportation Company Case Re: Income Interest on Bonds: Cases in Public Accounting Practice,* Volumes 3 and 4. Chicago: Arthur Andersen, 1961

GILBERT, L. D., *Dividends and Democracy*. Larchmont, N.Y.: American Research Council, 1956

HATFIELD, HENRY R., *Surplus and Dividends*. Cambridge: Harvard University Press, 1947

HOLLAND, D. M., *Dividends Under the Income Tax*. Princeton: Princeton University Press, 1962

LITTLETON, A. C., AND V. K. ZIMMERMAN, *Accounting Theory: Continuity and Change*. Englewood Cliffs, N.J.: Prentice-Hall, 1962

PREINREICH, GABRIEL A., *The Nature of Dividends*. New York: Ph.D. dissertation, Columbia University, 1935

SCOTT, W. R., *The Constitution and Finance of English, Scottish and Irish Joint-Stock Companies to 1720*. Cambridge: The University Press, 1910

SOLOMON, EZRA, *The Management of Corporate Capital*. New York: The Free Press of Glencoe, 1959

STAUBUS, GEORGE, *A Theory of Accounting to Investors*. Berkeley: University of California Press, 1961

Articles

BARKER, C. A., "Evaluation of Stock Dividends." *Harvard Business Review*, **36** (July–August 1958), 99–114

BROWN, HARRY G., "Division of Retained Earnings to Reflect Business Needs." *Accounting Review*, **XXXII** (April 1957), 258–263

Committee on Concepts and Standards Underlying Corporate Financial Statements of American Accounting Association, "Reserves and Retained Income." *Accounting Review*, **XXVI** (April 1951), 152–156

EHRLICH, H. B., "Theory of Factor Income Distribution." *American Journal of Economics and Sociology* (April 1957), 299–307

Eisner Versus Macomber, **252** U.S., 189 (1920)

FLORENCE, P. S., "Size of Company and Other Factors in Dividend Policy." *Journal of the Royal Statistical Society*, **122** (1) (1959), 77–98

HARKAVY, OSCAR, "The Relation Between Retained Earnings and Common Stock Prices for Large, Listed Corporations." *The Journal of Finance*, **VIII** (September 1953), 283–297

HORNGREN, CHARLES T., "Stock Dividends and the Entity Theory." *Accounting Review*, **XXXII** (July 1957), 379–385

LI, DAVID H., "Nature and Treatment of Dividends Under the Entity Concept." *Accounting Review*, **XXXV** (October 1960), 674–679

LINTNER, JOHN, "Distribution of Incomes of Corporations Among Dividends, Retained Earnings, and Taxes." *American Economic Review*, **XLVI** (May 1956), 97–113

PORTERFIELD, JAMES T. S., "Dividends, Dilution, and Delusion." *The Harvard Business Review*, **XXXVII** (November–December 1959) 56–61

SAGAN, J., "Toward a Theory of Working Capital Management." *Journal of Finance*, **X** (May 1955), 121–129

SIEGAL, I. H., "Some Problems for Index Number Workers." *The American Statistician*, **VI** (February 1952), 1, 21

SIMON, S. I., "Spin-Offs Versus Dividends in Kind." *Accounting Review*, **XXXV** (January 1960), 81–89

SINE, E. P. "Accounting for Dividends." *Accounting Review*, **XXVIII** (July 1953), 320–324

SOLDOFSKY, R. M., "The Cost of Capital Function for a Firm." *The Controller*, **XXVI** (June 1958), 263–268

WALTER, J. E., "Dividend Policy: Its Influence on the Value of the Enterprise." *Journal of Finance*, **XVIII** (May 1963), 280–291

WARING, W. C., JR., "Fractional Shares Under Stock Dividend Declarations." *Harvard Law Review*, **44** (1930–31), 404–426

CHAPTER 12

Books

ANDERSON, CORLISS D., *Corporate Reporting for the Professional Investor*. Auburndale, Mass.: Financial Analysts Federation, 1962

CERF, A. R., *Corporate Reporting and Investment Decisions*. Berkeley: University of California Institute of Business and Economic Research, 1961

CHERRY, COLIN, *On Human Communication*. Cambridge: Massachusetts Institute of Technology, 1957

HICKEY, JAMES J., *Reporting to Stockholders and the Financial Community*. Stratford, Conn.: Kevmar Publications, 1962

KEEZER, DEXTER M., AND OTHERS, *New Forces in American Business*. New York: McGraw-Hill, 1959

KENNEDY, RALPH D., AND STEWART Y. McMULLEN, *Financial Statements*. Homewood, Ill.: Irwin, 1962

LEWIS, R. B., *Accounting Reports for Management*. Englewood Cliffs, N.J.: Prentice-Hall, 1957

LINSKY, LEONARD, editor, *Semantics and the Philosophy of Language*. Urbana: University of Illinois Press, 1952

OSGOOD, C. E., G. J. SUCI, AND P. H. TANNENBAUM, *The Measurement of Meaning*. Urbana: University of Illinois Press, 1957

SCHUTTE, W. M., AND E. R. STEINBERG, *Communication in Business and Industry*. New York: Holt, Rinehart and Winston, 1960

SHANNON, CLAUDE, AND WARREN WEAVER, *The Mathematical Theory of Communication*. Urbana: University of Illinois Press, 1949

Articles

Accounting Practice Report No. 16, "Departures in Communicating Accounting Data to Foremen." *NAA Bulletin*, **XLIV** (January 1963), 3–21

AMEY, L. R., "Business Efficiency: An Interfirm Comparison." *Productivity Measurement Review* (May 1960), 32–45

ANDERSON, D. S., "Communications Problems of Financial Reporting." *Journal of Accountancy*, **115** (April 1963), 59–64

BEDFORD, NORTON M., AND VAHE BALADOUNI, "A Communication Theory Approach to Accountancy." *Accounting Review*, **XXXVII** (October 1962), 650–659

BYRNE, ROBERT S., "Control Charts to Measure Sales Performance Within the Month." *NAA Bulletin*, **XLIV** (December 1962), 43–52

LaFRANCE, J. W., "Communication with the Client and the Public." *Journal of Accountancy*, **113** (May 1962), 39–44

Research Series No. 28, "Presenting Accounting Information to Management." *NACA Bulletin*, **XXXVI** (December 1954), 595–647

RICE, M. Y., "Sketch for a Universal Accounting Statement." *Accounting Review*, **XXXVII** (January 1962), 6–21

SHILLINGLAW, G., "Leasing and Financial Statements." *Accounting Review*, **XXXIII** (October 1958), 581–592

SHILLINGLAW, G., "Problems in Divisional Profit Measurement." *NAA Bulletin*, **XLII** (March 1961), 33–43

STANS, M. H., "Modernizing the Income Statement." *Accounting Review*, **XXIV** (January 1949), 3–14

THACKER, RONALD J., "Income Statement Form and Classification." *Accounting Review*, **XXXVII** (January 1962), 51–55

TRUMBULL, W. P., "Disclosure as a Standard of Income Reporting." *Accounting Review*, **XXVIII** (October 1953), 471–481

Index

Index

235